BOWHUNTER'S DIGEST

by C. R. Learn

Edited by   Jack Lewis

Digest Books, Inc., Northfield, Illinois

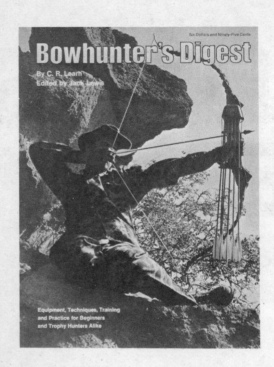

Produced by

Charger Productions

ON THE COVER:

Bowen Weems, maker of Weems predator calls, comes to full draw while perched on ledge under overhanging rock somewhere in northern New Mexico. Attired in camouflage suit by Ten X; he is equipped with a Pearson bow, Bear bow quiver, and Forgewood arrows tipped with Black Copperhead Magnum broadheads. Photo by C.R. Learn

EDITORIAL DIRECTOR
BOB SPRINGER

RESEARCH EDITOR
MARK THIFFAULT

RESEARCH ASSISTANT
CHERILEE ELLIOTT

ART DIRECTOR
PAT HOPPER

STAFF ARTISTS
ANDY GRENNELL
KATHERINE MALONE

PRODUCTION COORDINATOR
JUDY K. RADER

PRODUCTION ASSISTANT
WENDY LEE WISEHART

ASSOCIATE PUBLISHER
SHELDON FACTOR

ISBN 0-695-80451-0

Library of Congress Catalog Card Number 73-91589

CONTENTS

INTRODUCTION

During the 1973-74 hunting seasons, more than three-quarters of a million bowhunters purchased hunting and bowfishing or species' tags in the forty-eight contiguous states alone! Since certain states do not differentiate between those who hunt with the bow and arrow and those who hunt with a gun, an accurate total of the number of bowhunters in this country is impossible to obtain. Nevertheless, it is fair to observe that more and more Americans each year are taking up this intriguing and self-satisfying sport.

It is for this vast and ever-growing audience that this book has been written. And, in so doing, an attempt was made to move the reader progressively, chapter by chapter, from the basics involved, right through the proven techniques and equipment used by today's foremost bowhunters. In particular, such individuals as Jim Dougherty, and bowhunting's living legend, Fred Bear; to both of whom is owed a personal debt of gratitude.

When you have finished reading this book, it is our profound hope that you will have gained some knowledge and the desire to experience the close association with nature peculiar to the art of bowhunting.

C.R. Learn

The Beginning Bowhunter

CHAPTER 1

Some Sound Advice Before Going Afield.

IN AN AGE where man has the ability to send man to the moon or instantaneously transmit a baseball game played in Los Angeles to television viewers in London via a satellite, it seems almost anachronistic that there still are those who prefer to hunt game with one of man's oldest weapons, the bow and arrow. However, there are many such hunters and the ranks of enthusiastic bowhunters seem to grow each day.

To the thousands who have taken up this sport, the primary appeal seems to be the challenge that it offers, not only physically but mentally as well. Unlike many sports such as tennis and polo which traditionally have been associated with the wealthy, bowhunting draws its participants from all walks of life. Here, the banker and the mechanic, the professional and the store clerk all meet on mutual ground in a challenging sport that has no social, economic or cultural limitations.

The only prerequisite for bowhunting is the desire to match wits and skill with that wily creature, the game animal — an endeavor that is often frustrating, but never dull! Many bowhunters come from the ranks of rifle hunters who are looking for a new dimension to add to their skills in the field. Many of these also take up bowhunting in order to extend the time that they are able to hunt; rifle hunting seasons in most states are relatively short, while archers enjoy as many as thirty days in most cases and some states have seasons that extend over one hundred days.

There are some archers who prefer to shoot nothing but targets, but many of the most avid bowhunters are individuals who punch paper part of the year and switch to game animals during the season.

However, perhaps one of the biggest groups in the bowhunting field, if one can get them to admit it, are the converted rifle hunters mentioned earlier. Many of these hunters have become disenchanted with the fast bullets, flat

Bowhunters rendezvous to compare notes on where game was sighted, how it reacted and to map out their next moves. This exchange of information is standard throughout the bowhunting fraternity.

*Tree-studded draws
and rolling hills
offer a variety of
opportunities for
varmints and game
animals. Beginners
will spend many long
hours working areas
similar to these.*

trajectory and long ranges of rifle hunting. Downing game with a rifle has become relatively easy for them and they seek a harder, more challenging method to hunt game and turn to the bow and arrow. Most of these hunters already have hunted favorite areas with great success for many years. When they return to these areas with a bow, they often are the ones who become true addicts of bowhunting.

The range at which rifles down game can differ from a few feet to several hundred, but an average for mule deer in the Western states might be two hundred yards, give or take a few. When a newly converted rifle hunter first takes up the bow — without realizing that he no longer has the advantage of this long range — it often leads to a rather amusing series of events, and he does not down his game. To some this is so discouraging that they give up without further effort. However, more often than not, the hunter will take up the challenge and often never returns to his days of rifle hunting.

It goes without saying that the beginning bowhunter, be he a converted rifleman, a target archer or a complete novice to both hunting and archery, first must learn the basic fundamentals of the sport. As with any sport, there are many pitfalls for the beginner and we would like to discuss a few here. Often the worst enemy that a beginner can have, other than himself, is the well-meaning but moderately knowledgeable archer who takes it upon himself to give the beginner instruction. Without doubt, these individuals mean well and can be of some help, but the primary pitfall here is that this individual often passes on his bad habits to the beginner. What a beginning archer or hunter does not need are inherited bad habits passed on by his instructor.

Often one will find these well-meaning but inadequate instructors in a non-sporting goods store; many of which today do carry archery and bowhunting equipment. Although these department stores or discount outlets may sell bows, arrows, leather goods and all the other paraphernalia needed for bowhunting, they do not have expert bowmen as salesmen. Their primary job is selling and often, in their enthusiasm to make a sale, they attempt to appear more knowledgeable than they really are. Anyone who is seriously considering taking up bowhunting should visit a regular sporting goods store, where the personnel are much more knowledgeable and familiar with the equipment and can provide the beginner with sound, and in some cases expert, advice.

Another fine place to learn about archery, both hunting and target, is in an archery shop which specializes in nothing but archery and bowhunting equipment. Unfortunately, oftentimes there is no local archery shop readily available to the beginner, so he must turn to books such as this one and magazines featuring archery and bowhunting articles.

However, here again looms a pitfall. Many of these books and articles are written at a level that is far above the

Large groves of trees shelter many varieties of small, nongame animals, such as rabbits and squirrels, and provide shade and concealment for the hunters. Hunting for these smaller species is excellent practice for the fledgling bowhunter.

beginner and are apt to use terminology that is totally foreign to him. One of the most common mistakes that beginners who rely solely on books and articles for their information make concerns the selection of a bow weight that would be most suitable for them. Many authors — usually expert archers and bowhunters — will mention bow weights that they use; these are normally far too heavy for the beginning bowhunter or archer. The inexperienced beginner reading the article or book automatically assumes that, since the author is a well-known archer and successful in his field, he should know what he is talking about. He does, but he is talking about himself or other experienced archers, not a beginner.

Without taking this into consideration, the beginner will rush out and buy himself a bow of the same weight and end up being overbowed. An experienced bowhunter with many years of hunting under his belt can handle a sixty-pound pull, but there are few novices who can.

This book, therefore, is intended to take the beginning archer or hunter from the basics up to the more complicated and advanced techniques and practices of bowhunting. It also hopes to offer hints and ideas for the more experienced bowhunter who seeks to improve his present skills.

Archery, like any sport, has its own special language and anyone hoping to master the sport needs first to master the language. Archers use some expressions that go as far back as the Middle Ages, but for the most part the terms have, through the years, been updated and standardized.

The first thing that a potential bowhunter needs to learn about is the bow itself. The national average for hunting bow draw weight is fifty pounds. However, to understand this, one first must understand what the draw weight of a bow means. The term, "draw weight of fifty pounds," means that the actual strength, measured in pounds, to pull the bow from brace height, where it is strung, to twenty-eight inches will require a pull weight of fifty pounds. For the average person, this sounds simple, since most people can easily lift over a hundred pounds. However, the muscles one uses to pull a bow are far different than those used to lift weights. A bow with a draw weight of sixty pounds requires an archer with considerable strength or experience or both.

Various manufacturers offer bows that vary from a mere twenty pounds to more than one hundred pounds. Very few archers use the hundred-plus, but these bows are available. A beginner should spend many hours practicing with a light bow of possibly thirty or thirty-five pounds. Some beginners can start with a fifty-pound draw weight, but most are better off sticking with the lighter bows until they have developed their skills.

Another term to consider is the mass weight of the bow. This is the actual weight of the bow in hand, as you lift it or carry it in the field. This usually varies from a low of two pounds to a high of five pounds. The mass weight usually varies according to the materials from which the bow is constructed. It is determined with only the string attached and no other accessories.

It was stated earlier that the average hunting bow draw weight was fifty pounds. However, we advocate buying a light thirty-pounder with which to learn. This could mean that the beginner needs to purchase two bows. At one time this was the case; however, with today's modern bow construction it is not always necessary, since there are several styles of bows from which to choose.

The first is the old-style construction that laminates a hardwood center section, the riser, to a fiberglass material made especially for the archery business and the end product is a bow of one length and it can't be varied. This often is called a single-unit bow and the draw weight cannot be varied. If you buy a thirty-pound, single-unit bow, it will always be just that, a thirty-pound bow of sixty inches length or whatever other length it may be. You can pay as little as thirty dollars or as much as several hundred for a light bow of this construction.

Sometimes confused with the single-unit bow is what is called a self bow. The difference is that the self bow is an extremely old construction method using yew, orangewood or other hardwoods and is carved from one piece of material. This type of bow is still available, but has many problems in comparison to the modern laminated bows. It is mentioned only to prevent a beginner from purchasing one thinking he is getting a single-unit bow or other type of modern bow.

The third type of bow construction is the two-piece bow. It is made to disassemble, usually in the handle section, into two pieces for ease of transportation. It is still basically a single-unit bow, with the difference being that it has been modified to be more portable. Here again, this type of bow cannot be varied in length and draw weight.

The newest style of bow on the market is the three-piece take-down bow, which has become quite popular in recent years. The big advantage to this three-piece system is that an archer can buy the handle — or riser section in archery terminology — and as many sets of limbs of varying draw weights as he wants.

For example, a beginner might want to buy the riser section and a set of thirty-pound limbs. As he becomes more proficient, he can buy other limbs with a heavier draw weight. This type of construction also has an advantage for the experienced archer who likes to use bows of varying

The sides of draws, creek banks and similar areas offer many hours of good practice for the beginner. This bowhunter has picked out a spot on a stump, stepped off the distance, and is checking his accuracy.

draw weights. By purchasing one riser section and two sets of limbs of varying draw weights, he can have two bows for much less than he would have to pay for two single-unit bows of the same draw weights. Another advantage is that it gives one an extra set of backup limbs for hunting. This advantage will be discussed in some detail later.

The beginner who purchases this type of system should practice with the thirty-pound limbs until he feels he has gained sufficient skill in handling the bow to try his hand at game hunting. However, once he feels he has reached this point of proficiency, he should switch to a heavier draw weight of fifty pounds or more. There are those who have killed big game with light bows, but these usually are extremely talented hunters with many years' experience behind them. Using a light bow is comparable to a rifle hunter using a .22 rifle for shooting deer. It can be done, but it isn't recommended. The best policy is to shoot the heaviest bow weight that one can draw comfortably and shoot accurately.

One of the best target materials for practicing, whether a beginner or experienced hunter, is the standard straw bale. These can be set up in your back yard provided you have some type of backstop for those arrows that miss the bale. It is not necessary to have a hundred yards or more to practice in at first. In fact, the beginner is better off using shorter ranges, until he reaches the point where he hits the bale more often than not. Too often a beginner will attempt the long ranges and become so discouraged by misses that he will become sour on the sport before he has even given it a chance.

What the beginner must concentrate on is his form, release and technique, which can be done just as well, if not better, on short ranges rather than the longer ones. The novice can learn as much at ten or twenty yards, or even feet for that matter, than he can on the longer ranges where he is apt to become frustrated by his percentage of misses. All he has to do to change from ten yards to fifty yards is to raise the bow for sighting the longer distance. After hitting a nine-inch pie plate five times out of five at shorter ranges, the beginner then can begin to think about the longer shots, but he should not rush into them until he feels

A heavy snowfall alters terrain features and offers a real challenge to the beginner as well as to the advanced archer.

totally comfortable handling the bow and his accuracy is good.

The novice visiting an archery range for the first time might be appalled and somewhat awed by the gadgets and equipment used by experienced target archers. There are stabilizers on the front of the bow, finger gloves, finger tabs, exotic releases, sights, an infinite number of types of arrows and quivers, levels, peeps...the list goes on and on.

All of these items can be used for bowhunting, but all that really is needed is the bow, arrows tipped with razor-sharp broadheads, a quiver and perhaps an arm guard to keep the sleeve off the string, plus finger protection such as a glove or tab. Some bowhunters don't feel that the last item is necessary, since the three fingers used in drawing the bow toughen after a while and they feel it gives them a cleaner release. The equipment a bowhunter uses is a matter of personal preference and he can use as much or as little as he wants.

When a target archer and a bowhunter get together, it's apparent from their conversation that they do have some things in common, but it also becomes obvious that their two sports differ considerably. A target archer stands in one place, shoots at the target which is a known distance away and about the only outside influence he has to worry about, other than pressure, is the wind. It is certainly not an easy sport and requires a great deal of skill and practice to become proficient, but it is certainly a far cry from being in the field matching one's wits and skill against that of a wild animal.

Rather heated arguments arise between the two groups as to which is the more demanding sport requiring the most skill. However, it is really rather a moot point since both belong to the same fraternity and require considerable skill. Both have their own standards and both should be respected by the other.

In the selection of arrows, the bowhunter has several types from which to choose. Before making a selection, the beginner should test all types, then decide which is best suited for his purposes. There are times when a bowhunter may want to use one type and another type under different circumstances. Therefore, the novice is wise to become familiar with all of the varying types.

Cedar shafts are perhaps the oldest on the market. They have been made for years by the same method, with the majority of the wooden shafts sold today coming from Oregon and Washington. This type of arrow is called the Port Orford cedar and many highly successful bowhunters prefer these to the more modern fiberglass and aluminum shafts. Many manufacturers offer the Port Orford cedars and they are perhaps the least expensive of the three types.

A number of years ago, the advent of plastic technology brought about the modern fiberglass arrow shafts. They are offered by many manufacturers at a slightly higher cost than the cedars, but have the advantage of greater durability than the wooden shafts.

In the late 1940s, a gentleman by the name of Doug Easton began experimenting with aluminum as an arrow shaft material. He was told that it couldn't be done, so he set out to prove that it could and eventually built this "impossible" material into one of the leading materials used in modern arrows. Today, Jim Easton carries on the work of his late father and the shafts manufactured by the Easton company can be found on almost any target range, as well as in the quivers of many expert bowhunters. Aluminum shafts, at one time, were the most expensive arrows on the market, but they now can be bought for about the same price as fiberglass shafts. We will cover the advantages and disadvantages of these materials in more depth in a later section of this book, but the beginner should be aware that all are available in both target and hunting arrow configurations.

When purchasing his first arrows, the beginner should insure that they are matched to fit his bow draw weight. There are charts for this purpose and these usually are found in any store that sells archery equipment. If the arrow doesn't match the bow draw weight, it never will fly properly and all the practice in the world is not going to help your accuracy.

Most bowhunters will use a glove in the beginning. These are made of lightweight leather and fit over the first three fingers of the shooting hand. The bow is drawn with the right hand if right-handed and conversely, if left-handed. There are other methods and equipment that can be used, but for the novice it usually is easier to begin with the glove and change later after becoming more proficient in the sport.

For the beginning bowhunter primarily interested in

There are some aspects of target archery that are not found in the hunting field. There are many women hunters, but they seldom appear in the field in such pleasing costumes as this target archer is wearing.

backyard practicing, it is not necessary to have a quiver for holding the arrows. They can be carried in the hip pocket for practice and later, when he begins to hunt, he can purchase a quiver that best suits his individual needs. The various types of quivers will be covered in a later section.

Once the beginning archer has acquired his basic equipment — bow, arrows and a glove to protect his fingers — he should be ready to begin the many hours of practice that it is going to take him to become a successful bowhunter. It sounds simple enough, but there is more to it.

When he walks to the bales with the new bow, new arrows and the proper nocking point, with the stop put on the string for the arrow to rest on, the novice suddenly is faced with a startling problem — how to aim this ridiculous assortment of materials. With a rifle there are sights. A shotgun has a bead in front, but most ignore this and point the barrel, keeping both eyes open.

This method is perhaps the best method for the beginning archer, also. Keeping both eyes open, bring the bow up in the left hand (for a right-handed archer), extend the arm until the elbow locks and place the arrow on the string against the nocking point and on the arrow rest of the bow.

The bow at brace height, all you need to do is pull back as far as your arms will allow and shoot it downrange. It is really that simple.

In a little more detail: Hold the bow in the left hand, using a firm grip and bring the string and arrow back together, using the first three fingers of the right hand wrapped around the string to the first joint. Your left arm may quiver a bit at first and the right shoulder will subtly remind you that you are using muscles you didn't even know you had. However, with practice the muscles will loosen.

With a rifle there are front and rear sights for alignment. With a bow, this can be duplicated by using the corner of the mouth for the rear sight or, in this case, as a constant draw check. Bring the first finger of the right hand back, until it rests in the corner of the mouth. This is a constant position and is called the high anchor, which is favored by many hunters. With the finger in the corner of the mouth, you have one problem solved, but where do you get the front sight or reference? The tip of the arrow, either a target tip or a field point, will act as your front reference. Place the tip of the arrow on the center of the target, relax the right hand and let the arrow go. Hopefully, it will hit the center of the target.

Although relatively simple, for the beginner it can be a rather complicated procedure. The first problem will be the

Former movie Tarzan Jock Mahoney was introduced to the sport of archery through portraying the lengendary hunter on the screen, and maintains a high degree of enthusiasm for the sport.

arrow wanting to come off the arrow rest of the bow as you draw back. This comes from an unconscious action of the thumb trying to get into the act. Fold the thumb back into the palm of the hand and forget it. If you have too heavy a draw weight in your practice bow, the left hand and shoulder will shake, as well as the right, as you come to draw. This will cause you to want to turn the arrow loose when you get the arrow back to the corner of the mouth before you have steadied down on the target. This action causes you to flinch and pull the arrow off target, releasing the arrow before you are ready. This is called snap shooting and is a difficult habit to break.

If snap shooting becomes a problem with you, the best remedy is a lighter bow. If you feel you can't afford to buy another one, then borrow one to practice with, until your muscles build up to the point where you can hold and shoot the heavier bow properly.

This heavy bow problem, perhaps one of the greatest pitfalls for a beginning archer, is termed being "over-bowed." It forms bad habits that are difficult to correct since you can't hold the bow properly at a draw, even to learn the basic principles. The beginner is better off doing it

Equipment for small game hunting is minimal; single bow, pocket quiver and comfortable attire. Essentials magnify for big game hunting, but for practice the simplified approach is just fine.

Style and shooting techniques used by bowhunters vary from the more traditional vertical draw to the canted form being demonstrated by these archers during a practice session.

the easier way by learning the basics with a light bow, then going on to the heavier bow as he becomes more proficient.

One of the big mistakes that a novice often makes is allowing himself to be conned into the old bit that it takes a man to pull and shoot the heavy bow. There are some mighty small women who have made grown men shudder when they pulled, held and shot a heavy bow with deadly accuracy. They were able to do this not because they were

any stronger than the men, but because they had practiced until their shoulder muscles were better developed.

There is a story of a hunter who ordered a seventy-five-pound bow for the coming season. When it arrived, there wasn't a man in the shop who could pull and hold it. A young lady from the college archery class stepped forward and asked if she could try. With grins, the men told her to go ahead and handed over the bow. She pulled, held the heavy hunter at full draw, let it down and placed it back on the counter. It wasn't strength that pulled that bow as much as it was the girl's knowledge of how to pull it.

Hopefully, by the time you finish this book, you too will have that knowledge.

CHAPTER 2

AFTER THE BEGINNING archer has served his apprenticeship, hopefully conquering his initial faults and problems, he should move into the stage known as the advanced bowhunter. The advanced bowhunter is easy to spot in a crowd of archers or hunters. He handles his equipment with confident ease and more often than not, when he returns from the field, he has his game.

However, to reach this peak of proficiency, the advanced bowhunter has spent many hours practicing on bales and trying out his skills in the field. He also has spent endless hours testing equipment and has settled on one bow with the best draw weight for his individual style of shooting. His other equipment — or tackle, as it is called in archery terminology — has been selected with just as much care.

The one outstanding characteristic of an advanced bowhunter that sets him apart from the midrange archers is that he knows, not thinks, that he can hit a target of paper or an elusive game animal at a normal range.

However, it is most apparent that he has that certain quality that cannot be bought, but only comes with

the ADVANCED Bowhunter

Achieving The Skills Which Separate The Expert From The Neophyte.

Seemingly open terrain is deceiving, as archer is drawing on bird partially hidden in the bush on the opposite side of the bank. Kneeling position assumed by bowhunter will allow arrow to pass under limbs of tree on its flight to target.

practice, experience and knowledge. He not only knows archery, but he also has read of and studied game animals and their habits.

Reading is a great source of information, not only for the individual who wants to become a successful bowhunter, but for anyone undertaking any type of endeavor. However, nothing compares to actual practice and application in the field. You can read volumes on bowhunting and become knowledgeable, but first-hand knowledge gained in the field is what separates wisdom from general knowledge. The only way to become an advanced bowhunter is to hunt; no other way is possible.

Not only is the advanced bowhunter relaxed and confident with his tackle, he is curious. He is forever reading about and testing new products and ideas in the field of archery. He follows developments in his hunting areas as to available feed or possible closures due to fire hazards. He expands his field to include more than just the physical task of releasing an arrow at a game animal.

The true bowhunter not only has selected a bow that is comfortable for him to shoot all day, if necessary, but he is thoroughly familar with the cast, speed and the amount of elevation needed for different ranges. He will have selected a type of arrow material that he has determined after many hours of testing to be the best suited for his individual needs. The fletch or feathers on his arrows will be of a color that appeals to him for one of many reasons. Perhaps the color is easier for him to follow in flight or it is mottled to be less conspicuous in the field. He has tested and settled on the type of material for the fletch, turkey feathers or plastic vanes. This choice is primarily a matter of personal preference and only the individual bowhunter can determine what is best for him. He also will have determined whether he wants a right or left-wing fletch, spiral or helical and can tell you why he has made this choice.

Surprisingly, more archers qualify in the advanced bowhunting stage than the beginning archer might imagine. In fact, there are probably more advanced bowhunters than target archers. True, many of these hunters are also target archers, giving overlapping statistics, but if one were to compare the number of hunting licenses issued and the number of registered target archers, chances are there would be more hunters.

The tackle of an advanced bowhunter will indicate whether he is high or low in experience. If his bow is painted and mottled for camouflage, chances are he is a serious hunter. Many less experienced hunters are hesitant to paint a beautifully finished bow, so will use glare-preventing socks instead. However, sooner or later, if they stick with the sport, they will paint the limbs and riser after spooking one or two trophy bucks.

Experienced bowhunters prefer the bow quiver. This type of quiver comes in many shapes, sizes and capacities. The average quiver used most often by hunters will carry around eight arrows and will be the type that protects the tips or broadheads. The true bowhunter will prefer to shoot broadheads rather than field or target points. When practicing, he usually will use only those ranges and tournaments that allow this. In fact, there are those who will pass up a good tournament if not allowed to use broadheads.

Clothing of an advanced bowhunter will also reflect his sport. In many cases the bowhunter will go so far as to test materials on his own, since most camouflaged clothing on the market is designed with the rifle hunter in mind with a floppy sleeve on the bow hand or pockets that catch the

Game has a way of making an appearance when least expected and the advanced bowhunter is one who is capable of shooting from the most awkward of positions; such as this archer who immediately stopped in the act of stepping over a log to silently and quickly come to full draw and proper hold before releasing the arrow.

string on release of the arrow. Most bowhunters will come up with a combination of clothing of personal design that is specifically for bowhunting.

The best way for a hunter to improve his skills before actually going after the big game is to practice shooting rabbits, prairie dogs and other small varmints with a light bow. These usually are pests and, if you approach the farmer or rancher in the right way, he may prove happy to have you come on his property to practice. Many farmers and ranchers are hesitant to allow rifle hunters on their property for fear of accidental shooting of livestock. However, few object to the bowhunter and are even happy to have help in eliminating the pesky varmints.

There are many frustrating aspects to bowhunting and one of them is retrieving discharged arrows. It makes little difference whether they are the cheaper cedar shafts or the more expensive aluminum or fiberglass. Unless you have an unlimited source of funds, bowhunting can become a rather expensive pastime, if you lose too many arrows. In fact, the beginning hunter may find himself spending more time hunting arrows than game, until he gets the knack of watching the path of the arrow in flight. The best method for keeping track of an arrow is to watch its flight path and look for landmarks. Distinctive colored shafts or fletches

Hunting from tree stands is a popular preference of bowhunters throughout the Midwest and on the East Coast; another approach in which ability to handle the bow in various positions and at odd angles, plus learning to shoot down on game with accuracy, is important.

Shooting positions are not always the simple vertical styles used in target practice. The bowhunter must learn to shoot from positions that occasionally cramp the style, but produce results.

The scrub oak and quaking aspen area of Colorado offers prime deer country for the experienced bowhunter who takes advantage of the natural cover which is particularly appealing to deer.

also help. However, these also can spook the animal, so many hunters will not use this method.

As mentioned earlier, books often will save one time and money, as well as help increase his knowledge, but only by getting into the field and shooting at game will one become experienced in judging range, wind velocity, drift and all the other variables that must be taken into consideration in bowhunting. The beginner likely will miss more times than hit. However, one day he will start to hit more often than miss and he will know that he has moved up to the advanced bowhunter category.

After many sessions and months in local fields shooting

Just getting the bow and body through some hunting areas can be somewhat of a problem. South Texas (right) features wide variety of brushy areas intermingled with cactus. Deer seldom enter the bottom of washes and draws (below).

This hunter would have been wiser to move toward the distant quaking aspens using the cover of the oaks on the right. When moving into open spaces like this, the advantage is all on the deer's side; they can see the hunter, so the hunter never sees them!

Sparse natural cover makes hunting in rim rock country of West Texas especially challenging. Advanced bowhunters stay back from edge of rim, then move up cautiously to look over and check for game.

Plaid-shirted bowhunter, with arrow in nocked position, gingerly picks his way through a dense thicket in the Colorado scrub oak country. If camouflaged attire is not available, dress in clothing which resembles in color the surrounding hunting area.

Rugged sections of Arizona like this are haven for javelina as well as mule deer. Making one's way through this type terrain without being spotted by game necessitates picking a route along the brush or tree lines.

at small game, the beginning bowhunter begins to think big. He will begin to eye the bigger game and become anxious to get out and try his hand with these animals. The most-hunted large game animal in the United States is the deer, which comes in many sizes and types. The East Coast and Southern states offer the whitetail, while the Western states have both whitetail and mule deer. On the West Coast there are also blacktails, along with the other two types. A few other types such as the Coues deer of Texas and Arizona are good game for the bowhunter, but for the most part it

is the whitetail and the mule deer that draw the most from bowhunters.

If you are fortunate enough to live in an area that offers game hunting, it is simple to set up a hunting trip. However, for those who don't, part of the fun is traveling to a new area where game is plentiful and hunting is allowed. Finding a new place that offers good hunting, good campsites and possibly a good trout stream is all part of the enjoyment of bowhunting.

Locating a good hunting spot is one area where the

Maneuvering through loose rocks and shale-covered hillsides and draws, where game is likely to be found, poses the additional aspect of spooking game with noise.

More often than not, it is when the bowhunter finds himself in a position like this that the particular game he is after makes its appearance. But, it's all a part of this exciting sport.

Somewhat humorously called the "Texas crouch," it's the only way to move through the low brush country in parts of the large Southwestern state; a favorite of bowhunters.

converted rifle hunter may have an advantage over the novice who has never hunted at all. Most rifle hunters already will have at least one favorite hunting spot where they know there are some good bucks. However, there is a problem. Most archery hunting seasons open before the rifle season, usually in the early Fall months of August and September. Many of the mule deer that the rifle hunter is used to seeing in an area are there because the area is a Winter feeding range — big bucks are not yet there during the months of August and September. This is just one more

Larger bush at right is a Junco (Crucifixion Thorn), a great place for pigs, but certainly no place for a bowhunter to attempt moving through. Procedure for hunting in country like this involves finding a trail and waiting out the game, while fellow bowhunters try to flush the porkers from the impenetrable brush.

A double pleasure is available to those bowhunters who also enjoy wetting a line. While waiting for game to make its appearance at a watering hole, this nimrod has broken out a telescoping rod to pass the time.

piece of information that comes with experience.

The whitetail deer, as another example, lives an entire lifetime within a small radius of several miles of where he is born. Only man encroaching with development or a blight of forage will force the whitetail to change his location. This is an advantage to the hunter, except that these critters love heavy brush and downed timber where they can hide. Moving through heavy brush with a bow is a problem in itself and trying to do so with little or no noise makes it even more difficult.

Trying to shoot a bow in heavy brush is still another problem the bowhunter has to overcome. In heavy brush, stand hunting from a tree or a blind can be an advantage; however, it's up to the individual hunter. Some will prefer to sit and wait, while others walk their game down. The advanced bowhunter will know the odds in favor of either technique. He has spent many hours studying the habits of game animals and will put this knowledge to use in the field.

The advanced bowhunter has learned the problems of his

sport, mastered or overcome most of them, then has proceeded to new ones and found solutions to these as well.

Once he has mastered the technical problems connected with his bow and equipment, the bowhunter has the problem of finding his game. This only comes with time and practice. There is that lucky hunter who walks into an area on opening day, stumbles across a big buck or whatever other type of game he is seeking, places his arrow with deadly accuracy and heads home with a trophy only after a few hours of hunting. It does happen and there is nothing to explain why except that he happened to be in the right

place at the right time and had the skill to place the shaft where he wanted it.

However, this type of luck is the exception, rather than the rule. This same lucky hunter may spend years in the field before he gets another game animal to his credit.

There is a certain amount of luck associated with any sport, but the advanced bowhunter trusts luck less than his own personal skill. He knows that luck is fickle and prefers skill and knowledge as his hunting companions. He leaves luck to the beginner or the less serious hunter.

Here is what all the toil and trouble is about: the game animal. Known as the collared peccary, this toothy critter is more commonly called the javelina, one of the smallest animals in the big game series.

THE TROPHY HUNTER is yet another category of bowhunter. In every sport, there is the ultimate plateau, the top of the list and that is where the trophy hunter belongs in the field of bowhunting.

This is an individual who is almost always successful in getting his quota of game animals. He has studied the art of hunting and bow marksmanship, until he is a true professional in both lines. He has finely tuned equipment and could drive nails with it, if that were needed. He has something just a bit beyond the advanced hunter in bow skills and, when he shoots, he normally finds his target.

There is nothing to equal the thrill and exhilaration of bagging the first deer or other large game animal with a bow and arrow. This and the thrill of the chase is what bowhunting is all about. As you progress in your skills and become successful at normal game hunting, chances are you will not become bored with the sport, but you will begin to strive for bigger and bigger game. When we mention bigger game, we are not speaking of a larger species of animal, but larger individual members of the species you are hunting. Hopefully, you will one day bag that really big one, the trophy animal.

CHAPTER 3

The TROPHY Bowhunter

The Challenge Of Bagging The Best Of A Species; And What It Takes!

Beto Gutierrez displays the tusks of his Texas-killed javelina. One of the most difficult specimens to collect with a bow because of dense foliage the javelina calls home, any hunter can be well satisfied with such a pig.

Bowen Weems can be justly proud of the Corsican ram he bagged with a single arrow while shooting on a preserve in northern New Mexico.

The definition of a trophy has many interpretations. To target archers it may be a marble or bronze plaque or cup. To the bowhunter, however, the trophy animal is the biggest ever recorded of that species. For deer this would be the largest in the several different deer categories. They are also broken down into categories of natural and nontypical trophies. The natural would be that deer that has the biggest measurements as judged by the Pope & Young Club, the bowhunter's equivalent to the rifleman's Boone & Crockett Club.

These are what many call buster bucks, big daddies or other terms used by hunters to describe the oldtimers who have outwitted all hunters, both bow and rifle, for many years. These bucks don't become trophies by being careless and to garner one, the hunter must work harder, go higher into the wilds and use the ultimate in technique.

Where do these big bucks roam and hide during the hunting season? Trophy mule deer often can be found high above the timberline where they have almost unlimited vision to all approaches to their hiding place. For the hunter to get close to these big bucks it takes a great deal of skill. By close enough, I mean fifty yards or less. Be closer if possible, but they are pretty wily creatures and don't allow just anyone to blunder across them.

Whenever there is a mention of a large buck, there will always be someone who has seen or knows where such a monster is hiding. The difference between the talker and a trophy hunter is that the latter listens, files the material away for future reference and often checks out the rumor. A truly serious trophy hunter will go to any altitude, any area, if he feels there is a chance of bagging the buck that will take over the Number One position on the trophy lists.

Many feel they don't live in an area where there are any trophy animals. However, you never know. A trophy white-

Left: Guide Jack Niles inspects the razor-sharp tusks of his Texas javelina. Bowhunters must make the first shot count, as wild pigs may charge attempting to make escape.

Charlie Farmer nailed this fine Arizona javelina, which also favors dense brush. Note spiked growth behind hunter.

Bearded author poses with downed fork horn muley taken in Colorado at a distance of twenty yards. Antlers still have velvet covering (above).

While the forkie isn't of trophy standards, it satisfied author's meat requirements — one of toughest bowhunting decisions. Here he drags the gutted carcass to a road.

Testament of the whitetail's wiliness has come from many lips, and bagging one is a supreme achievement. While Curt McClanahan's four-point won't set any records, he will be good table fare and the source of many memories.

tail was killed behind a barn in Iowa after having fed in the farmer's cornfields for years.

A good way to find an area where the trophies dwell is to work with an experienced hunting guide. They are not hard to find, since a guide who has helped a hunter bag a trophy animal uses this as good publicity for attracting other hunters. Sometimes these individuals can be expen-sive, but their price is sometimes well worth it, if you bag that really big one.

Trophy hunting isn't easy. The beginning bowhunter may have thought it difficult bagging that first deer and chances are it was, but when he starts for trophies, he is opening up new vistas to explore. Many hunters don't feel it necessary to carry optics in the field when deer hunting.

However, a hunter looking for trophies would be wise to invest in a good pair of field optics. The average hunter looking only for a deer may not need optics, since he can normally see a herd of muleys on a hillside without them. He then can calculate the wind, determine the feeding path and intercept their line of progress. Chances are that he will get his deer.

However, the trophy hunter wants to know if there is a trophy animal in the herd or one slightly over the hill. With optics he can determine this much easier. Many trophy hunters will carry a spotting scope of high magnification so that he can actually count the tines on a buck's rack. This piece of equipment weighs little and should be one of the first items added to the serious trophy hunter's gear. Otherwise, the normal archery tackle used for any other type of hunting is adequate for trophy hunting. The ultimate factor in whether or not you bag that trophy is, of course, your ability to use that tackle.

In states where it is legal, many bowhunters will pass up shots at bucks to bag a fat, barren doe. Some claim that during the rut the buck's meat is tainted. Author likes all venison, and took this plump doe in the low areas surrounding New Mexico's Sandia Mountain Range.

New Mexico's long hunting season paid off for Jack McDowell (right), who gets an assist from Doug McGraw in dragging out a fair-sized forkie taken near the Sandia Range (above).

McDowell (below) poses with his muley just prior to having tags validated by in-the-field game warden who drove up. Bowhunting in snow calls for warm, appropriately colored clothing like the white overshirt hunter is wearing. Insulated, waterproof boots also are nice!

A New Mexico preserve provided the Corsican ram taken by author during a period when no bow seasons were open for other game. Preserve hunting is growing in popularity among bowhunters, who pay for their kill but sharpen their skills for upcoming deer and bear hunting sessions.

One other factor that enters into whether a trophy hunter is successful is his physical fitness. One certainly can't go after trophy mule deer at 12,000 feet when fifty pounds overweight. A trophy hunter must be in good condition physically and he must also have endurance. Sometimes a trophy hunter may find that he has to camp out overnight with very little shelter in order to stay with the animal he is tracking. Since trophy animals don't stay around road areas as do some deer, many trophy hunters will invest in a complete backpacking outfit. This allows them to go anywhere that the game may lead them without having to worry about shelter and other supplies necessary for survival in the field.

However, many other bowhunters are perfectly satisfied with the regular hunting method of setting up camp and hunting from it. Many times one will be successful with this method and may even be fortunate to bag a trophy, but the chances are quite slim.

A beginner may scoff at the idea of putting forty or fifty pounds on his back in addition to his archery tackle and

Texas whitetail don't get as large as their Eastern cousins, as demonstrated by this hunter's over-the-shoulder packing, but are just as wily and perhaps more delicious after feeding on pecans and acorns.

setting off for high country. However, to find the really big trophies, a hunter has to get off the beaten track and away from other hunters.

Trophy hunting requires more work in all areas. The trophy hunter must know the area that he plans to hunt and must be able to get off the beaten track to find the big ones. In order to do this, he must be in top physical condition, which takes extra effort on his part. Perhaps he may not have hills or mountains around his home where he can practice hiking, but something as small as running up stairs instead of walking or taking the stairs instead of the elevator helps condition him for the field.

The mule deer is one of the most hunted game animals by the average, advanced and trophy hunter. However, many bowhunters who have bagged innumerable species of game will state that they feel the most sought and highly prized game animal to add to the list is the whitetail deer. These are found just about all over the United States, except for sections of the Southwest. They are different

The end of the dreamed-about hunt: Two Texas bowhunters dragging fine whitetails back to camp after a successful morning hunt. Camo clothes and patience are key needs.

from the mule deer and are definitely more difficult to hunt due to their habits and keen senses. It takes time, patience and skill to bag any game animal, but the whitetail ranks high in most hunters' books as one of the most challenging species.

There is an unending list of other animals, any of which can and do fall into the trophy category. Included are the black, brown and grizzly bear; elk; moose; caribou and many more. To take a trophy in any category, one must work harder and longer than he would to just get game of any type to fill the tags.

The trophy hunter begins to think like the animal he

A camo-clad hunter blends into the shadows where Texas whitetail bucks and does hang at an outlying camp. Such good luck is rare, but indicates much study and bowhunting skill.

Trying to make like a feathery clump of leaves, this guinea fowl is just seconds away from the stewpot. Archers should practice such shots to be ready in field.

Wing shooting at exploding fowl can really sharpen bowhunting skills and is a fine way to spend Summer dog-days. After losing many arrows, hunters will watch arrow flight, which helps later when after game like deer or bear.

hunts. He studies their habits, observes them from a distance to see how they move, when they move and how often they move. He actually becomes a specialist in the game he decides to hunt. This is above his proven ability as an archer.

If we were to describe a trophy bowhunter, we would have to say that he is the true professional of the bowhunting fraternity. He is the star of the sport and has obtained accolades for his achievements, not only from the general public, but from his own kind. There can be no higher gratification than to be rated among these expert hunters and marksmen.

If you are a beginner, you may never become a trophy hunter and, in fact, you may never even meet one personal-

Hunting from horseback can be different, a practice which sometimes even results in downed game. However, before embarking on the horse, bowhunter should ascertain whether it is even possible, or he may end up walking back to camp! Some horses will spook at the bow's twang.

Whitetail does take after their antlered counterparts in the wiliness department, especially after being shot at a few times. Author ears a doe that will hang on meatpole.

ly. However, if you stay with this challenging sport, the chances are one day you will begin to strive to place yourself in this elite group of bowmen. There are many things that money can buy, but a trophy animal is not one nor is the status of recognized trophy hunter.

One must get out and work and this work starts with the beginner who diligently practices until he has mastered his sport, hoping that one day he will reach the rank of trophy hunter. This is the top, the ultimate in bowhunting and it only comes with practice, hard work and patience.

Author filled half of his either-sex tag with this New Mexico mule deer doe. After hitting her, author spent time following blood trail, until coming upon dead carcass (left). Bowhunters need skill in this area.

bow bets for DISTAFFERS

If You Think Bowhunting Is Too Tough For The Light Of Your Life, Look To Your Laurels!

BOWHUNTING CERTAINLY IS not the exclusive sport of men and, in fact, the supposedly weaker sex often has proved herself better in the field than her male counterparts. There has been more than one chagrined male who has come home empty-handed, while his wife or girlfriend has bagged herself a nice buck.

The only possible limitation for female bowhunters is that a few states require a certain minimum bow draw weight of forty pounds or more. For the beginning distaff hunter, this sometimes can prove a little heavy, but for most, a little practice and muscle toning will overcome this handicap. Almost all states require that a hunting bow be able to shoot a prescribed distance, so the beginner, whether male or female, needs to practice with a lighter bow before taking to the fields with a heavier hunting bow.

A word of warning to those males who may be slightly thin-skinned: If your ego is such that it may be damaged by being outhunted by a female, then it's probably best that you and your female companion join a mixed bowling league instead of taking up bowhunting. There is bound to come a time when she may bag a bigger buck than you!

Surprisingly, women have several factors in their favor when it comes to hunting. For one thing, most are not as anxious to see "what lies over the hill." They have the patience to sit on a stand in a blind and wait for the game to come to them. Most men begin to fidget, move and, sooner or later, give up the blind and do some wandering. Many women also have the ability to move through the timber and hills slowly and quietly, whereas a man — in his impatience — may be noisier in his movements.

To be good hunters, women have to forego certain niceties in the field. For example, they should avoid wearing perfume and hair spray while hunting. It may seem a minor matter, but the odor of these products is not a normal woods smell and often will spook the game if worn. However, women who like bowhunting — and there are many — gladly give up these frills for the fun and excitement of the hunt.

One disadvantage that women have is that, when they do down a buck, they do not have the strength to lift it and pack it back to the camp. However, most women hunters are accompanied by male companions or a guide, so this doesn't present too major a handicap. When it comes to field dressing, they do as well, if not better, than many men.

Many women hesitate to go on a hunting trip with a bunch of men, because they feel they might be saddled with the cooking and washing of the dishes, but this doesn't need to be the case. When a woman goes along on a hunting trip, she should share the chores, including cooking and dishes, with the rest of the party. If she weren't there, the men would take turns with these tasks and the same should apply when there is a woman in the party. She is there to hunt as well as the men and should not be saddled with all the dirty chores around camp. However, if she enjoys roughing it and cooking out over the fire, that's another matter. Most women can whip up a meal that is a real welcome change to the usual deer camp fare.

When it comes to handling the bow, women are just as deadly as many male hunters. It's a known fact that when a woman gets fired up about something, she will attack the project with much zeal. Bowhunting is no exception. Women who take up bowhunting practice just as much and learn the proper procedures as well as men.

Many husband and wife teams have been successful in garnering their share of big game. They work as well as a team in camp and in the field as they do at home. One advantage to a team like this is that they never have to worry about a hunting partner, since most of the time they are free to hunt at the same time.

A good way to introduce your wife or girlfriend to bowhunting is to take her on a carp shoot sometime. This is an easy way to get her started and once hooked, you'll have a hunting partner for life. Carp bowhunting is relatively easy and gives a beginning bowhunter excellent practice.

When hunting with any new bowhunter, one should insure that the individual has some knowledge of map and compass reading. This is especially important when taking a woman along for the first time, since often she will not have the experience in the field that a man may have. It is

CHAPTER 4

Raccoon treed by hound dogs proves to be elusive target for author's wife, but she scores successful shot.

wise to hunt together for the first few days, until she has learned the area and has built up her confidence in finding her way with a map and compass. This holds true with any beginner. Proper precaution is always good hunting policy.

So far, the ladies haven't taken any trophy animals to move men off the trophy lists. However, the day soon may come since many more women are taking to the fields with bow in hand.

One who already well knows the frustrations and rewards of bowhunting is Midge Dandridge, who recalls a certain black bear hunt, as related here in her own words:

I tried to match the snow-tracking pace of my guide, Ed Vance, but I couldn't come close. At each step I broke through frozen crust and was nearing exhaustion. Vance, who told me to follow his tracks, was far ahead of me. I could barely hear the sound of his hounds in the distance.

We had been trying to get together for a bear hunt for months. The prime time to hunt black bear in the areas he prefers is at the beginning of the season, but delays kept holding us up. My husband, Holt, and I refrained from heading out for the Glennville, California, home of Ed and Mary Vance, until a hurried call about a cattle-killing bear hastened us.

Vance said we would hunt on a few local ranches where the killer bear had been reported, so we loaded our gear into his truck and watched as he loaded his hounds into the specially designed box on the back of his pickup. Most of the dogs were blue ticks and in beautiful condition.

We spent all that day and part of the next looking. We found the bear's tracks and set the dogs out, but after a few hours of fruitless tracking we gave up for the day. The next afternoon, as we drove the many miles to our destination, Vance kept us entertained with wild stories of his hunts. One of his best tales involved a lady hunter who shot and wounded her bear. To his dismay, he discovered that the shells to his gun were in his jacket at the truck and his huntress had lost hers out of her shirt pocket. As the story goes, he ended up by killing the bear with his knife.

We found tracks where a bear had headed up a steep hill and when the dogs got a whiff of the scent, they

Flanked by dog handlers, successful and serious-faced distaff bowhunter lugs out raccoon trophy personally.

immediately started to howl and take off. We listened carefully, but finally couldn't hear them anymore. Vance decided they'd gone over the top, so we started up the mountain, and I mean up the mountain! As I gasped for breath during one of my frequent stops, I wheezed something about never knowing that bears were such good mountain climbers and was assured they can make it up the steepest hill with little effort.

After hiking for some time, we still couldn't hear the dogs, so we decided to go back to the pickup. We drove to another point and could just hear their faint sounds. Suddenly, we heard a dog from a different direction, which Vance readily identified as Mindy, off on another track and lost from the others.

Mindy was a 10-month-old pup on her first bear hunt. We started through the forest looking for her, but after an hour's time could no longer hear her, so we headed after the other dogs, leaving one of Vance's jackets at the spot where we had let Mindy out of the truck. A dog usually will return to the original area it started from and if you leave an item of clothing with the owner's scent, it will stay there and your chances of finding him are good.

We could hear the other dogs clearly now, and Vance said they definitely were on the trail of a bear, a mean bear, and we were gonna have trouble. Sure enough, his prediction came true. We hiked for endless hours and miles. When we seemed to be getting close, the sound would start to move again, indicating the bear had not treed but was fight-

ing the dogs on the ground, then moving off. We were beginning to worry about the condition of the dogs. It had been many miles since we started after them but they sounded like they weren't going to give up. Finally Vance told us to head back to the truck. He was going to see if he could get the dogs back, but couldn't catch up and arrived back at the truck without them.

We stopped at a lodge to call his wife, who had just received a phone call from a woman who found the dogs four miles away. When we arrived, the dogs all greeted us happily, although one female redbone had been chewed on her hind legs.

We decided to go back to the house and get a good night's rest before starting out again early the next morning to look for Mindy and try to pick up the bear's trail.

When I had first brought my archery gear into the house, Vance was quite interested in it. I was to be his first woman bowhunter, so he wanted to make sure I had all the right equipment. After examining my Jennings Compound bow, he remarked that he'd had some hunters use this particular bow on bear and lion with no trouble getting their game. My compound was cranked up to forty-five pounds.

A friend of mine had reworked some of my Pearson-Easton aluminum arrows. The 2016 shafts would have plenty of knock-down power. For broadheads I went to see Hugh Rich, whose archery store has been in Glendale for thirty-nine years. He suggested I use the durable and reliable two-blade, Black Diamond Delta broadheads. I put in many an hour with a file on those heads and they were sharp enough to shave the hair off your arm. I am a firm believer that the most important item in your bowhunting equipment is a sharp broadhead.

The next morning there wasn't much conversation on our way out. Everyone was concerned about Mindy, but our grim faces turned to smiles as we drove up and saw her lying on Vance's jacket. She jumped up wagging her tail with joy, none the worse for wear from her overnight outing.

We then went to where we had seen tracks the day before and drove down the dirt road, passing a few deer hunters on the way, soon spotting a track Vance thought was just minutes old.

Vance put the dogs on the track and they immediately took off in hot pursuit. We watched as they zigged and zagged through the trees, following the path of the bear. They topped the far ridge and we listened. Suddenly, they came back over. They had split. One of Vance's best dogs, Sue, was going one way and the rest of the pack another. Figuring they must be after two different bears, Vance jumped into the truck to try and head off the pack while we tried to keep tabs on Sue.

As Holt and I stood watching across a large ravine, we could hear Sue's howl clearly. Then we heard two rifle shots. I'm a gun hunter myself, but it sure made me nervous standing out there in the open listening to someone fire a gun.

A few minutes later Vance came back, and we told him about hearing the rifle shots. Another loud shot went off a

Ed Vance loads hounds — mostly blue ticks — into special-built carrier on rear of his pickup truck.

After long, up-and-down-hill chase in sub-freezing weather, wily bear finally is brought to tree by dogs.

few yards away and Vance told us to stay put while he went to investigate. In a few minutes we could hear him talking to someone and breathed a sigh of relief when we heard him call Sue and put her in the truck. He drove the truck back, jerked it to a stop, got out and slammed the door as he told us a deer hunter had just shot my bear — a big record class one, too! I was bitterly disappointed, even more so when Vance said the deer hunter reported he didn't see or hear any dogs, although Sue was standing over the bear's carcass when he got there.

The news wasn't all bad, though. Vance told us the other dogs had picked up the trail of the same mean bear they were onto yesterday. He had recognized its track and from all indications, it didn't show any signs of treeing. As we took off to try and find the dogs before they got too deep in the woods, Vance explained that occasionally you run into a bear that won't tree, making it rough on the dogs and hunter. Usually young bears act this way, and they often tear good dogs to pieces.

We managed to cut the dogs' trail and in a couple of

hours had them safely in their box on the back of the truck.

After we told our hard luck story to his wife, Mary, that evening, we wishfully decided that our bad luck was gone and we'd get a bear the next day. Mother Nature postponed our activities for a couple of days with rain and snow.

After the storm we hunted futilely for two more days. On our last afternoon Vance drove to another spot to check the area for tracks and we found two separate, fresh sets. Knowing how badly I wanted a bear and because of the bad weather we had encountered and the unfortunate incident with the deer hunter, Vance invited me back for the following weekend, noting we'd hunt this area where we had found the fresh tracks.

When I arrived the following weekend, Vance was working on a new snowmobile. Because lion hunting has been closed in California for several years, Vance goes to Nevada to guide mountain lion hunts in the Winter. The heavy snows there make it impossible to drive through the back country, so the snowmobiles are used to drive back roads looking for lion tracks. When tracks are found, the dogs are released from their box which is pulled behind the snowmobile. The hunter and guide then make their way through the snow on foot, because it is against the law to pursue any game with the snowmobile. We planned to use the same strategy for local bruins.

Vance said it had snowed quite heavily in the area that we planned to hunt, so we were taking the snowmobiles along in case we couldn't get the truck through the back roads. That evening I applied an extra thick coating of sno-seal to my Red Wing Hunter boots.

The next morning was bitterly cold. The wind bit and

A good guide is especially appreciated by the ladies, particularly when it comes to packing out trophy enroute to taxidermist.

Male bowhunters — who had not even seen one — gather 'round to admire Midge Dandridge's black bear trophy.

stung our ears and faces. I popped on my ski cap and turned the truck heater up another notch as we made our way to the predetermined hunting spot. The area was fresh with new snow, but the freezing temperature had frozen the crust and we knew it wouldn't be an easy task finding fresh tracks and making our way in the knee-deep drifts. The snow was not too deep on the roads and the snowmobiles were not needed.

We drove for hours, straining our eyes for sign before Vance spotted a fairly fresh track. Flipper and Sue, his two best dogs, were released and they took off immediately. Within minutes they had picked up the track and we could hear their excited howls as they began the chase. The rest of the dogs were released and soon we could hear them all, hot on the bear's trail.

Then began our trial of tramping through the snow in pursuit of the wily bruin. Off we went, with Vance far ahead and me in what is laughingly referred to as hot pursuit. After some time, I found I was following not only Vance's track, but ones belonging to the dogs and the bear. There was blood on the snow from the dog's feet and the bear's, too.

Finally, after hiking up canyons and over countless ridges, Vance emerged over the one I was struggling to conquer and made the announcement that the dogs had treed the bear. When I arrived at the top, he pointed down below us a few hundred yards away, explaining the dogs and bear had taken us for miles in a semi-circle, the bear finally going to tree several hundred yards from another

part of the road. He suggested we hike back to the truck and drive over there.

All I could do was nod. The cold air stung my lungs and had nearly frozen my fingers on the hand that held my bow. Returning to the truck would give me an opportunity to thaw out a bit before I had to do the shooting.

When we reached the area, Vance cautioned me not to alarm the bear anymore than he was already. My excitement was high now that I was nearing the apex of the long hunt, and I was anxious to see what the tree held. We approached carefully and Vance pointed to my trophy high in the tree; an average bear with a good-looking dark brown coat. As Vance tied up the dogs, I moved into position to take my shot.

There was only one good angle, with lots of shadow, so when I released the arrow, it penetrated his left leg and angled into his stomach. The bear moved to the other side of the tree. I was nocking another arrow as I ran to the other side. I let fly with my second shot and hit a small branch. The arrow flipped up and landed on some branches in the huge pine tree. With that, the bear headed to the top of the tree.

Muttering some about the darn limb, I reached for another arrow as Vance motioned me down the hill and pointed to the top. I looked up to where he was pointing and saw a narrow space between two limbs, framing the perfect shot. I raised the bow, concentrated on the spot and released, scoring a perfect hit.

The bear spun around and started to fall. We watched

50

the branches break as he crashed through the tree. When he hit the ground he didn't move. Later examination showed that the second arrow had penetrated the liver and heart and he died instantly.

While we were filling out my tag we heard the dogs bark and, in turning, came face to face with a game warden; the first time in all the years I've hunted that I've run into one in the woods. He was accompanied by a wildlife biologist, and they had come over to investigate after hearing the dogs. They congratulated me on my success and the game warden validated my tag as Vance told them he thought my bear was extremely small bodied in relation to its head. It was obvious the bear would make the record book, but according to the head size it should have weighed fifty to seventy pounds more.

The game warden explained that the area had a bad crop of pinons and acorns and he thought the bear probably would not have survived the Winter. The Department of Fish and Game had trapped twenty bears in this area during the Summer and transferred them to other areas where the feed was more plentiful.

As I stood admiring my trophy, Vance pondered how I would go about telling my finally successful bear-hunt story. It's simple, I told him, all we have to do is start out by saying, "If at first you don't succeed...."

A second trophy of the bear-hunting expedition was this photo of a fawn, snapped by Midge Dandridge while scouting for sign.

Selecting The Proper Bow

This Most Basic Part Of Your Hunting Equipment Should Match Your Intentions, Capabilities And Pocketbook.

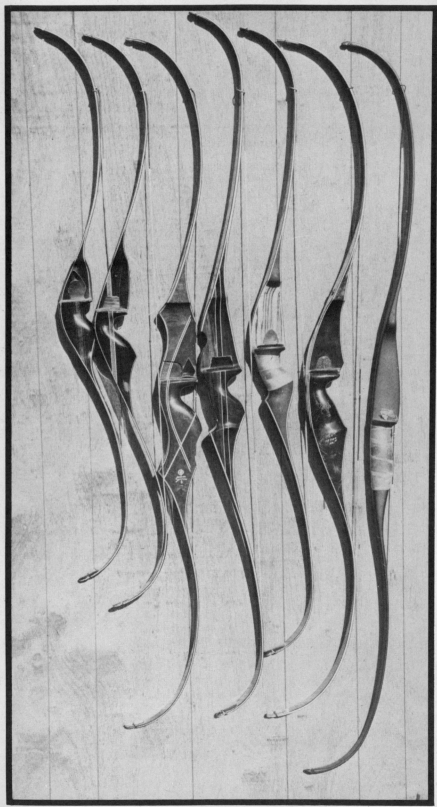

Don Gordon of Gordon Plastics checks fiberglass filaments as they are fed through grates in first production stage of Bo-Tuff, a unidirectional fiberglass used for laminated bows.

SINCE THE MOMENT a caveman bent a stick and tied the ends with a section of vine or hide, the bow has been undergoing variations in style, manufacture and design. The first practical models were the so-called self bows. These were carved from one section of yew or other suitable wood. They did cast an arrow but presented problems. They would become very stiff on cold days and very limber on hot days. This was something bowhunters lived with until the late 1940s.

During the WWII years, chemists developed a new material they named fiberglass. With certain modifications, this material adapted itself to the needs of the archer better than any other man-made or natural product had in the past. This was the advent of our modern laminated bow. Many variations of laminated bow designs were made centuries ago. The Turks, the Eskimos, the Chinese and Japanese all made laminated bows of different materials. The laminated bamboo bows still are a work of art, as are the Turkish bows.

The construction of a modern laminated bow is not extremely difficult, but it does require special equipment. Most of the bows made today are made in the same style from pretty much the same materials but with certain modifications in design to obtain a faster bow, perhaps a more rugged bow or whatever the manufacturer feels will appeal to the hunting archer.

The single-unit bow is made of laminated items, constructed to a certain length and will always be just that length unless you break it. These have been in the hunting field for many years and have several advantages.

The first advantage is the basic cost of the bow. The single-unit bows can be purchased from a low of about $30 to as high as you care to go. There is one on the market now at over $150.

What makes a bow cost a hundred dollars more than one that might look just like it from the beginner's viewpoint? There could be several factors involved. The first basic reason would be the type of materials used. If the bow is an

To construct a bow, the riser section is placed in the center, between long strips of hardrock maple laminates, which in turn are flanked by fiberglass. The thin sections are joined by using epoxy or other type of cement.

ultra-fancy model with hand carving in the riser, more for a collector than a bowhunter, it can and does cost more. The type materials used vary by manufacturer and are pretty much the same as far as the average bowhunter is concerned. There are technical details but that is more involved in the production systems rather than the shooting.

The laminated bow consists of a center riser section that can vary from the less expensive but excellent maple to exotic hardwoods imported from Africa, South America or India. These might include shedua, rosewood, bubinga or others of a continuing list.

The reason for the choice of woods is to change the

actual bow weight in the bowhunter's hand. Rosewoods are dense and heavy and weigh more. This would be for the hunter who likes the weight to keep him steady while holding on target. Others who prefer a lighter bow are happy with the less expensive maple risers.

Most modern bow manufacturing plants are similar. Each company has a process or a machine that saves time, increases the cast of the bow or makes it a better product. These trade or manufacturing processes could be classified as industrial secrets. They don't advertise the process and often won't allow any outsider to see it.

The riser is first rough cut on a bandsaw to a determined

bow model pattern. Next, it goes through a series of sanding machines that feather the edges down to a paper thin section as well as roughing in the basic shape of the handle. Some companies utilize specially designed sanders and carving machines to make each handle section have the exact same grip and weight, each duplicated and controlled by a master unit.

The riser is next joined with a backing of unidirectional fiberglass. This is a special type of fiberglass material designed for the bow manufacturer. You can buy fiberglass in single fine strands or in woven clothlike material. The woven variety will not allow the fiberglass to stretch under the pressures placed on them when the bow is pulled to full draw. The manufacture of the unidirectional fiberglass — the filaments run only the length of the material, not across as in woven fiberglass — is done basically for the bow companies.

After the fiberglass backing is on the boards, the next material added will be some sheets of finely sanded hardrock maple. This is nothing more than a spacer in the bow construction. The riser next is placed in the sandwich that is forming and on top of it is placed another section of the hardrock maple and the final layer of fiberglass facing. This sandwich is held together with special epoxies and the entire unit is glued up on a bench.

The lumpy looking mess is placed in a bow press where the basic shape of the bow will be formed. The press has controlled pressure and temperature and the unit is left there for a specified time.

After the curing process, the rough bow passes through many stages of hand and machine work until it emerges in the packing room where it is boxed and shipped.

The entire process requires special skills all along the way. Execution takes years of knowledge. For example, the thickness of the fiberglass used in the two sections — the back and face along with the thickness of the maple laminates — will determine the actual draw weight of the finished bow. A good bowyer will be able to measure the thickness of these units and know which thickness to use for a fifty-pound bow. A craftsman will come within one or possibly two pounds of the desired bow draw weight.

The most expensive part of any bow is the time it takes to make it, as time involves people. The most time-consuming step is the hand rubbing to impart the glossy finish to the wood.

There will be variations in the manufacturing process. One company may use a special epoxy glue for the laminated limbs. Another may improve the limb design. This is what makes one bow perform differently from another; limb design and construction. As a beginner, you will be

When the cement has been added, the bow is placed in a pressure/temperature-controlled unit for curing, which binds the components together solidly. The temperatures and pressures used are trade secrets of the bow companies.

interested mainly in draw weight and price. Later you will look for a thicker limb for rugged dependability or a thinner, narrower limb for speed. Maybe you will shop hoping to find one maker who puts a rugged limb on the bow that has speed, too — the ideal hunting bow.

After a few hunts — or when you really become serious — you no doubt will camouflage your bow by painting it. If you plan to paint it, buy a bow that is protected with an epoxy finish. This will save you some money because the bow doesn't require extra steps during production.

The idea is sound and has been tried by many of those who make bows for hunters. There have even been some made with the camo already on them; but here's what happened. The archers thought they might be buying a lower grade of bow and the maker had covered the flaws with the paint. This wasn't the case at all, but the idea fell like a punctured balloon and now the companies are content to make the usual bow with the high gloss finish at the same price where any archer can see what he is buying. He can paint it later if he so desires.

Regardless of the type of bow, they are still classified into two styles. The first is the older style longbow. Perhaps the best known still being made is the Howard Hill model utilizing laminated bamboo and fiberglass on a "straight stick" principle.

The modern recurve bow is the more popular and is readily available. The standard recurve bow has a straight handle or riser section with a hand grip in the center of the riser; the tips of the unstrung bow curve away from the handle, as you hold it. This recurve is where the modern bows gain their speed.

The term, stacking, may be heard, if someone is trying to nitpick at your tackle. If a bow stacks, it will draw smoothly, up to say twenty-six inches. To pull twenty-eight, you have to literally horse the bow back to get to full draw. This bow isn't comfortable to hold and, on release,

If the handle section also rises above the table at an angle, the bow is deflexed.

The deflex addition to the bows reduced, and in most cases eliminated, the stacking and kick on release common to some of the early laminated recurve models. When the riser is deflexed it also has a tendency to rob speed from the bow. The bowyer must arrive at a design that incorporates enough reflex on the limbs to give speed and just enough deflex in the riser to reduce the kick and stacking tendencies without robbing the essential speed factor. When you add one thing, you sacrifice another and a compromise usually is the answer.

While the semi-finished bow still is rough-looking, the tiller is checked by eye and with a ruler. Upper limb usually is deeper toward string than lower. If not, a skilled craftsman can tiller it to meet required specs.

tends to kick the bow arm. You may have a fast arrow, but continued shooting will be tiring and the kick on the arm will become annoying. Most bows today don't have this problem, as it was more common during the early development of the laminated recurved style.

To eliminate the stacking tendency of the bow and eliminate the kick in the bow arm, designers have deflexed the handle or riser section. To determine whether your bow has a reflex-deflex design all you need do is lay it out on a table, unstrung, with the tips or recurves facing up. If the handle is almost parallel with the table top, it isn't deflexed. This doesn't mean that it will necessarily stack or kick.

One basic factor to remember about the hunting bow: You won't shoot it several hundred times a day as you might a target bow. The hunter seldom takes a dozen shots in a day. You will shoot much more than this during practice sessions. If in shooting condition and the bow is right, you can shoot it on field courses all day, too.

Should you find a bow that has the speed you like but might kick a bit, maybe even stack during the last few inches, keep in mind that a few shots during a hunting trip are all that you will obtain normally. The main objective is to place that first shot in the vital area; that may be the only shot you take, if done right.

Some of the ultra-short bows, say in the forty-eight-inch length, are extremely deflexed. This adds to some extent in relieving the finger pinch that is hard to avoid with shorter bows. When you brace the ultra-shorties and place a shaft on the string, you may notice it appears almost half shot already.

The next idea that came out of the bowmakers' think factory was to make a bow that could be dismantled for

Prior to packaging the bows for shipping, the finished products are inspected for quality again, as each has been during the many phases of production. Sometimes even company presidents do it, like Bob Lee of Wing Archery (left)!

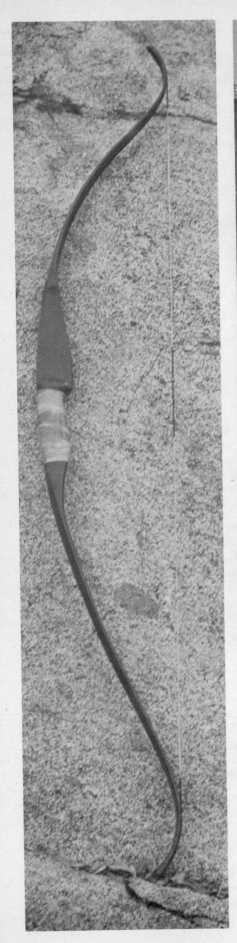

There have been many bow designs which never surfaced on the market, like this double-limb specimen dubbed the Tarantula (above). While the author confesses it did shoot, it never found its way to the shelves of dealers.

This ancient relic (left) is out of tiller. Note the distance between string and upper limb just above the riser, then compare with lower limb below the riser. Curves are radically different, and bow could break!

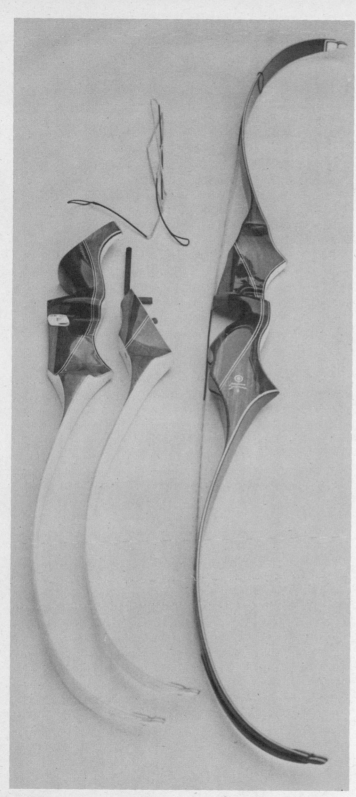

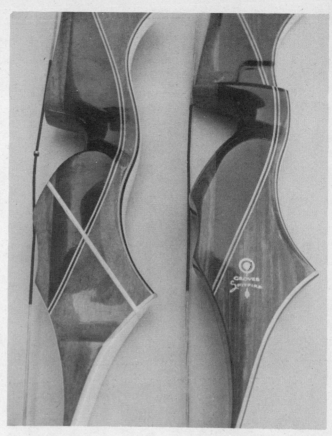

Another view of the two Groves' products reveals similarity in riser design. Keeping up with changing trends, Groves now offers a three-piece take-down unit that's popular.

carried it to and from hunting areas in a car. After you have carried some of the long seventy-inch single-unit bows a few times, you will realize why they thought up this take-down style.

When the modern laminated models came into vogue, the same idea was applied by Harold Groves in New

The take-down Spitfire features an allen bolt through the riser and two guide pins to assure a tight bond .

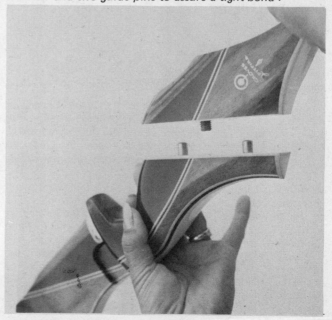

Either assembled or broken-down for easy carrying, the Groves Spitfire is a neat piece of equipment! The lock system is so tight that it appears a single unit.

easier carrying. The first of these were made many years ago by a gentleman named Pearson. His bow was much the same in design as any other, except it came apart in the middle at the handle. The upper section telescoped into a socket in the handle on the lower limb and you had a two-piece take-down bow. This made it handy when you

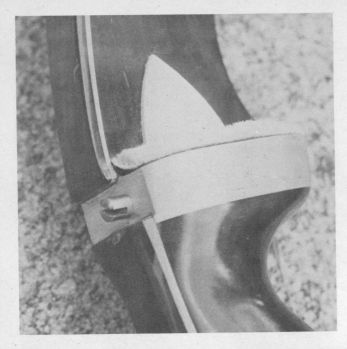

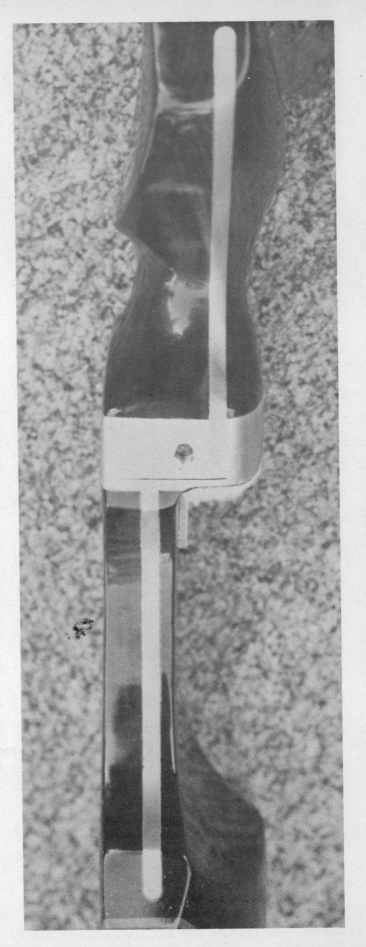

Top: Another rigid take-down is from Pearson Archery and doesn't appear to have a joint! Above: A twist of the attaching bolt and the aluminum notches are visible. Right: Both upper and lower limbs have aluminum extension deep into the riser for rigidity, along with pins.

Mexico. He has made a two-piece take-down bow for many years that comes apart with the aid of an allen wrench. The cut for dismantling is made on a diagonal in the lower riser section. There are placement pins for proper alignment so the bow will be set up precisely each time.

Ben Pearson Archery introduced a modification of the first socket style two-parter by making an aluminum keyed or slotted section that would fit snugly every time and could be assembled in minutes and centered with a bolt. This has been in the product line for several years and is one of the

Another good feature of the Pearson take-down in the ease with which it can be disassembled. A quarter or similar object is all that's required to loosen bolt.

As the attaching bolt runs all the way through the riser, the bowhunter is assured of a solid lock-up. The use of aluminum helps to keep the bow light in weight.

firm's more popular products. Other companies also make these two-section take-down styles.

The two-part take-down bow has been overshadowed to some extent since bowmakers came out with the newer three-piece take-down units. When assembled, these look like any other bow, but when you take the string off you have a variety of attachment methods. Each company is in the race for the most practical and convenient method of taking the limbs from the riser section. This bow style has many advantages. First it breaks down into a total length

that is now shorter than the length of your arrows. The three-piece take-down bow costs more than the single-unit or two-part bow, but if you break a limb on either single-unit or two-part take-down, you have a bow that is done for. Break a limb on the three-part take-down and you can purchase a new set for a fraction of the cost of a complete bow. A three-piece take-down might cost in the neighborhood of $125, but a new set of limbs for that bow costs about $50.

This has another advantage, too. Buy a three-part take-

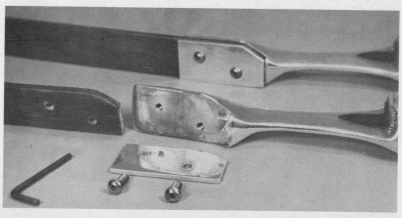

Plas-Steel's Bushwhacker take-down is assembled (below) and disassembled (right). It is a three-piece model with fiberglass limbs, full metal riser with a padded grip, sight window, mohair rest and side plate. Allen wrench is used for disassembly, and bow modestly retails around the $30 mark.

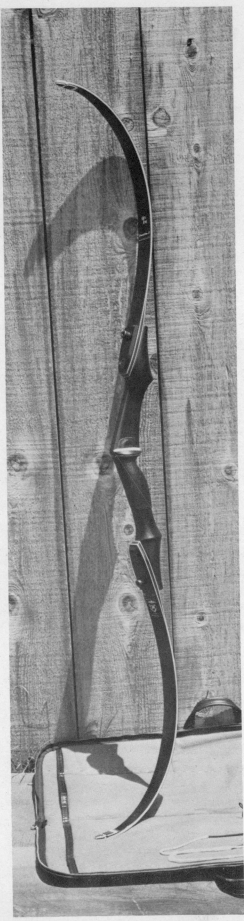

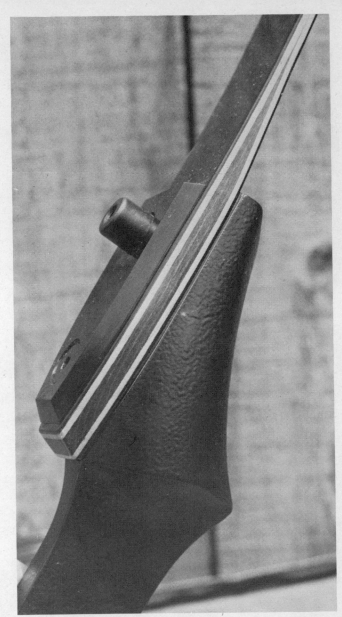

A closer look reveals the Competition II has metal riser. Limbs are held by a milled and grooved channel, which allows them to be slipped into place. Lock-up is firm.

down bow and, before going on the hunt, purchase a second set of limbs. They might be the same draw weight, lighter or perhaps heavier. You could have a set of fifty-pound limbs for deer hunting and another set of sixty-five-pound limbs for elk or bear. This gives the equivalent of two bows, but you will be shooting with the handle to which you are accustomed.

There are many methods of attaching the limbs to the riser. The riser sections are of formed wood, similar to that on any other bow, or are cast and moulded from light aluminum; epoxy, in one case, and ultralight and strong magnesium. Each company has designed a limb attachment system to draw the archer to that bow and there have been few problems with any of them. What they desire is a method that requires no bolts, nuts or screws to become lost in the field. Most use a modified socket with a clamp-

One of the newest take-downs on the scene is Wing's Competition II which utilizes slide-lock design.

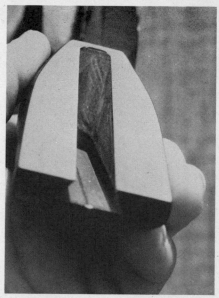

Ball bearings located on riser are visible as the limb is removed from the channel of the riser. They supply slight pressure, through spring construction, but move readily when pulled or pushed. Limbs can be permanently mounted.

When held toward camera, the grooved slot in the Competition II's riser is visible. It provides rigid support.

ing system to retain the limbs until the bow is strung. Once the bow is braced, about all that could separate the limbs from the riser would be to run over them with a truck!

The limbs for the three-part take-down bows are made in much the same way as the single-unit bows, except they will be laminated to the shorter section of hardwood used in the mid-section for strength at the riser joint. They will be laminated of fiberglass and hardrock maple, as are the others and about the only variation will be in the base of the limb, where it attaches to the riser.

If you are a budding bowhunter with a budget for equipment, the three-piece bow would be an excellent choice. The first set of limbs might be forty pounders, or even lighter and you could purchase anything later on that you desired. The heaviest limbs draw in the seventy to ninety-pound area. These have advantages the lighter bows don't, provided you can handle that much draw weight.

Another advantage of the three-piece unit is that, in many models, you also can vary the actual length of the bow. This is one factor many archers never consider. They think that, if they will be stand-hunting in trees, the shorter bows will work better at avoiding tree limbs that will be in the way. However, a bowhunter with a long draw, say thirty inches, trying to shoot a short bow of fifty-four inches, will find problems he wouldn't experience with a longer bow.

As you draw the bow from brace height to full draw, the angle of the string to fingers changes from almost flat to a varying angle according to the total length of the bow itself. If you have a short bow, the angle at full draw will be acute. The resulting finger pinch from the sharper angle will create sore fingers instantly. About the only remedy for this angle length problem would be to go to a mechanical device, where you don't use the fingers.

With a sixty-six-inch bow, about standard for many models, the angle when at full draw will be much shallower; less finger pinch will result, shooting will be more comfortable and accuracy will improve with the added comfort.

For an example of the three-piece take-down that will offer a variety of poundages and limbs, take a look at the Fred Bear take-down model. They offer two risers to the

bowhunter, A and B. A is fourteen inches long, B is eighteen inches. With these two risers are available three different limb lengths to make up a bow of the desired length and draw weight.

If you had riser A and a fifty-pound set of limbs, they would be forty-eight pounds in the longer B riser. Using the No. 3 limb and A riser, you can make up a bow that will be sixty inches long. With the B riser and No. 3 limb, the bow will measure sixty-four inches. One also can go the other way and make a shorter combination of the A riser and No. 1 limb at fifty-six inches.

With this system, you would need a chart from which to work, but could tailor the limb-riser combination to fit the needs of the hunt. A short bow could be created for stand shooting, with another bow of similar poundage but longer in length for roving shooting and the convenience of the wider angle for the fingers to have less pinch. This is just one of the many advantages with the three-part systems.

The newest approach involves the advent of what is called graphite glass. It is expensive, but has properties that the unidirectional fiberglass does not. When considering cost, it will run about $90 per pound compared to $.50 per pound for the more available glass filaments.

One problem we have been plagued with since the laminated bows came on the market has been twisting of limbs. If the limb becomes twisted through improper stringing or leaving a braced bow in the sun with weight on it, the bow becomes useless; the bow will never be the same again.

This new graphite glass might just be the answer to this age-old problem. One company at present offers a series of bows, ranging from the single-unit models to a new three-section take-down model. These bows will be in the upper price brackets, but reportedly have great cast and unique design that wasn't possible with the other materials. You might call it a marriage of the old Turkish recurve tip with the newest of materials, graphite glass.

Before a bow is sent to the finishing section of any plant, it must be tillered. This process involves cutting some string grooves in the tips of the bow so a string may be put on. When the bow is first braced — the term used for placing the string in the string grooves and imparting the basic shape of

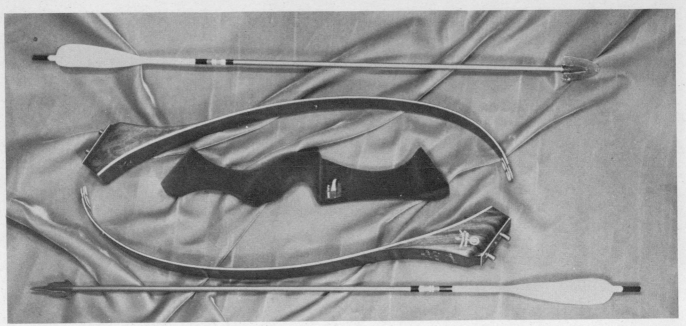

Groves Archery of Albuquerque produces this three-piece take-down unit for the bowhunter. The riser is of light aircraft metal, which is flocked with a special compound for camouflage. It uses same lock-up as two-piece models.

the bow — the limbs will not be balanced properly. The technique of balancing is simple to a craftsman, but not one you should ever attempt in your shop.

When the bowyer looks at the limbs of the braced bow he will note whether they are balanced or not. If it has a tendency to twist a bit to one side, he will place the opposite side on the belt sander and carefully remove a bit of

Once tightened into the riser of Groves' three-piece take-down, the allen bolt shown disappears. Because of the allen bolt, it pays to carry a spare wrench!

limb material on that side. Too much and it is ruined, so this is a careful and exacting process. When the limbs are sitting true center on the bow, the next item he checks is the tiller, the difference in the depth between the string and the upper limb at a certain point and the same on the lower limb. This must be different on the two limbs.

Remember, we shoot with the three-finger release method as a general rule, so the bow must be set for this procedure. Two fingers are below the arrow, one above it. This puts added pressure on the lower limb. This is measured by the bowyer in fractions of an inch. It might be as little as one-eighth inch or as much as one-half inch, depending upon the design and use for the bow.

Once the bow is tillered it shouldn't be changed. This would have to be done with a file and most hunters wouldn't know what to do anyway. This is mentioned in case you should note a bow in a shop or at a swap meet for a special low price. If it doesn't have a string or they can't find one, forget it. The limbs may be twisted from improper use and it never will shoot an arrow accurately. The tiller could be erratic. Some companies sell reject bows as seconds under another product name. Such a bow could be radically out of tiller.

One bow picked up on purpose because of the radical tiller proved to be an excellent bow, but this was the exception and a limb could break anytime. If the upper limb and lower limb look similar in distance from the string to the limb, the bow probably is all right, but if they vary a great deal, beware.

The handle of any bow is important. If it fits comfortably in your hand, you will shoot it better.

If the handle is uncomfortable, you probably will fight the grip of the bow and shoot differently each time since you will hold the bow in a different fashion each time. A comfortable grip makes for better shooting all the way.

There are three basic methods of holding the bow. The first is the open hand with the fingers extended and you draw the string back to the anchor point and release. When you release, you either have a sling connecting the bow and the wrist of the bow hand or you grab like mad to prevent the bow from flying across the area.

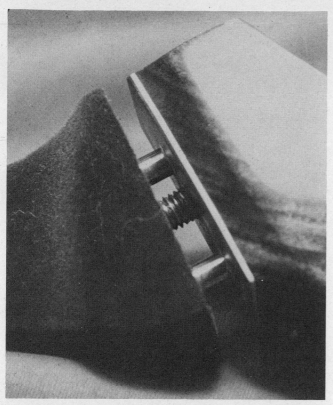

When purchasing a take-down of either two or three-piece design, check the lock system. If it has allen bolt construction with guide pins like this Groves model, it usually will prove rigid and dependable.

The second method would be with a light, but firm grip on the bow, which prevents the bow from flying.

The last method was advocated for Turkish archers and still is popular. This solid firm grip on the riser has some advantages and offers some problems. The greatest advantage is in the fact that, if you grip the handle until the knuckles turn white, you are, in turn, stiffening the entire arm, including the shoulder. This makes a rigid system and, if you grip the same each time, you will have a solid bow arm, the first aid to good shooting.

But, if you grip a bow too tightly you have a tendency to torque the bow, twisting it to the right or left or up or down. This torquing won't happen if the handle fits properly, but if it has a high section in the palm, you may push the bow forward with a tight grip. This torquing, if it occurs, will tend to cause an erratic arrow. You won't hit the same spot two times in a row since you might vary the grip and the twist on the bow and the resulting torque will vary, also. If the handle fits properly — and many bows now have small circumferences on the handle where gripped — you will have no torquing problem. How to grip or not to grip is still being argued among archers and there are advocates of all types, so it is just another of the variables you will have to test prior to deciding.

The Bear Archery Company thought of this handle problem when they made their magnesium riser for their three-piece take-down bows. They offer three different styles of handles to fit the basic straight section of the metal riser. This gives you a choice of a high, medium or low riser handle and you can test each, if uncertain which you like. You also can take the moulded handle off and shoot from the bare metal, if you prefer.

One final item you might consider when you go to buy a bow is whether it will take a sight. You may not use a sight

Another view of the locking system of a take-down bow shows the guide pins and allen bolt even more clearly. It's a durable design.

now and perhaps never will, but again you might want to try one. If the window, the section above the shelf where the arrow rests, is long enough, you could mount a sight for an aiming aid. If the window is short you can't, it is just that simple. The sights will be discussed later.

The described bows have been termed longbows for many years. Perhaps this is a method of separating them from crossbows in making game regulations in the different states. All states allow bowhunting with the longbow but few approve any type of crossbow hunting. The crossbow is a system that marries the stock of the rifle hunter to the bow of the archer. The bow lies horizontally on the stock in what can be a deadly combination for accuracy.

A few years ago, there was introduced what has turned out to be the most controversial bow of the century. This is called the compound bow. It looks like the standard longbow in that it has a handle, a short limb and a string for the arrow, but from there it varies drastically. Instead of gaining speed and cast from the design and materials used in the limb, the compound bow uses a physics principle with a system of cables and elliptical wheels for propulsion.

To put it simply, the bow has a handle, short stiff limbs that have a round wheel on each end with grooves into which aircraft cables fit. These cables are extended to a section on the riser that allows adjustment of draw weight. When you pull on the string with the arrow on it, the wheels on top start to roll over. They are not drilled in the center as with most wheels, but are off-center or elliptical.

As the wheel moves over it lets down and the actual draw weight of the bow changes from say fifty pounds at peak draw to a holding weight at your anchor point of thirty-five pounds or so.

This bow has created considerable controversy in the archery field. Most states now have accepted the compound bow as legal for hunting during archery season, but target societies still outlaw it.

The greatest advantage is the reduction in the holding weight of the compound bow. Many archers have a tendency to snap shoot with the heavier bows, since they can't hold them at draw at the peak load of, say fifty pounds. If you use a compound bow, the peak weight will occur be-

The notched limb base sits over the metal rod at front of riser and spring pressure holds it in place until the bow is braced. Once braced, it can't come apart.

Herter's, Incorporated, has a three-piece take-down unit that is utter simplicity. The short riser has a section on each end with a spring clip system that the limbs click into easily. It has a moderate price tag, too.

The heavy take-down bracket hides the simple spring clip system used on Herter's bow. With care, this model will be around long after its initial purchaser!

fore you come to full draw at twenty-eight inches, for at the actual draw length, you will be holding only thirty-odd pounds, as you follow the game on the trail. It makes it much easier to hold and has aided many bowhunters who have arthritis or bursitis afflictions.

A disadvantage of the compound would be the weight of the unit in the field. The compound is heavier than the longbow in physical weight and, if you are considering a compound, carry it in the field with a bow quiver full of hunting arrows for a day. If you want the advantage of the lighter draw-holding factor and feel you can carry the extra weight for the advantages offered, it might be the bow for you.

If you go to an archery group for an opinion you certainly will get one. There are many advocates who strongly recommend the compound and there are many in the other camp who feel the unit isn't a bow but a contraption!

There have been some who state that a specific bow isn't accurate, others who claim that all short bows are faster than

With both the notched limb and riser shown together, it's easy to see how the design comes together into a functional, easily-transportable single unit, handsome in looks. New designs are surfacing all the time, some finding application.

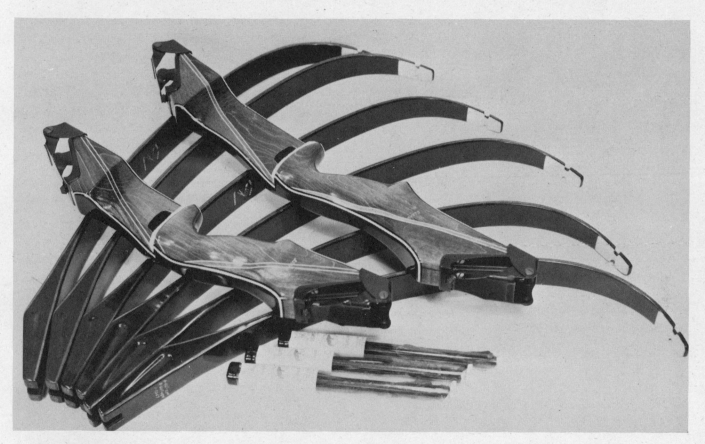

Bear Archery, long devoted to improving the bowhunter's equipment, has built an entire system around a simple take-down design. With the system, a bowhunter has his choice of three risers and three sets of interchangeable limbs. Shown above are two Futurewood risers and three sets of limbs that will fit either riser, varying in weight and size. Below is a close-up look at the Futurewood riser with a set of the limbs attached. Note the method of attachment.

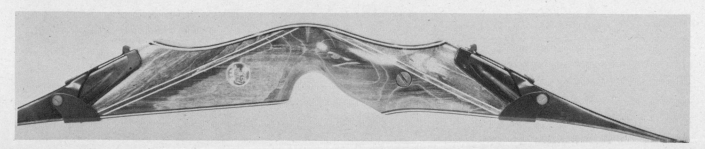

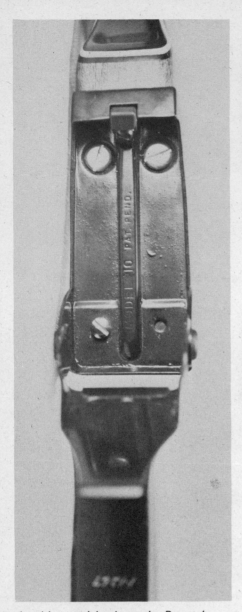

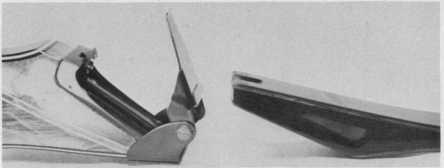

To assemble the Bear take-down with interchangeable limbs, the locking lip on the riser is raised and the limb inserted. The riser has a locator pin to prevent attaching the wrong limb in the riser, saving problems.

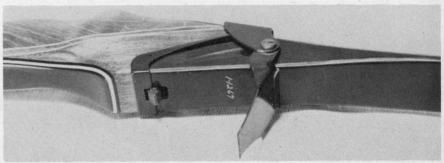

With the limb installed, it's easy to see the locator pin at the edge of the riser. If improper limb is attached, the pin will prohibit seating that limb all the way, so that the metal locking lip can swing downward.

Looking straight down the Bear take-down system, the locator pin at the top of the shoe base becomes visible.

With the proper limb attached to the correct end of the riser, the locator pin allows the limb to be seated to the correct depth. The locking lip then is folded down and the tip of the locator pin is grooved to catch it snugly.

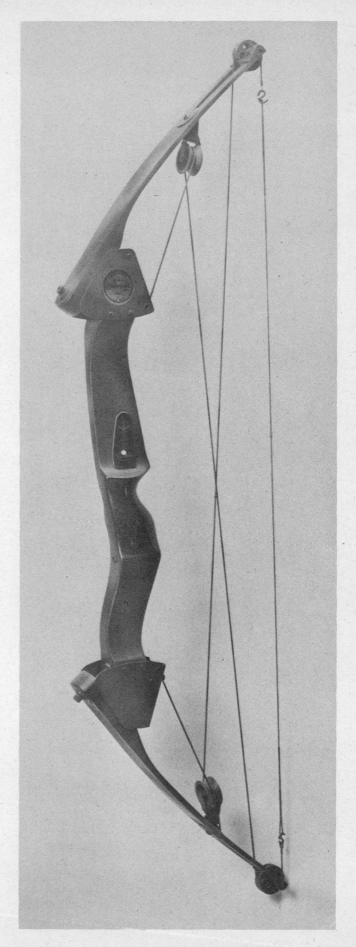

When first introduced, the compound bow started a heated controversy among archers. The Jennings at right uses a series of pulleys, elliptical wheels and cables to increase draw weight with less effort. This model has been factory-camouflaged for hunting, has a brush arrow rest and plunger side plate. It's proven effective on game.

longer bows. There aren't any inaccurate bows on the shelves, but there are a large number of archers who can't shoot a specific bow style accurately, so they blame their shortcomings on the bow.

The longer the bow, the better the cast or speed is a general statement of fact. The shorter bows are designed for close work and are just as accurate and fast up to a certain range. This will vary with different bows, but if you don't think so, take two bows of different length of the same draw weight and shoot them at twenty yards. You won't be able to see much difference at that distance. Take them to fifty or sixty yards and you will probably note the longer bow has a slight edge in the speed department at the longer ranges. If you plan to shoot from stands or move in close to thirty yards or less, speed isn't a factor as much as ability to shoot properly. If you feel you can't get that close and will take longer shots, consider the longer bow.

When we mention arrow speed, cast or speed of the bow, we are talking about low velocities in comparison to rifles or even pistols. The average bow will shoot below two hundred feet per second. It is an exceptional fifty-pounder that will make two hundred feet per second. If you go to a heavier draw weight of sixty pounds you will pick up speed at the same time. This added speed will be an advantage in the hunting field. You will have less elevation angle as you shoot at that deer. The lower angle means that you have a lower trajectory due to the higher speed. This will allow you to shoot under that limb you might hit with a lighter, slower bow. This added flat trajectory requires less calculation, since you know you can hit the game at a point-on distance of sixty yards or more.

To determine point-on distance of any bow, take the arrow length you will shoot in the hunting field, the bow you want to test and go to a marked range. You place a target of some type — a coffee can lid or something similar — on the bales and back off, until you can hit the center of the target by placing the tip of the arrow on that center. This is point-on for that bow at that draw length and will never vary, unless you change arrow weight or length.

If you hit high, at say fifty yards, you back up to fifty-five or farther, until the arrow hits the target center. If you

Dubbed "the bow of the future," the compound is adjustable to either increase or decrease its draw weight, with a corresponding reduction or increase of effort required to pull back an arrow. Its appearance looks strange.

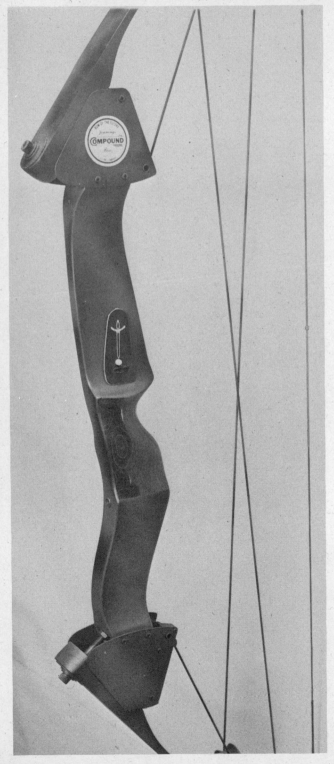

Cables crisscrossing in different directions does make the compound appear confusing, but the angles and use of the pulleys are what make the bow what it is. Note the "S" hook used to attach a bowstring to the aircraft cables.

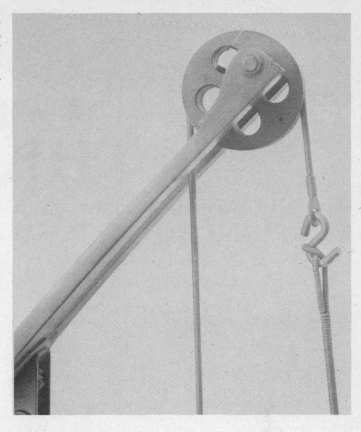

The elliptical wheels aid the compound in its weight reducing feature. Changing the position of the hole placement on the limb bolt changes the roll-over of the ellipse and draw length of the bow. It's a real help to handicapped archers and ladies who have bowhunting bug.

hit low, below the target, you are too far and must move forward. Your point-on distance might be an aid, since you will know how much trajectory you will have and whether you can clear or go under a jutting limb that might be in the path between you and that buck. Every edge you can find now will help you later in the field.

The bow is a basic part of your hunting system. How you use it will be determined partly by how much you practice. The best, most expensive bow won't perform, until you make it work for you.

Buy a bow you can afford in a style you like. It may be short or long, single-unit or three-piece take-down, but it will be your bow. Practice with it, learn to literally drive tacks and you will have little problem with the hunting side of the game.

You may want to experiment with the different methods of holding the bow and find you prefer the solid, hard, white knuckled grip, it feels good and you shoot better with it. You may prefer the open hand since you can't torque the bow.

These are all decisions only you can make and it will just take time and shooting to decide. Friends can make suggestions — and they probably will — but sift and sort from the good and bad information you will receive.

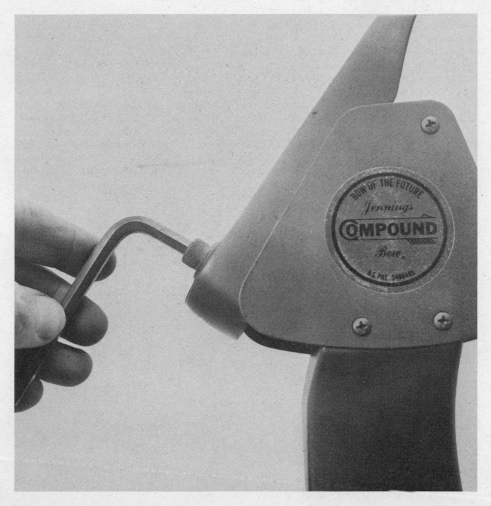

Allen wrench is used to raise or lower limb tension and draw weight at same time. Both limbs must be adjusted equally or bow won't shoot accurately.

CHAPTER 6

A STRING FOR THE BOW

You Can Buy Or Prepare Your Own, But In Either Case The Bowstring Is An Essential Element.

IN THE DIM history of bowhunting, the bowstring was made from natural materials. They could be twisted sinew, fibers of grass or whatever could be found that would hold up. In our modern age, we have the advantages of technology.

One of the popular materials used to be Flemish flax, but archers began testing different materials as they came out of factories, trying to find one that wouldn't stretch under tension. Nylon was out, as it really stretches, and the strings that were attempted weren't worth the time to put them together. Brownell's, Incorporated, makes many items of chemical origin; their Super B43 dacron is used in bowstrings. Brownell's dacron strands not only were compatible for archery bowstring use, but now are the basic material. The firm has tried several variations, but the current material in use is classified as Super B43 dacron.

There are two basic types of strings. The older style is often called a Flemish twist, but is more properly termed the handlaid string. This is made by measuring three sections of string material. These strands are twisted, then the loops that fit over the ends of the bow are twisted and the end product makes a rugged, serviceable string. The advantage of this string is that it can be made in the field with minimum materials.

Several years ago I met Fred Wilson on a pig hunt in Arizona. I noted his string was the old style handlaid type, not often seen in these days of the endless stringmakers.

"I like them since they have strength and, if I cut one strand, there is no way for the string to unwind or to slip out as an endless might," Wilson remarked. "Drop over someday and I'll show you how to make one."

That someday stretched into a few years, but a recent call from Wilson reminded me of the advantages of knowing this little-used technique. He had called to remark that he had lost one string while deer hunting in Utah and tried to make one of the handlaid types, but had to make several since he had forgotten how. It was a piece of information that jogged the memory into action.

The handlaid string, often misnamed the Flemish string, is strong and reliable when made right. Actually, one can goof and still have a good string, although it might not look as pretty. Perhaps the biggest advantage is that it can be made right in the hunt camp with one small board, some small nails and one big nail or other anchor system. You will need dacron bowstring, a knife, some beeswax and patience. The first string may look horrible and probably won't even fit the bow, but you might be pleasantly surprised.

Using a ruler, mark the taper board at three-eighth-inch intervals, then pound in the small tacks or small nails purchased.

When these are attached to the taper board, a notch is cut to hold starting string. A sharp knife is a necessity!

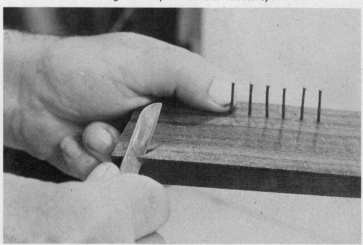

If you plan to try this, you could make a pattern board and place it in your tackle box, as it is small. The only other item needed in camp would be a ruler of sorts and a base nail or peg.

The basic board can be of any material. Wilson made his from a piece of oak flooring. I made one from walnut cut eight inches long and three inches wide, but didn't need that much. You need a center line, so mark that with a pencil. Allow 1¼ inches between the pegs or nails you will drive. Start on one side and drive one nail, brad or other permanent peg. Measure down three-eighths of an inch in line with the first one, then pound in a second.

Continue down the board at three-eighths-inch intervals till you have six nails or brads in a straight line. Check your measurement, move to the other side of the board and drive a brad opposite the first one, but 1¼ inches from it laterally. Place five more brads down the board opposite the ones on the other side.

This will give you an eighteen-strand string, if you fill all the nails as will be explained. Eighteen strands will handle up to and including one hundred pounds of bow draw weight.

At the upper end on the inside move up from the top brad about one inch and drive another for the string starter. Opposite this nail you can cut a slash into the wood to hold the string as you start the handlaid bowstring. I modified my board by placing a brass screw there to wrap the string around for starting; either will work.

This will give you the tapered strands required to prevent the bowstring from balling up, as you twist it; the end product will be a clean, even twist and a good looking string.

Place the board on your workbench, or camp table if you have to do this as an emergency task, and measure a dis-

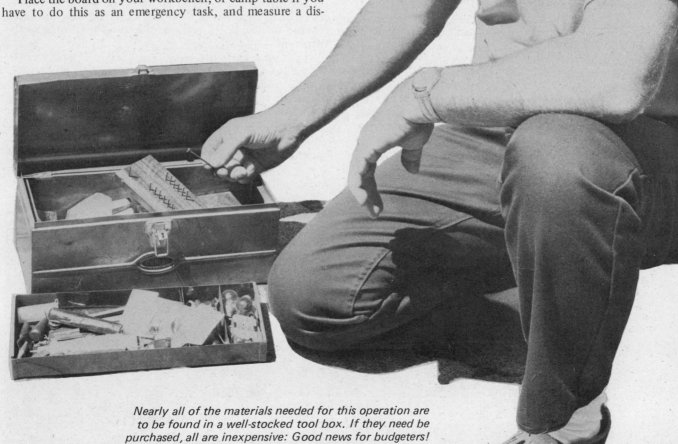

Nearly all of the materials needed for this operation are to be found in a well-stocked tool box. If they need be purchased, all are inexpensive: Good news for budgeters!

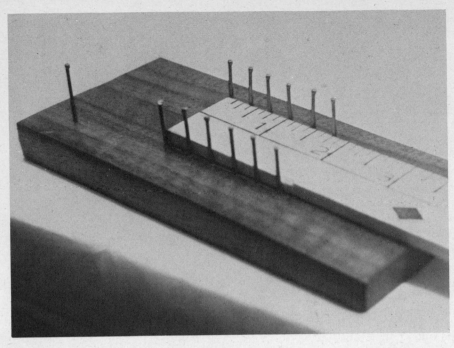

This is how the completed taper board should appear, with nails tacked, a notch and starting nail.

tance to drive the base nail. This is where the variables will enter into the string method.

If you want a string for a sixty-inch bow, measure from the top nails in the board thirty-five inches to the base nail. When you finish with the twisting, that should give you a string to fit your sixty-inch hunter. The variables would be how tight you twist, how many twists for the bownock loops and basic technique in general. This is a starting point.

Other measurements in case you don't use a sixty-inch bow would be as follows:

Peg or nail distance from top nails in board to achieve the following lengths: 37"=5'4" (64"); 36"=5'3" (63); 36"=5'2" (62); 35½"=5'1" (61); 35"=5' (60).

As you can see, a change of one-half inch in the nail-to-board distance equals an inch change in the finished string length. If your hunter is shorter than sixty inches, you can continue down the scale to arrive at the proper distance to drive your nail.

To make a string to fit a sixty-inch bow, clamp the board and measure down thirty-five inches from the top nails and drive an anchor nail. The next phase is to take your dacron string and place it in the holding slot or screw. Move over the top single nail to the outside, and down around the anchor nail and up the inside. Drop one nail to the second set of brads in the board, across and down the outside around the nail and up the inside to the next lower set of brads then across. Continue until you have four nails covered on the board and one strand up the inside to the fifth brad.

Take your knife and cut all strands down the center-line of the board, holding the loose end you have just brought up the inside on the board. Lift the five strands of string in your left hand, holding at the same point as when they were cut, then twist them slightly to keep them together. There will be two ends of this section with tapered strings of different length on each end. That is what you want.

Lay the section to one side and do this operation twice

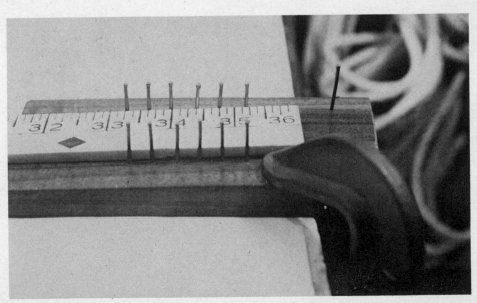

When making a string, clamp the taper board to tabletop. For sixty-inch string, measure 35 inches from top nails.

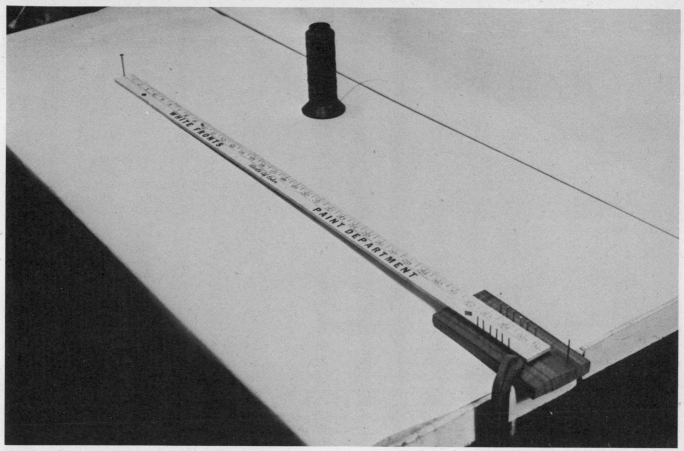

After measuring the 35-inch length needed for a sixty-inch bowstring — one of the more common sizes found on bows built today — pound in the base or anchor nail at the opposite end. While a yardstick is handy, a tape measure can be used.

more to end up with a fifteen-strand string when twisted together for the finished product. If you want thirteen strands, just eliminate the last wrap. If you aren't certain of the number of strands on each side, they must be even. You can lift them and count before you cut them.

After you have all three string sections cut and lying in one area, pick them up in your left hand — for right handed people, that is — and measure 8½ inches from the bitter end of the strings and place your left hand at this position. You now are ready to twist the strands. What you will have at this point is fifteen single strands of dacron. In three sets, they vary in length to form the proper taper.

Hold the strands in the left hand, take the uppermost strand with the right hand and twist it away from you and,

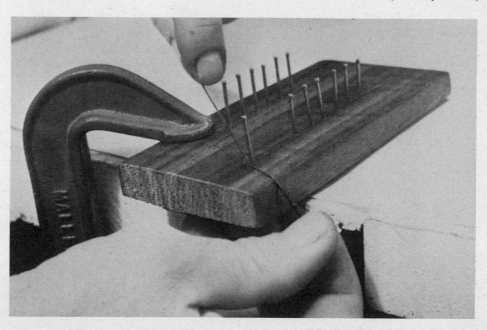

With these steps performed, take your dacron string and attach it to the taper board by pressing it into the previously-cut notch.

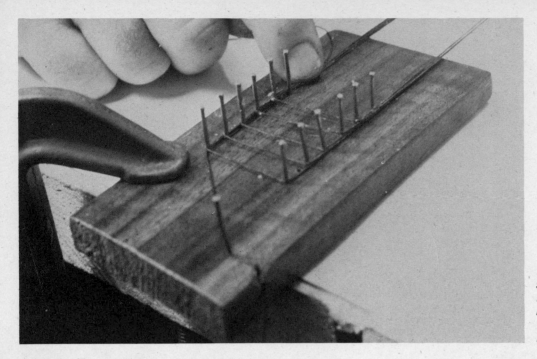

For a fifteen-strand string, the dacron line is wound around nails and looks like this. Follow concise instruction in text.

at the same time, bring it over the other two strands so it is closest to you. You must count these twists at this point, so keep track. Take the next strand at the top, twist it away from you with the right hand as you bring it over the other two toward you; so it goes for twenty twists. This will form your lower bownock loop.

When you have reached the twenty count, you will have a twisted section of string about two inches long. The tighter the twist, the neater the string. The secret, as I found out, is to twist with the right hand until you feel the strands start to buckle or knot up. That is enough, as you don't want them to buckle.

As you twist and bring it over with the right, you will pull back with the left hand at the same time to keep tension on the twisting strands. It sounds complicated, but is really easy — after you goof the first one.

Now you are ready to form the lower bownock loop of the string. The twisted strands that are loose must have one strand over the top of the other two strands. This is the way the string comes over as you twist and pull toward you.

Make a loop of the twisted strands toward the longer section of the string where one strand must be over, two under. Match the one strand over with the one over on the

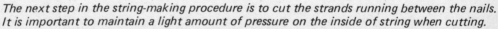

The next step in the string-making procedure is to cut the strands running between the nails. It is important to maintain a light amount of pressure on the inside of string when cutting.

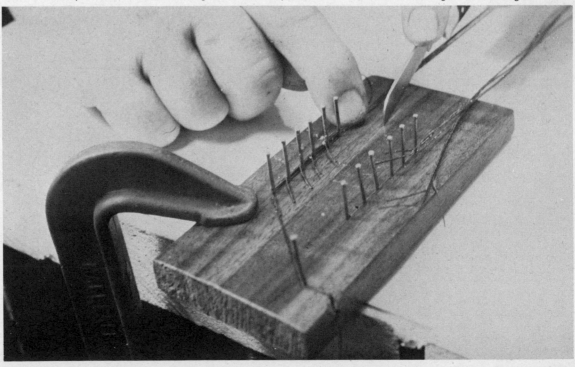

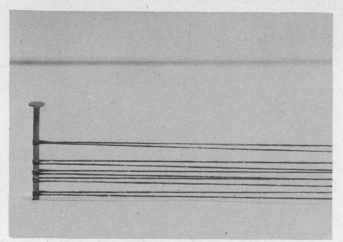

Prior to cutting the strands at the board, the anchor or base nail should look like this. Note that none of the wound segments of dacron overlap any of others.

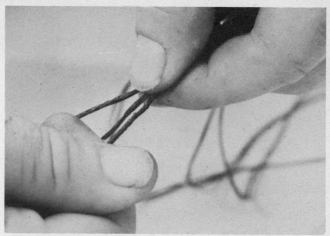

After cutting, all three strands are held in the left hand. The top strand then is brought over the other two with the right hand, as shown in the photograph.

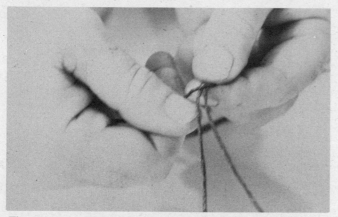

The top strand then is twisted over the other two. This twist is continued for approximately another twenty or so times, the top string being brought over other two.

long section; the two under with the long sections hold together. Now you can start twisting these thicker strands.

The method is the same. Take the top section, twist away from you and pull over toward you; take the next one at the top, twist away and pull over toward you and on down the string. Continue until you reach the single strands of the tapered section. These won't lay over too well. You can either continue to work them in or leave them and trim later.

You now will have the finished loop for the lower end of the bow formed, twisted and it will surprise you how neat it looks. If you err you probably will see a section where you didn't get the top strand, but the middle one. It won't lie flat as the other sections but that won't hurt the function of the string; only the looks.

Place this formed loop on a nail or other point to stretch the string. Measure down 9½ inches from the bitter ends of

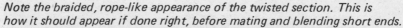

Note the braided, rope-like appearance of the twisted section. This is how it should appear if done right, before mating and blending short ends.

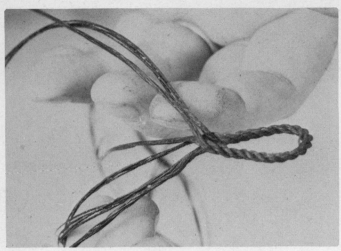

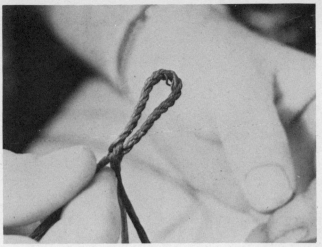

The one overly-short section, caused by repeatedly wrapping over other two strands, is now matched with the one over on the main section. Get the right pairs.

The lower loop, or the one which will attach to lower limb that is smaller in size, should look like this before it is twisted to finish production on that end.

the strands. Keeping them taut and even, this will be the bigger upper loop that must fit over the bow limb for stringing, so you want this loop bigger; hence 9½ inches instead of the 8½ for the lower loop.

Grip the strands together at this point with the left hand, take the upper strand, twist away and bring over and toward you just as you did the lower section. This time, count twenty-six twists before you form the loop and again match the one over and two under strands to form that loop.

Here is another variable for you to work into your string. If you have a wide-limb bow you may find you need more than twenty-six twists. Trial and error is one method, but if you use a bow stringer you can forget the upper loop problem. Learn to make the bigger upper loop in case you forget the bowstringer, too. With the push and pull method it is hard, if not impossible, to string the bow without the string being on the upper limb so you can slide it up the limb to the nock. Keep that in mind.

Now that you have the one over matched on the short

Below is a finished fifteen-strand bowstring, less the serving which will be applied. Note the difference in the size of the loops, which is a must for stringing the bow. This is an area where a bowhunter can same money, by making his own.

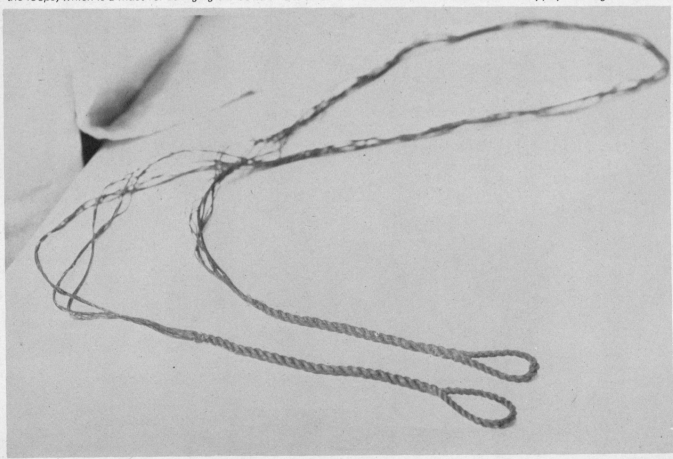

section and the long section, the other two strands matched, you may begin twisting and bringing over just as you did for the lower loop.

One thing that worried me at first was how to prevent the snarled mess I knew I would have when forming this upper loop, since the lower strands were held in place. Don't worry. It won't happen. As you twist the strands, bring them over and continue down the string. The string moves with you and there are no snarls.

Remember that, when you measure the upper loop after forming the lower one, keep all three strands even when you measure the 9½ inches. That is why you place the loop over the nail: to keep them in line and even when starting the upper loop. If you don't you will have uneven strands and a string that will never work. Just keep them even.

When you twist the upper loop to the small ends, you will have both ends finished. The center section of the string will be fifteen strands held top and bottom with a twisted, even loop.

The next phase is to place one loop over a strong nail or peg and a piece of wood or arrow shaft in the other end near you. Pull a bit of tension into the string against the nail and start twisting the entire string in a counter-clockwise twist, counting twenty twists.

As you move into twisting the entire string, increase pressure on the string by pulling back. If you apply too much pressure at first, the loops will pull out, since there is nothing to hold them together. By twisting in the counter-clockwise rotation, you will tighten the twists in the loops and make them permanent.

When you have the required twenty twists, you can take a piece of leather, double it over the string and, applying pressure, work it up and down the string to heat it up, giving the twisted strands a unity and bringing out any stretch that may be in the string.

All that is left to the project is fitting the string to the bow. The first string I made came out far too long for the sixty-inch bow. My next string, under the guidance of Fred Wilson checking over my shoulder, fit the bow. The factory string had measured a brace weight from the pivot point on the handle of 9½ inches. My string came out a bit shorter at 8¾ inches, but would be a shootable string, although it braced higher than I like.

Wilson made a string to the same measurements as I had, but he had a tighter and neater twist, so his string came out 9½ inches. This would be much better and it could let out to about the right brace height with some shooting and further flexing with the leather.

This working of the string with the leather creates heat and will lengthen a string to its maximum. If you don't burnish the string with the leather, but merely start to shoot, it might let down on you more than your nocking point.

One advantage of this bowstring is that, if you are a bit low on brace height, you can give it more twists to bring it up. I twisted my string, then let it out a few twists hoping to get better height, but didn't. Wilson's technique was far better than mine, but we both made shootable strings without much equipment and both would be better than giving up the hunt due to a broken string with no spare. A little practice and careful measurements, along with records of brace heights obtained, and one can make a string that fits right the first time.

Some archers who have used the handlaid string object to the bulkiness of the loops. Others feel this string is more durable than endless strings. It is a fact that, if you cut one or two strands, you haven't lost the entire string. By making a fifteen-strand string that will handle an eighty-pound bow and you shoot fifty-five, you have a couple of strands to lose if you cut them with a sharp broadhead and still will be safe to shoot.

The big advantage of the handlaid string is that you can

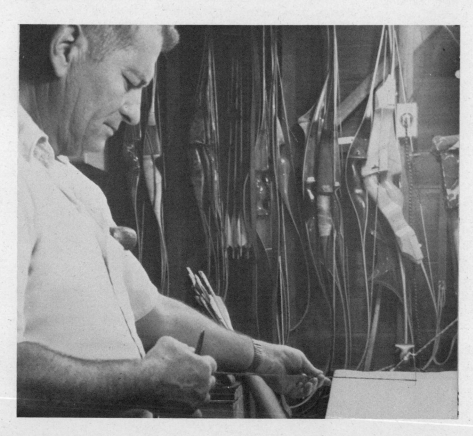

With your string built, all that remains to be done is add the serving and rub the twisted strands with leather.

build it almost anywhere. If you don't build a board and put it in your tackle box you could make a string on a camp table, a log or any surface. If you don't have a ruler you might have a dollar bill or other folding money. Bills measure 6-1/8 to 6½ inches, which aids an educated guess.

I am playing around with a crossbow and recently came up with a new bow style, but no string to fit. I made a measurement of the bow limb at forty-five inches. I guessed at the required string length, made a handlaid string that came out far too long. My second string braced the bow a bit too high, but the third was right on the button.

The big advantage was that my string jig for the endless type wouldn't come close enough together to allow me to make the shorter string. Now I can make a string for any length bow, from the long monsters to the short crossbows, with nothing more than one board that fits into my tackle box.

The endless style string is more popular and easier to make, especially for the beginner. The materials can be bought from the archery shop or mail order houses. You will need a string jig, which can be made or purchased; dacron Super B43; some nylon serving thread and a serving device.

The string that fits the bow when you buy it may be right for that bow. After shooting a few years, you may prefer a string that is higher or lower than that supplied by the factory. This is a personal item and takes time to be certain. The string is measured in two ways. First, the number of strands used to make the string are determined by the draw weight of the bow you plan to shoot.

The second measurement will be the length of the string and this is determined by the brace height as recommended by the bow manufacturer and the length of the bow itself. If you buy a bow of sixty inches, the string will not measure the same length. It will, as a rule of thumb, be three inches shorter than the sixty inches of bow length. You can measure this by bracing the bow, then checking the actual string length under tension. If you use this as the method of measuring to make a new string, you should add three-quarters of an inch to the physical measurement. This will allow for the turns on the posts of the bow stringer and the wrap around the string nocks on the ends of the bow.

The brace height is measured according to a standard established by the Archery Manufacturers Organization. This group got their heads together to try to standardize some of the many variables found in the sport. Bows were made in many different lengths and supplying strings for all these odd lengths became a dealer's headache. To help both the dealer and the archer, the organization established certain specifications and the brace height is one of these. (We will refer to this group often as AMO.)

The brace height is the distance between the lowest section of the grip at a right angle to the string when it is on the bow at both ends; "braced" is the usual term. This can vary from seven to eleven inches, depending on the style of the bow. Some bows have what is termed a deflex, the bow actually having a curved section that is in front and angles away from the string. To measure the brace height, place a square on the string and measure to the small section of the grip. This will be standard for that bow as recommended by the maker.

Another method is to measure to the forward section on the arrow rest, the point where the broadhead or hunting point would hit the bow were it pulled all the way back. This is sometimes used as the measuring point and there is a difference. The dealer or bowmaker usually will specify, but if in doubt, you can check both methods.

The higher the brace height, the more the bow will sing or vibrate on release. This is one thing we don't want in the hunting field. Many shots have been missed due to game "jumping the string." This term refers to the fact that the bowstring sings as the hunter releases the arrow. The noise of the singing or twanging string in turn spooks the game and it is gone before the arrow gets there.

There are several ways to alleviate this problem. The first is to lower the brace height, but when you make a new string to lower the recommended brace height, you will run into some new problems.

Again, a basic rule is that a one-half-inch longer string on the jig will lower the brace height three-quarters of an inch. Hence, a one-inch longer string achieves an inch-and-a-half lower brace height.

Lowering the brace height stops some of the twanging of the string on release, but if lowered too far the string becomes mushy and will slap the arm on every shot. That is too low, so bring it back higher.

The ideal string height is that which gives you the fastest arrow speed, least amount of string noise and will not slap the arm. You can prevent arm slapping by wearing an arm guard of leather or plastic. It fits over the inside of the bow arm to prevent ugly welts from popping up on the arm. String slap can be uncomfortable and will result in flinching if you allow it to continue without protection.

After attaining the right string height, you still may have a noisy string. String silencers can be placed on or in the string to prevent most of this.

A release device also may cause excessive string noise. The release may vary in design from a chunk of wood called a bowlock to one of the string and pin methods. We will discuss these later, but they can cause more string singing due to the cleaner, faster release, compared to the standard three-finger method. If you find string noise minimal with finger shooting but excessive with a release, the only remedy is string silencers.

String silencers are made of many materials, but can even be fashioned of simple rubber bands. These are placed on the string about half-way between the finger section and the upper and lower limbs. Two silencers are needed, one above and one below the center serving. These silencers dampen the vibrations and, in turn, lower or even eliminate the noise factor. You place the silencer on the string and move it until you obtain the quietest noise factor. Too big a unit will tend to slow down the cast of the bow and arrow speed along with it, however.

Anything you put on the string other than the bare essentials will slow the speed of the arrow. The string is the propulsion system that marries the bow design to the propelled object, the arrow. If you tie on a bunch of gadgets — and there are plenty of them on the market — you may have a silent string, one that won't bruise your fingers, but for each item hung on that string you sacrifice feet per second in arrow speed. The cleanest string, one free from devices, is the fastest. Brush nocks, finger stalls, silencers, peeps and other items will help do what they are meant for, but the sacrifice may be more in arrow speed than they are worth.

If you are handy in the shop, you can make a bowstring jig in a matter of a few hours. These are simple in design and execution. You can also purchase a jig from an archery shop or dealer, but they may not have what you want and, if you have no dealer handy, you almost have to make them.

The materials used for a string jig range from pine two by fours to machined and tooled components, but you can make your string jig with a hacksaw, file and a three-eighths or one-quarter inch electric drill and two drill bits. You

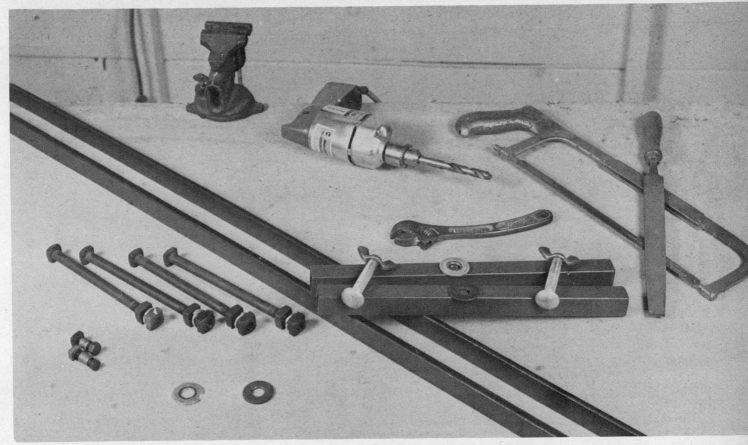

Should you desire a somewhat more formal string building apparatus, the string jig is just the ticket. Inexpensive to construct and almost indestructible, it will pay for itself in a short time. The needed materials are shown above.

might want to add some paint, maybe a wrench and some half-inch bolts about eight inches long with two nuts. You also need the basic frame.

For the main base section of the frame, purchase two pieces of angle iron about one-inch wide, and for the crossarms purchase two pieces of one-inch square formed iron. The length of the angle iron will be five feet, the crossarms will be fourteen inches each. It might be easier to

If angle iron was purchased uncut, you must pare it to proper size with a saw, then file ends smooth to prevent snagging clothes, string.

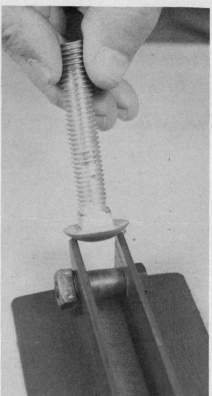

The next step is to drill holes on both ends of the angle iron and use any size of bolt for rigidity. Cut a section of copper tubing as a spacer between rails, add the washer and nut. See text for details.

Gap between rails is designed to fit half-inch wing bolt with a round head. One end is movable.

have the shop cut the lengths with power tools they usually have, or you can buy the longer lengths and cut them at home. Cost is around $5.

The angle iron base will be strong enough for any string

With crossarm bolt in place, note snug fit on base of bolt with washer to allow pivoting on the rails. The crossarm now can be placed on the rail when finished.

system you care to make. Take the five-foot lengths of angle iron, file the edges smooth from the saw cuts and, if you prefer, paint them to prevent rust. A spray can or conventional brush method will protect the iron many years.

To space the two angles you can use a series of washers, a block of wood or, if you have some scrap copper pipe or tubing on hand, it can be cut about one-half inch long and used for the bolt spacer. Drill two holes, one on each end to fit the main beam bolts. Don't make these too big, about one-quarter inch on the low side and maybe three-eighths on the upper dimension. No problem if you have two odd bolts, since the idea is to hold the two sections of angle iron apart to allow the crossarm to adjust back and forth for string lengths.

After the holes have been drilled on the two ends of the main beam take the bolts, pass one through one side, place the copper tubing or washer spacers on the bolt, slip the other angle iron onto the bolt and tighten them down. Follow through the same way on the other end. The finished main beam will have about one-half inch clearance running the full length of the five-foot sections. This completes the work on the main beam.

Take the one-inch-square formed iron pieces and cut them to fourteen inches, if you bought one long section. These will form the crossarms of the jig. File the edges smooth so you won't cut fingers or worse yet, a partially made string. Mark and drill the center of the crossarm at seven inches. Drill both arms with a half-inch bit through both sides.

Move to the ends and measure in about one inch, drill another half-inch hole and do the same to the opposite end, both arms. The finished product will have two holes in the ends, cut only through the top section on the same side, the center hole being drilled through both sides of the arm. You don't want the ends to go completely through as they must pivot on the main beam when making the string.

To attach the upright half-inch bolts, you merely place one nut on the upper section of the threaded end, place it through the one-sided hole on the square arm, place the other nut on the inside of the arm and tighten until the bottom nut is flush with the surface of the bolt. The upper nut then is run down and the entire bolt tightened on the arm. This makes a rigid system, but one you can change if you want higher or lower risers on the string arms.

You will need two half-inch round-headed bolts, with one washer and a wing nut for attaching the crossarm to the main beam. Place the round-headed side through the beam. The half-inch-square inner surface of the bolt should fit snugly against the two sides of the beam. Place a washer on the bolt, then the crossarm and finally the wing nut. Do this on both ends and you will have the required two arms that can easily pivot when making strings. By tightening the wing nut you can position the arm wherever you need it and it will pivot on the beam when serving the ends.

The finished jig will have a main beam five feet long, the fourteen-inch-square iron crossarms will be centered on the main beam and held in place by the half-inch wing nut bolts. The tops of the upright arms will still have the half-

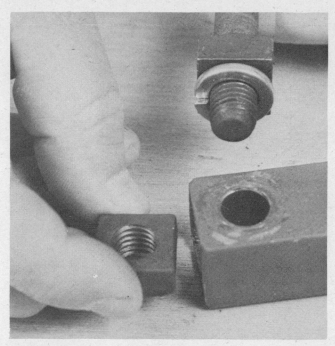

Cut the one-inch-square iron crossarms fourteen inches long. Measure in one-inch from the end and drill a half-inch hole through upper metal only. Run a nut up the threads of the half-inch bolt, place a washer, then put the bolt into the drilled hole and fasten with another nut inside the crossarm.

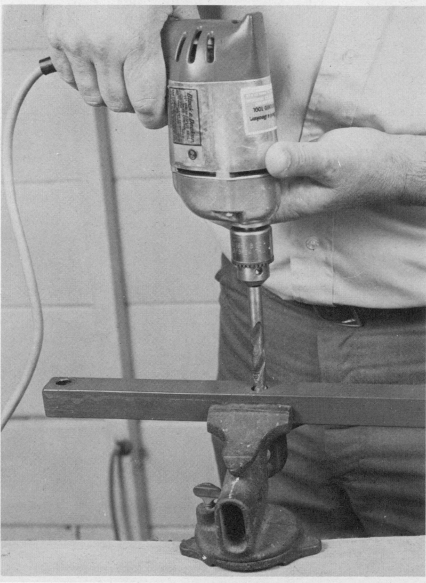

Taking a rule, measure half-way down the length of the crossarm — seven inches — and mark this spot. Then, using a power drill and half-inch bit, drill a hole through both sides of the angle iron. It is important to make sure drill is centered exactly.

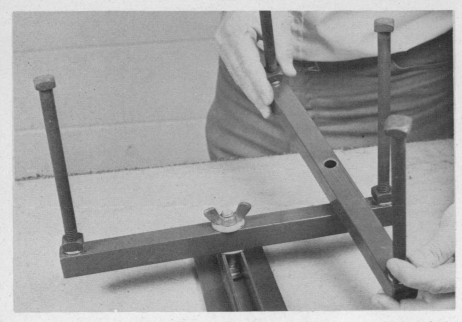

This is how the movable crossarm looks attached to the jig with the wing nut. Arms around which the string is wrapped are bolted firmly to the adjustable crossarm. It will work this way, but loops on string will have to be large enough to fit over the one-half-inch bolt heads.

inch square or hex head on them. You can make strings with these bolt heads still in place, but they might be awkward when removing the finished string. You can try using the uprights with the bolt heads on or you can cut them off with a hacksaw. You must have a string groove or ridge to prevent the string material from slipping up and down and possibly off the arm while moving the arms and running the serving.

If you cut the bolt heads off, cut them so you will have six inches above the crossarm surface. You will need this distance to allow the string server to swing as you serve; any lower and the server will strike the arm and you'll end up hand-serving instead of swinging the server.

Round off the tips of the cut bolts with a file or a sanding belt, if you have one. A power grinder will work well, too. Make the upper surface clean with no snags to cut a string. Move down about a quarter of an inch and cut some grooves into the bolt. These can be cut with a lathe, if you have access to one; a file, by using the edge and care-

fully cutting as you rotate the bolt; or by grinding on a small stone with a power grinder. The lathe works best but the other systems will cut the required groove.

Clean up the edges after the groove is deep enough to hold a served string. You can easily check this by taking a string from a bow and noting the depth as you cut it into the bolt end. These surfaces must be free of snags or they will cut the individual strings as they are wrapped around the arms.

The finished jig will work two different ways for making strings. If you have no vise, you can place the arms on the

Gene Chandler adjusts small vise holding inverted jig. The crossarms have been removed and turned over so the wide side of angle iron is uppermost, making jig more movable. You can duplicate this method if desired.

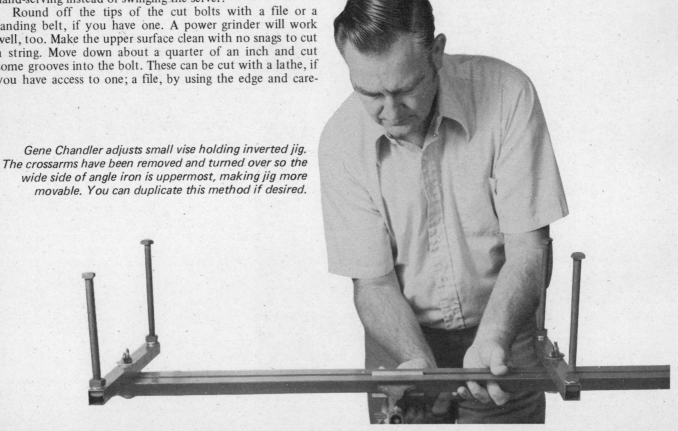

small side of the jig, the one-inch beam on the base side and clamp the jig to a table while making strings. You must have a solid base from which to work.

If you have a small vise you can turn the arms over to the wider section of the base, take a spacer of wood to prevent the beam from being bent, place the narrow section into the vise and clamp it down. This will place the wider base of the beam on the top and give a stronger and more substantial surface for the crossarms.

One end of the jig — one of the crossarms — usually is kept in a fixed position. You can tighten the crossbolt on the main beam to hold the half-inch round-head bolt in that position. The copper tubing, if used, will squeeze as tightly as you like to grip the bolt inside area of the crossarm bolt.

The other crossarm is kept movable so different-length strings can be made by moving that crossarm back and forth on the main beam. You can make a string from six feet — seventy-two inches — down to one about twenty-six inches long by moving the one arm back and forth on the beam.

The finished jig can have the upright bolt heads in place or the grooved cut-off ends. You can paint the entire unit or, if you want to be extra-fancy, send it out and have it all chrome plated. You should have a protective coating on the iron components to prevent rust.

The main feature of this jig is rigidity. It will be strong enough to make a good, tight string. You will be able to make them the same length and have the same tension on each. It is simple to make, requires few tools and perhaps two hours in the shop to complete.

Rig a jig from these iron components — it will last a lifetime.

To make a string of the endless style you would proceed as follows:

We noted earlier that, if you measure the string you plan to duplicate when braced on the bow, all you need do is add three-quarters of an inch. Turn the arms of the jig to the widest side and, using a tape measure, set it up for this distance. Turn the arms at right angles to the main section and take your Super B43 in hand. This string material is usually on small spools of one-quarter pound and should last for many strings. The next item to determine is the number of strands. This has been figured for you also, and is printed on the wrapper that comes with the dacron.

Assuming you plan to make a string for a fifty-pound hunting bow, this comes out on the charts to be fourteen strands. Some archers feel they get a faster bow with a lighter string of fewer strands and this is true to a point. Too light a string will stretch and nothing will be constant. Another method is to make all strings for fifty pounds and up to eighty pounds all sixteen strands. If they recommend fourteen strands, why sixteen?

The heavier string obviously will slow arrow flight. Also, it will be thicker in diameter and usually will fit the nock of the arrow much tighter. But, should you become careless and move a razor-sharp broadhead near the string and slice one or two strands, you still will be within the minimum strand requirements, according to the manufacturer. Cutting a string or a few strands is easy to do in the field, so this is one of the major reasons for the sixteen-strand hunting string.

Last, the thicker string will fit any bow weight you care to put it on and not be too light. Most hunters never go beyond sixty to sixty-five pounds in draw weight and the string you make with sixteen strands for the fifty-pound bow will work on the sixty-five pounder, if it is the right length.

Tie the end of the string to one arm of the jig to prevent

A hunk of wood used as a spacer is a good idea, and is what the vise should be clamped to. This prevents any bending of the metal as vise pressure is applied.

it slipping and hold the dacron under tension, as you wrap the strands on the jig arms. Count sixteen strands and you will end up at the same end you started. Tie the end off and you will be ready to serve the nock loops.

The server is a metal or plastic unit that holds a spool of heavy thread. This usually is heavyweight nylon, or it might be heavy cotton. Nylon wears better, so purchase that if you have the choice. The server is made to hold the spool under a tension you can adjust, yet feed the thread onto the strands of the bowstring. They lock the strands together in a tight, close wrap.

Place the end of the thread on the area you have marked off for the serving, about five inches at most from the center of the two arms. Make the first few wraps with the fingers pulling it tight. When you have a half-dozen or so wraps, pull the tension on the spool to allow the arm or indented area of the server to fit the string strands.

Turn the server in the direction you have been wrapping and, with the tension properly set, the serving will go on easily. You may prefer merely to move the server around the string by hand at first, but as you progress in string-making, you will learn to swing the server to obtain a twirling motion that will serve the string in a few minutes.

After you reach your stop mark, pull the server out to obtain some excess thread. Cut close to the server and you are ready to tie off the end. This is simple in theory. Take the thread and move up about two inches on the string. Wrap the thread on the string in the opposite direction in a loose wrap for about six turns. Then pull the loose end thread back along the served section. Wrap the thread over the loose end and, as you wrap onto the string, the other loosely wrapped end will unwrap and disappear.

When you have one loop left, hold it in one hand and pull the loose end tight against the string. The finish is a hidden, tightly held end that seldom comes loose. This is the same technique used in wrapping ferrules on fishing poles.

Cut the loose ends of the dacron to clean up that end of the string. Move to the opposite end and repeat the process. When both bow nock ends have been served, take the arms in both hands and rotate them in the same direction to have a single post with the string held tightly between them. Pull on the string to move the served sections over the posts so they are equal where they meet down from the posts.

Taking the server again, pull the two sections together and, starting at the end closest to the post, serve down the string for six or seven inches. Tie this off with the same wrapping, pulling through as before. Move to the other end and repeat.

When finished, you will have a string with the two end loops and the serving that goes down the limb of the bow. All that is lacking is the center serving. You can add this later, but first check the brace height of the new string. If you measured this with the string on the bow before, you should be very close with the new string, unless you made some sloppy turns with the dacron material as you wrapped it on the posts.

Place one end on the bottom string nock of the bow, brace with a bracing device and slip the upper loop over the upper bow limb nocks. You now can measure the string brace height for comparison. You might be a little high. If so, burnish the string with a piece of leather. Rub its full length with some pressure on the string as you do so. With the older string materials you made your string short, burnish it like mad and it might stretch as much as one-half to a full inch. You might stretch a half-inch with the Super B43 dacron material, but no more.

If you are too low, remove the string from the upper bow nocks, start twisting and count about six turns of the string. This imparts a twist the entire length of the string and one can take up as much as one-half inch with this technique. If you need more twisting than that, it is better to make a shorter string as too much twist will result in a sloppy job.

Many archers make the string a bit long and twist six to twelve turns, since the twisted string will tend to be more quiet. This is due to a certain amount of stretch the twist imparts to the string.

When you arrive at the desired brace height or the one

For easier jig operation, cut off bolt ends on uprights and file the crown smooth. Then cut a groove in each of them with a lathe or file, which holds loop easily.

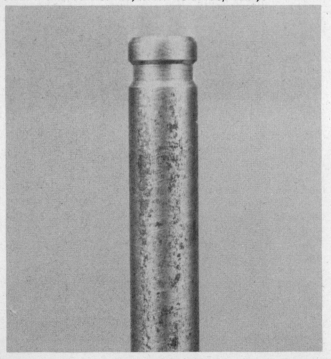

you may want to test with the bow, mark the center serving area with a pencil for upper and lower stops. The center serving should go high enough to provide protection to the string strands above the finger on the arrow and low enough to protect it from the arm, when carried in the field. This usually will be ten inches or so.

If you are shooting a right-handed bow, start from the bottom and turn the server away from you. This will put the center serving on so that, when you pull the arrow back, you will tend to twist the bowstring tighter in the fingers. If you turn the server away, you will tighten the serving when you draw. If you turn the server the other way, this tends to loosen the serving as you shoot the arrows from the string.

Start the serving in the same manner; spin the server to the upper stop mark and tie off with the same method. Use twelve or so wraps by hand for the upper serving, since this is the section that receives the maximum whip when the bow is shot. As a finishing touch, place a drop or two of good cement at the ends of the string on the center serving and the upper and lower sections of the nock servings. Rub the cement into the string serving ends with the fingers and they will last as long as the string.

There also is electronic wrapping material; wax impregnated nylon tape about one-quarter-inch or so wide that makes an excellent upper and lower nock serving material. This is wrapped on by hand and is serviceable, but not easy to locate.

The center serving also varies as to materials. The one mentioned was cotton or perhaps nylon, both easily found, but you might want to use the newer monofilament for the center serving. This material is tough and makes a good serving, but if you use it, you must retain tension at all times or it will unravel and you have to start over. Tricky at first, this is no problem after you have done one or two.

One of the newest materials and the slickest available is Saunders Archery's teflon tape or thread for center serving. This is impervious to weather and is tough. It makes for a clean, fast release, when used for center serving material.

One of the first things to be added to the string after you place it on the bow is an arrow nock. This is a small reminder knot or device to allow you to place the arrow on the string the same way each time. Without it, you never will achieve any degree of accuracy. This is a measured distance and is simply done as follows:

Place a bow square or regular shop square on the string and allow the right angle to rest on the string, the long edge dropping to the arrow rest on the bow. When the long arm on the arrow rest is snug but not depressing the rest, mark the string at the right angle formed by the square at that position. Remove the square and measure up about one-half inch from the right angle mark. Make another mark as a starting point for the nock position.

Here we again run into variations. Some hunters like the nocking point below the arrow, some above the arrow and some on both sides of the arrow. A majority prefer the nock above the arrow. With it in this position, you can remove the arrow from the quiver, place it on the string and move it up to the nocking point, come to draw and shoot without taking your eyes from the game. It is done by touch.

This is the position we have marked; an upper nocking point. You can use the handy Noc-Set made by Saunders or tie one on with the serving thread to make a small raised knot on the string.

To determine whether you have the proper distance for the nocking point, move to a bale. Shoot a few arrows from under ten feet into the bale. If the arrow enters the bale

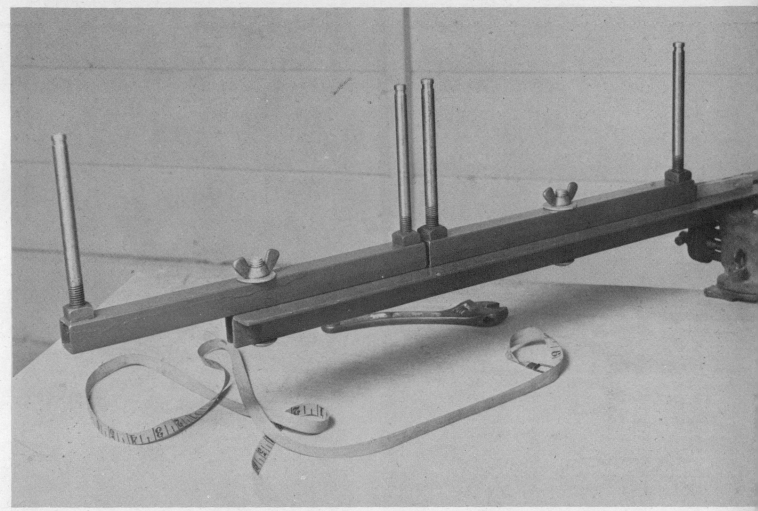

This modified jig by the author has shorter uprights sans bolt heads, with grooves cut and the upright polished. If the bowhunter/jigmaker wants to avoid the polishing segment of the work, he should purchase new, coated bolts at hardware store.

and has the nock end of the arrow high, lower the nocking point on the string a small amount. If the nock on the arrow is low, raise the nocking point a bit. These adjustments will continue until the arrow enters the bale with the nock of the arrow straight in relation to your position. When you have the proper setting, either crimp the Noc-Set or cement the knot.

Another item hunters often add to the string is a set of brush buttons. These rubber buttons, one inch or less in diameter, are placed over the ends of the string. Move them up on the string, then brace the bow. With the bow in braced condition, move the brush buttons to the ends of the string till they almost or just barely touch the limb of the bow. These are designed to fend off twigs and weeds that will catch in the string-bow gap as you move around in the field and woods. You will sacrifice a small amount of arrow speed but not much.

If you feel you need a peep in the string to match the sight on the bow, you can add it. If you prefer not to wear a glove or use a tab, you can add rubber shooting sections that slip over the string. String maintenance should not be overlooked. A piece of paraffin will last for many years and a pound costs about fifty cents in any grocery store. Rub paraffin on the center serving to prevent it from fraying or getting too soft. You also can use it on the entire string, but many prefer beeswax. On the center serving, beeswax gets sticky and will hang up your release if it builds up too

much. While you are in camp after a few days out, take the paraffin and rub it on the serving. Rub beeswax on the rest of the string and burnish this in with a section of leather to make a tight, neat string, without fuzzy ends sticking out all over it.

There is one fuzzy end you may want to add to the top tip of the bow. You can make this from a section of the nylon serving thread or pick up a small feather in the field. Tie this bit of fluff (fuzz out the nylon thread if you use it) to the upper limb of your hunting bow. This will give you an instant wind locator. The lighter the fluff, the more it will work in light breezes.

There are variations of serving materials and if you find something that looks possible, try it. Beware of rough materials on the bow nock ends. Never use monofilament, for example, as this will wear into the string grooves due to the bow action. Experiment, but remember to take two strings into the field when hunting. They should be identical in length and both should be shot many times so they will respond the same, if you should break or cut one.

You can tape the spare onto the riser in a small camo pouch. Have it shot in and the nocking point set, as you won't have time or materials if caught in the field. Leave it attached to the bow for emergency use. It will last for years, but while practicing you could shoot it to be certain it still shoots the same as when you made it. If you change string lengths for any reason, change the spare, too.

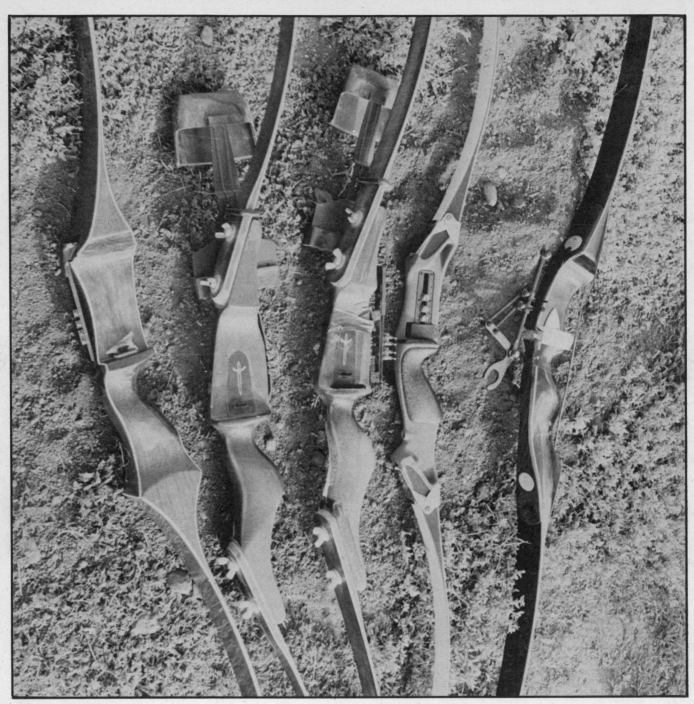

CHAPTER 7

BOWSIGHTS

*Placing An Arrow In A Pre-Determined Spot
Is Somewhat More Complicated Than Aiming A Rifle*

When you buy sights, they will be packaged in a manner similar to this Browning model. You will have to mount them yourself or have it done.

Here, the Browning sight — as shown in upper photo — has been mounted to the bow, with rangefinding grids to the right and sighting pins to the left.

THE BEGINNING BOWHUNTER may have problems, but he will have advantages over the rifle convert. Hunters accustomed to looking over sights to line up their firearm on game will wonder how they are supposed to hit anything without a sight.

There are several ways of hitting game with bow and arrow. Point of aim is used by taking a reference point which may be on the ground or a tree top depending on the distance at which you aim.

This doesn't mean that you will hit that point, but you hopefully will hit the target you are aiming at by using that reference point.

The first thing learned in shooting a bow is that the arrow doesn't go where you think it will. If you want to hit something close, you aim under it. If the target is farther, you aim over it. Each case has the problem of trajectory. This is one place where the faster, heavier bows have an advantage. Each has a faster arrow, flatter trajectory and makes shooting easier. If you want to hit a coffee can lid in a bale, you might drop a piece of paper ten feet in front of

To use the Browning sight, first set up the sight picture, as here, with the area simulating a deer's torso in the brackets. Here, aiming point fits within 20-yard wires.

and use that gap distance between the target and the tip of the arrow. Some archers use one or the other and still more use a combination, but aren't aware they do. You may have to try several methods before you find that which works best for you.

When you work with the gap or point of aim system at a known distance, it will help in the learning process. But when you go into the field, you won't know the distance the game is from your stand. You could shoot a few practice shots from the blind to determine just where to hold when that buck ambles along the path to the waterhole.

The simplest, yet hardest, system is instinctive aiming. If you have ever played baseball and thrown a ball from shortstop to first base, how did you aim that ball to reach the first baseman? You really don't know, when you stop to think. The ball is in your hand, you bring it back, pitch it as hard as you can and you will throw within reach of the baseman. This is an instinctive method; you do it, it works but you can't really explain it. There are some fortunate archers who can do this with the bow and arrow. A rabbit comes up, they swing the bow as they come to full draw holding on the rabbit and they don't even seem to aim. But when the arrow and rabbit come together they aren't surprised.

Many archers wish they could shoot this way, but if they don't have the computer in the brain cells or whatever it takes to achieve this seemingly simple aiming method, they never will hit anything but the ground, some rocks, a few trees and occasionally a deer or rabbit.

There is one bad habit that might be picked up by trying this technique: snap shooting. You think you are on target, you are coming to draw but never quite make it and the arrow falls short since you didn't have the full power of the bow at work.

Running targets are one way to determine if you have the instinctive touch. If you can come to draw, hold, lead and shoot in a smooth system that hits the target, you might have instinctive shooting ability. Don't try to work on this system too long, as it will develop bad habits; you will start missing more than you hit and become thoroughly discouraged about the entire game.

Before you can learn any system, point of aim, gap or the instinctive, you must work on the basics. There are many variables in the sport of archery. We can eliminate some of these and put them into the constant section. For example, if you come to a full complete draw each time, the first finger of the right hand is in the corner of the mouth, the thumb behind the right ear or whatever anchor you find works best for you, you will have eliminated one variable.

Each time you draw that bow and come to the same anchor point, you will develop the same amount of power and thrust to the arrow. If you come back part way, the power will diminish and the arrow won't go as far or will drop a bit lower in the target. A positive anchor is the first step on the road to filling the game bag.

Rifle hunters use sights. They can zero these sights in on paper and utilize this in the field. We can do the same thing as archers. Now that you have the draw-anchor system the same each time, we introduce two more variables. The first concerns elevation. If you want to hit higher, you raise the bow hand, arm and arrow higher. If you want to hit lower, you lower the combination. How much to elevate or depress will depend on the distance from the target and how small a target you will accept as hunter accuracy.

Assume you have elevation to the point that you hit the bale each time and could lay a ruler across the arrows but

the bale. When you come to draw, you actually put the tip of that arrow on the paper on the ground. The physics involved in the trajectory boil down to the simple fact that the arrow passes through an arc and, to control that angle of arc, one must aim above or below, depending on the distance. A bullet has the same complication, but is much less involved due to the speed involved.

The gap system is similar in some ways to the point of aim: You would pick a spot on the bale, hold the tip of the arrow on that spot and hit the target. Where do point of aim and the gap system separate? Actually the two systems tend to merge together.

If the target is close, use point of aim or, if you prefer, a gap below the target that you determine by trial and error. When you go to longer distances, you have no ground reference point, so you pick a spot on a tree or the hill behind

Here's a sight that's similar in principle, but using a circular wire ring instead of wires for bracketing.

The sighting system at left is in use, here. Largest ring is aligned with paper and sight is adjusted to center arrow.

none of them are in the target itself. This is the azimuth or left and right problem.

There are several reasons you might be hitting right or left all the time. The first is a possible mis-match of arrow spine to the bow. Another involves flinching, pulling or dropping of the bow arm before the arrow is off the bow. You tend to watch the arrow hit the target, you drop the bow arm to get it out of the sight pattern and the arrow drops with it, or perhaps moves to the left since you moved the bow a bit in that direction. Hold the bow solid, don't worry about hitting the target. The bow must be a stationary launching pad for that age-old missile you launch downrange.

Many successful archers use bowsights. There are many sights and systems on the market. Perhaps the simplest system is one that uses a series of metal pins that are adjustable both up and down and in and out. The bar these pins are positioned on is attached to the back of the bow, usually with a set of screws into the handle riser. This bar allows the pins to be moved up or down and a set position can be maintained by tightening a holding nut. They can be adjust-

ed (left or right) for the azimuth by moving them in and out. If you were to install one of these multiple pin sights on your bow, it would work like this:

First, follow the installation instructions sent with the sight bar. They will tell you where and how to position the bar on the riser. After you have it in position, place all the required pins — as many as five or as few as three — on the bar itself. The next step is to go to the bales and, using a tape, measure off a distance that you know is correct. Start with twenty yards. Place a target, a coffee can lid or similar aiming point on the bale, bring the arrow to full draw and anchor, place the dot on the end of the pin on the center of the lid and release the arrow. If you hit the lid where you aimed, lock the pin in that position. If you are lower than you like, lower the pin. If too far to the left, move the pin to the right. It is simple but could become confusing.

Back off to a measured thirty yards, move the next pin down to where you think it should be (it will be sheer guesswork at the first shot) and repeat the shooting system. Adjust the pin up or down, in or out by the way the arrow hits the target. This is why the full draw and constant anchor are so important; they make the bow perform the same each time.

When set, this pin will be lower than the twenty-yard pin. Back off to forty yards, repeat, then again at fifty and, if you like, at sixty yards. If you want more yardage markers on the bar, you can put on more pins, but you may not intend shooting at longer ranges.

The pins used for close shooting are the highest in the sight window, while those for the longest distances are the lowest in the sight window. These reference pins will allow you to put the pinhead on the desired target and, if you have judged the distance properly, the pins will put that arrow in the target. They do help, since you now have a reference point for the elevation and the pin will help hold the azimuth. You will be on target more often and probably will hit more.

Many archers don't like sights and they caused quite a

This Bear takedown bow has a magnesium riser with a center sight window built into it. There is a plate, or you can remove the plate and use the sight pictured below.

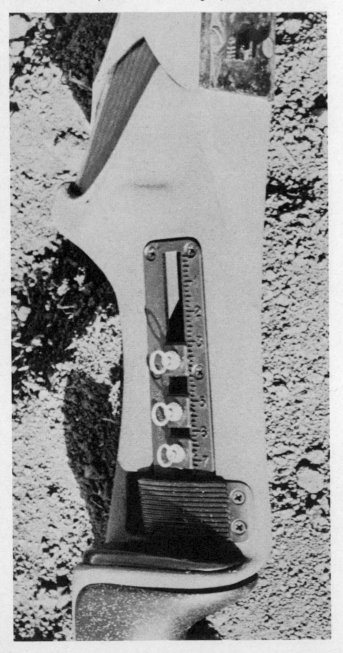

controversy when brought into the archery games. Hunters or target archers not using sights are termed barebow shooters. Since they have nothing on their bows for a sight reference, they use the gap, point of aim or a combination of both or shoot instinctively. The pin shooters, as they are often called, shoot in a different class on the target courses, but all sights are legal for hunting.

There are exotic sights on the market that not only give elevation and azimuth but have a system that can be used as a rangefinder. These have become popular with the entry of new archers in the hunting field.

One type uses a series of decreasing circles. The bigger circle on the top is for the close shots and the smaller circles move progressively down the sight window as the yardage increases. The basic size of a deer's chest from the bottom to the top at the shoulder is supposed to approximate sixteen inches. The twenty-yard circle will put the arrow into the center of the deer's chest if you hold the circle on the deer to break the chest, top and bottom. This is also true for the other sized circles.

With this system, you would sight it in the same manner, except you would use a measured distance — say thirty yards — place a sixteen-inch cardboard circle on the bale, shoot and position that circle on the sight until the arrow drops into the center. The same method is used for the smaller circle at longer ranges. Easy to set, they lock in.

This system does work and many hunters have brought home venison by using it, but what to do with a running deer? It is not foolproof, but it is better than guesswork, if that is your present problem.

Another system uses a large V sighting method. The acetate or plastic sight is installed on the bow by a prescribed method and one merely holds the V on the deer. When the chest area meets both sides of the V, all you have to do is shoot. This system works, also.

Still another type of sight has the pins on the left side

As these rings are all the same size, they're not intended to frame the target but should be adjusted so arrows strike in the center of the ring at distance corresponding to setting.

This Merrill sight has been on the market for some time and has won considerable favor among bowhunters. Here, the mounting bar is taped in place for preliminary tests, but it will be mounted solidly for later use. The pins can be moved up, down, to the right or left, as may be needed.

When using the Merrill sight, the tip of the pin is put where you want the arrow to land, after estimating the distance and selecting the proper pin sighted for range.

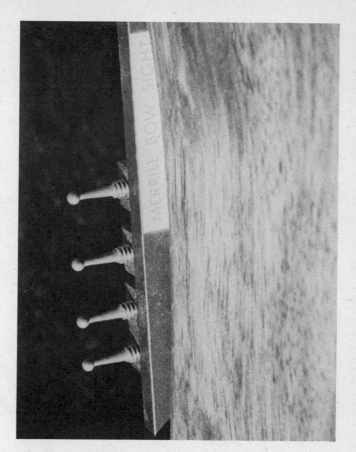

If desired, additional sight bars for the Merril can be obtained and installed for shooting at different ranges.

where they protrude into the sight window. On the opposite side is a plastic with lines scribed in different colors. This works as a rangefinder by placing the lines across the deer's chest area, picking the one that comes the closest to the top and bottom and using the color coded pin that matches the color of the scribed line.

This is a mere sampling of the wide variety of sighting systems you have to choose from on the market and more are being invented, produced and sold each year. If you have a problem with range estimation, the rangefinder style might offer a definite advantage. If you can get the range, but have azimuth problems, perhaps the pin alone should offer enough reference to put you on target. But what works for one archer may not work for another.

If you choose to shoot with a sight you are obligated to shooting with the bow held in a straight, vertical position. The other method of shooting is to cant the bow to the side. This method has some advantages, if you don't need sights, in that you can shoot under limbs, shoot more easily from a sitting or kneeling position and get a shot under or around brush that you couldn't get through with the vertical bow.

You could use sights with the canted bow, but the sight pins would have to extend farther out into the sight window to allow for the slant of the bow. The pins for short ranges would extend out while the longer range pins would be in close to the riser. Adding to that, you would have to cant the bow the same way each time. Most archers who cant the bow don't shoot with sights.

Whether you shoot with a sight, instinctively or whatever method, you will have to learn to judge distance to the

The Sprandel sight combines measure of range with integral sight. Simply press the operating lever with finger of bow hand until target is bracketed between the two range bars, then the white dot pin is moved to the spot you wish to hit and arrow is loosed.

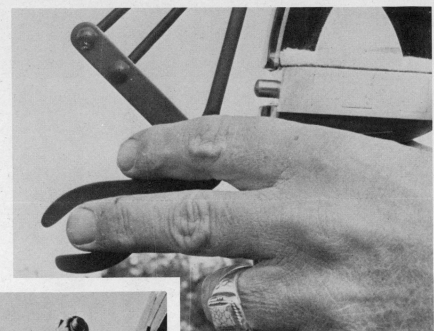

Naturally, it is necessary to calibrate the Sprandel sight to match the given trajectory of the combination of the bow and the arrows you're shooting.

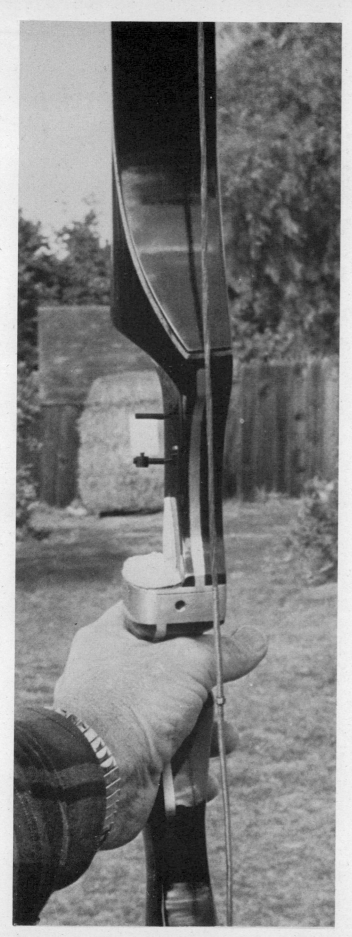

target. One method that works fairly well for most archers is to mentally determine how many football fields the distance would encompass. One hundred yards is farther than you will hardly ever shoot. A shot that distance would depend upon the luck factor, since few deer are killed at that range. But half the football field, or fifty yards, could mean a good shot if the deer is in the open with no brush or limbs to interfere with arrow flight.

You can go to a field range where the yardages are marked off. These will vary from ten to eighty yards but one also can compare bale sizes at these distances. Target archers use a different size face for the different ranges. The closer shots are on a small target, the longer shots are big targets and the ranges between have targets of comparable size.

There are rangefinders for use by golfers and riflemen that can be utilized as a learning process. Pick a target, guess the distance and follow up by checking your guess against the rangefinder. Some archers are poor at estimating ranges, but still hit what they look at. They don't even know how they do it if you ask them. Other archers can judge distance right on the button, but have trouble hitting due to the left or right azimuth hangup. For the beginner, a few sessions with a rangefinder would be of great help. It will at least let you know whether you can judge properly.

A shooter's-eye view of the preliminary rangefinding, as the two bars are aligned with top and bottom edges of the target, dimensions of which correspond to a deer's torso.

After the target has been bracketed, to establish the distance, a white knob on the lower bar is shifted to the intended point of aim, taking care not to change setting.

CHAPTER 8

STRAIGHT FACTS ABOUT ARROWS

The Materials Available And Some Techniques Used In Cresting And Camouflaging.

To THE BOWMAN who takes his archery seriously, the selection of quality arrows is as important and involved as choosing a bow. Arrows that lack exactness, strength and accuracy of flight make successful bowhunting impossible.

Archers have come a long way since the beginning days of bowhunting, when they spent weeks selecting just the right tree for carving their bow and arrows. Today's hunter lets machines do the initial labor for him. In fact, he can easily let manufacturers do all the production tasks for him, limiting his own efforts to a trip to the local sporting goods store, mail order house, discount store or hobby shop, where numerous styles of arrows await his selection.

However, there are still those bowmen, totally absorbed in the sport of archery, who seek the challenge of creating their own equipment. For most, this begins with the home-made arrow.

The first step in producing a handmade set of arrows is to select the appropriate shaft. It should be noted here that throughout this chapter the term shaft will refer to the long, narrow rod of the arrow only. The term arrow indicates the finished product with the colors, feathers, and possibly the tips installed.

There are at present three major types of arrow shafts offered: the cedar or wooden shaft, the fiberglass and the aluminum. As costs of production of materials decrease, manufacturers hope to add a fourth style — the graphite glass shaft, a strong, lightweight arrow. However, current costs make this shaft impractical to the bowhunter, and initial production is expected to be limited to development of target arrows exclusively.

For the novice bowman, it's wise to limit those first purchases to cedar or wooden shafts. This is especially true of the bowman whose loss rate runs high. These shafts are correctly termed Port Orford cedar, since they originate from a small section of the Oregon-Washington coast. Port Orford cedar is known for its straight grain and uniform weight-to-strength ratio, and has been a leading supply area for many years.

Great care is taken in the selection of the best cedar. The trees are then felled and the wood stacked in billets to cure. After a prescribed time they are taken into the mills and cut into squares which are, in turn, cut or sanded into round dowels. These dowels are sold to the arrow manufacturers for making the cedar shaft bought in local stores.

In selecting suitable shafts, the bowman seeks the characteristics of straightness, weight, spine (stiffness) and uniformity, all qualities that bear directly on arrow accuracy.

There are three sizes of cedar shafts popular today, including the more common hunting size of 11/32-inch diameter, the lighter spine and shaft size of 5/16-inch, and the in-between size of 21/64-inch. Another size, but seldom seen, is the big log of 3/8-inch, used for the extremely heavy bows. Most hunters prefer the 11/32-inch size shafts since they offer the heavier spines and mass weight. Most hunting tips are made with the 11/32-inch size in mind.

While the relatively low expense of using cedar for arrow shafts makes it one of the leading choices for beginning bowhunters, this particular shaft has its disadvantages as well. Working with cedar requires a greater degree of labor to produce the finished arrow than when using the fiberglass or aluminum shafts. First it must be dipped in a lacquer preservative, then crested, if that means of identification is preferred, and finally the fletch or feathers added for guidance. The cedar shaft is much more sensitive to humidity and temperature changes than are the other two shafts. However, working with cedar can be a much more enjoyable experience, and certainly a much more aromatic one. Cutting the nock taper or the broadhead taper on the cedar shafting yields a pleasant aroma not otherwise present. As one archer put it, there is a bit of nostalgia involved when working with the oldest arrow material available to us today.

Regardless of the romance or nostalgia involved, what type arrow does cedar make? Those who have stayed with wooden shafts over the years say that they cannot shoot any other type. Perhaps they simply will not shoot any other type, but they can offer many hours of reasoning for their choice. There are certain, indisputable facts about cedar shafts, however. The price of Port Orford cedar is the lowest of the materials offered in the arrow market. If working with a limited budget, it offers the highest quantity of shafts per dollar. Conversely, the wooden shafts

Many bowhunters who select aluminum or fiberglass arrows for use in the field purchase them without any fletching or tips attached, which saves money. As they often are oversized, they must be cut to the archer's proper draw length and a tool used for this process is Easton's Aluminum Arrow Cut-Off Tool. It cuts cleanly and evenly, two prime requisites.

have a higher breakage factor, especially in rabbit and small game hunting, than all the other materials.

If the cedar shafts are stored improperly, they will probably become warped. It's possible to straighten them to some extent with applied heat, steam and pressure bending and achieve a straight arrow, a must for accuracy.

If there is any one major drawback to cedar shafting it is the spine or stiffness available. With low-weight bows there is little problem. However, with bows weighing sixty pounds and more, it may be difficult finding shafts stiff

enough to match the hunting tackle. If it is possible to stay with the lighter fifty-pound bows, the cedars are fine. Heavier spined cedar shafts are available, but the supply is limited and manufacturers generally limit their sale to special orders.

There are two things to look for when buying arrows of any type: spine and weight. Try to avoid a heavy arrow; too heavy in mass weight, that is, for the spine being shot. The total arrow weight for a fifty-pound hunting bow should not exceed six hundred grains (approximately 1¼ ounces)

As can be visualized by the inch increments on the tool, just about any arrow length can be handled. The nock end of the shaft, either bare or with nock and fletching attached, is placed in a hollowed keeper (near the knob in the photograph).

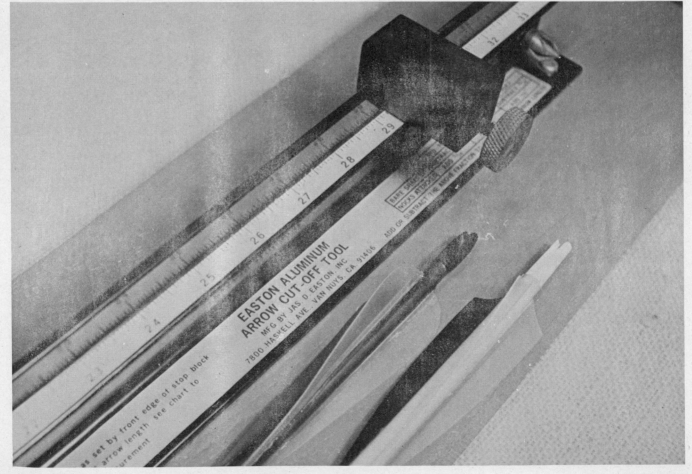

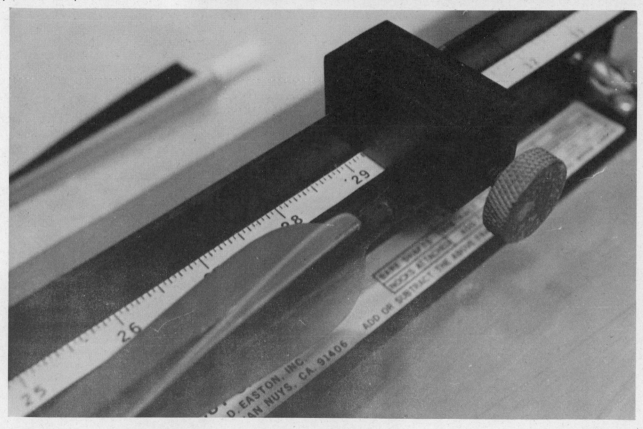

The handy chart on face of tool aids in determining proper cut distance, with either bare or nocked shaft. The guide then is set to distance.

BARE SHAFTS	MID-NOX SUBTRACT 1/8"	BJÖRN SUBTRACT 5/32"	INDEX SUBTRACT 3/16"
NOCKS ATTACHED	ADD 3/16"	ADD 1/4"	ADD 1/4"

ADD OR SUBTRACT THE ABOVE FRACTION TO OR FROM DESIRED ARROW LENGTH

This aluminum shaft, outfitted with Bjorn nock, is set for cutting at 29 inches. Remember to allow extra length for overdraw, so hand won't be cut by a razor-sharp broadhead.

when finished. In order to get this weight-spine ratio, all cedar shafts must be spined and weighed. Many plants offer electronically spined and weighed shafts, at a slightly higher price, assuring the materials to be within the specified limits of the machine. These limits usually are within five pounds or less of spine and within a few grains of weight.

The standard length of an arrow shaft is measured at twenty-eight inches. Standard length refers to the established average length of a bowman's draw, measured as the distance from his right eye, in shooting stance, to the knuckles of his left index finger, minus 1½ inches. However, draw lengths will vary from man to man. The usual length of cedar shafts has thus been set at thirty-two inches, allowing a four-inch variance to accommodate both longer draws and variations in point styles.

When hunting, the bowman is interested in just one thing: putting that arrow, preferably the first one, in the right place to kill the animal cleanly and quickly. Cedar shafts made into hunting arrows have been doing just this for many years.

For the bowman who prefers the cedar shaft, but also prefers to shoot a heavyweight bow, an excellent choice of shaft is the compressed cedar shaft, produced by Forgewood in Oregon. Bill Sweetland came up with a process a number of years ago that allows him to offer any spine and weight combination needed. If a tip-heavy shaft is required, he can make it, as well as the standard styles on the market. Although there are still a limited number of Forgewood sets around, those who have used them find them more than adequate. Forgewoods offer one item the regular cedars do not: a tailored shaft to meet specific requirements. For the archer who likes cedar materials and heavy bows, this may be the only answer.

In the late 1940s a new material was developed — fiberglass. Although the use of this spun glass filament material was hardly restricted to the archery business, it signaled a new era in the manufacturing of hunting and target arrows. Plagued by problems during the initial years, nearly all difficulties have since been solved.

There are two types of fiberglass arrow shafts on the market. They both use fiberglass-resin systems and a similar grinding process, but the method of making the shaft is varied. One system uses the fiberglass woven material which is impregnated with resin and cured under heat and pressure into a hollow tube. This rough exterior tubing is then ground to specified tolerances and the end result is a straight, hollow arrow shaft.

The second method involves the combination of whirling fibers of fiberglass around a mandrel or spindel, while laying a series of fibers along the mandrel. These are also ground to a smooth-finished, straight, hollow shaft.

The variety of shaft sizes is almost endless. The length of the shaft material, again, is usually about thirty-two inches, which allows for the long-draw archer. Transformation of these materials into finished arrows requires the addition of inserts which provide a method of attachment for the nocks and broadhead or field points. It is not necessary to dip or paint them, unless so desired. The color already is in the resin and many hunters shoot the shafts as they come from the dealer.

Fiberglass arrow shafts are either straight or crooked, and there is no straightening them. They will not warp due to normal heat or cold. Like any other material, they will break if not handled properly or if shot into rocks or other hard surfaces. They usually last longer in field use than do the cedars, but that depends mainly on the areas being hunted.

The spine-to-weight ratio in fiberglass is controlled in the manufacture. It is possible to add weight if needed, but the manufacturers usually are archers themselves and are aware of the problems involved. Shafts are available for both target shooting and hunting, and can be used with bows as heavy as the seventy-five-pound hunters. There also is a selection of aluminum or injection molded materials on some shafts. Gordon Plastics makes what they have termed a Nocksert. This incorporates the insert that goes into the end of the fiberglass tubing and the nock that goes into the string. These units are injection molded and fit the different tube sizes as needed. They are made of nylon and are extremely rugged. If damaged, the broken section is either shoved into the tubing or drilled out and a new one added.

Most inserts for the nock and broadhead adapters are made of aluminum and designed specifically for the tubing's inside dimensions. These change with the different sizes, causing some archers to often order the wrong size.

The woven, impregnated style handled under the trade name of Microflite, has been around for many years. To those who have used it, it is known as a good shaft material for hunting.

The only materials needed to make a completed arrow from the fiberglass tubing are a hacksaw with a fine-toothed blade, a miter box to obtain a straight cut and some two-solution epoxy for cementing the inserts to the tube. It isn't necessary to protect the material. It is made ready to shoot after fletching. It will not twist out of shape and the time involved in completing the finished arrow is much less than with the cedar. After the epoxy has set, fletch the shafts with the material of choice and it's ready to take into the field. It also can be dipped, crested or otherwise altered to personal desires, but it isn't necessary. Fiberglass shafts cost a bit more than cedar materials, but for many hunters it is the preferred material.

A little over twenty years ago, a gentleman by the name of Doug Easton started developing the aluminum arrow

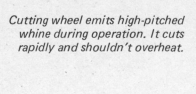

Cutting wheel emits high-pitched whine during operation. It cuts rapidly and shouldn't overheat.

MOTOR SPECIFICATIONS

115 V AC/DC _____ ⅛ H.P.
RPM _____ 23,000 NO LOAD
                  7,000 NORMAL LOAD
AMPS _____ 1.6 N.L .25 STALL
• DESIGNED FOR INTERMITTENT USE
      DO NOT OVERHEAT
• SEALED BALL BEARINGS-NO LUBE REQ'D

MANUFACTURED BY JAS. D. EASTON, Inc.
7800 HASKELL AVE. VAN NUYS, CALIF. 91406

Top: Another angle of the cutting operation, this one on a Swift shaft. Excess is at base of motor. Above: This white-colored fiberglass shaft also can be cut on the Easton machine, with good results. Right: A deburring tool is located at end of system. It cleans the inside of the cut aluminum shafts prior to insertion of a metal broadhead adaptor. No rough edges are desired.

Note the flat edge resulting from cutting with Easton's machine on this fiberglass arrow excess. It's as smooth as uncut end, not ragged.

shaft. As engineers who worked with that material vowed it couldn't be done, Easton proceeded to turn the impossible into one of the finest arrow materials we have today. Doug Easton passed on in 1973, but his son, Jim Easton, is carrying on with the production of the well-known Easton Aluminum arrow materials. Easton Aluminum doesn't make arrows, they make arrow shaft materials. They sell these materials to dealers, who in turn make arrows from them.

Many archers, especially the novices, will state that the cost of aluminum is too high. They prefer to use the less expensive fiberglass or cedar shafts. While it is true that they do cost more in base price, and that they can be bent or lost, surveys indicate that their frequency of breakage and loss is actually less than that of the other styles. They are impervious to any weather. Straight tubes of metal, if bent by a bad hit or ricochet, they can be trued with a bit of time and effort.

There are several grades of aluminum arrow materials made by Easton. The first and lowest in cost is the Swift grade, more than adequate for hunting arrows. The newest

To attach an aluminum insert for broadhead, all that is required are the tubes of epoxy cement, both resin and hardener, and the aluminum adaptor. All are inexpensive.

Another method of inserting the broadhead adaptor, in this case on a Swift shaft, is by using a hot melt cement. You must have a low heat source, like torch.

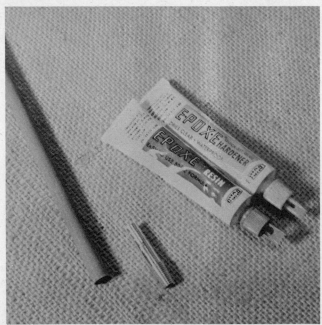

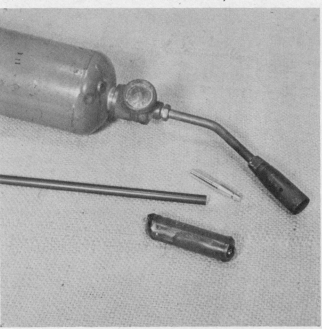

102

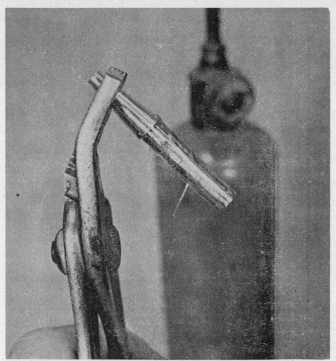

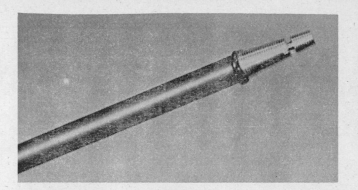

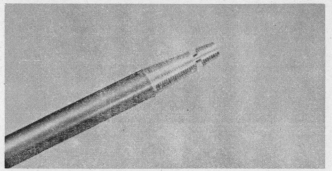

If using a hot melt cement, both the cement and the adaptor should be heated with torch. The cement should be spread on the adaptor, which is held with pliers to prevent burning the holding hand, thereby postponing any arrow building.

Top: Once shaft is heated slightly, the adaptor coated with cement is attached. Note ring of excess cement at base. Above: Once cement has cooled, the excess can be flaked off with a fingernail, leaving a smooth surface.

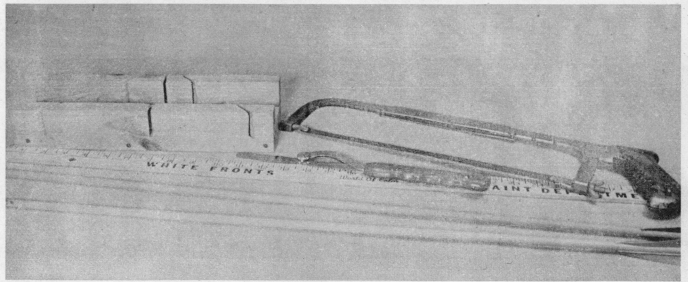

If purchasing the Easton tool for cutting shafts is out of your pocketbook range, fiberglass and wooden shafts can be cut just as neatly with a miter box and fine-toothed hacksaw. Aluminum also can be cut, but not as neatly, this way.

wrinkle in the Easton system has been to take the Swift shaft and anodize it to a buff green that is non-reflective, and will not wear off as a paint or dip will. They are an excellent choice for the hunter.

The next grade is the 24SRTX, a little more bend-resistant than the Swift. The 24SRTX has been highly popular on the target range and in the hunting field for many years.

The next grade would be the XX75, which is even more bend-resistant and makes a tougher hunting shaft for those who give their arrows rough treatment.

The top of the line is the X7, at present sold only through the Bear Archery Company in hunter grades. The X7 features an extremely high bend resistance and tough shafting. It also is anodized to prevent oxidation.

For the hunter who likes the ultimate, many prefer the metal shafts. They often object to the bright color of the metal, but this is easily solved by an acid etch or dip system that will impart any color, any shade or a buff coating to the metal to make it non-reflective in the field. It makes no sense for the hunter to camouflage his bow and himself and then carry a set of six or eight brightly reflecting arrow shafts on the bow quiver. Reflections spook game, just as bright colors do.

The one great advantage of the aluminum shafts is that the hunter can obtain any spine he needs for the bow he

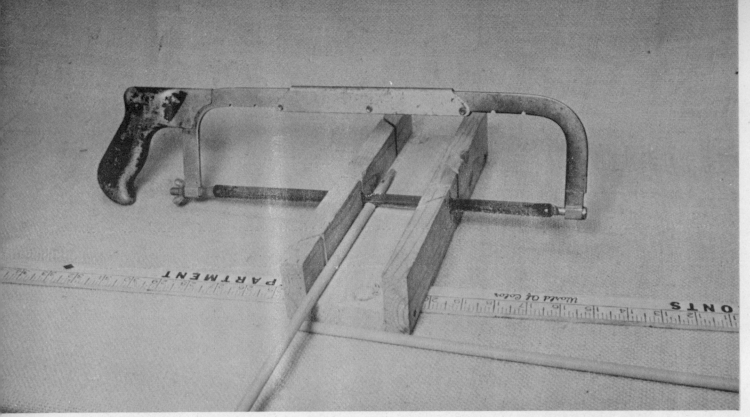

As can be seen above and at right, the wooden shaft is held against the square side of the miter box, then is cut with the hacksaw. This was measured at 29 inches.

carries. The manufacturing tolerances are very strict and have been maintained over the years. The wide selection of tubing, the wall thickness, the weight and many variables that the hunter can put together to make his arrows custom fit to his shooting technique and tackle make the aluminum an excellent choice. They do cost more than some of the other materials, but it is false economy to buy the best bow, spend many dollars on a hunting trip and have the entire project jeopardized by using the minimum in arrow material. A trophy animal is too hard to come by to sacrifice by a savings of a few pennies or at the most a dollar or two for the less expensive materials.

The hunter who converts to aluminum shafts for hunting will find himself watching where he shoots as well as what he shoots. Wanting to retrieve the arrow for future use, he watches its flight more closely, calls his shot a bit tighter and in turn becomes a better hunter.

A hunter should always retrieve a shot arrow, not only because of the cost of the shaft itself, but because it is also the best way to verify a hit. If he finds the arrow stuck in a quakie, with no traces of blood, the animal was missed completely. If there are some traces of blood or some hair on the shaft or fletch, he knows he has wounded the animal and must look for and find it.

Regardless of the arrow shaft material selected, the bowman may prefer to add his own colors to the shaft for identification, ease of sight or camouflage in the hunting field. There are several ways of doing this, and the easiest is by dipping the entire shaft in a tube filled with the proper paint material. The most popular system uses a dip tube made of copper pipe components, one made of PVC pipe components or the commercial models that are of teflon or other similar materials. The main idea is to fully immerse the shaft into the lacquer solution to impart a drab, full-length color to the shaft.

Automotive lacquers are one of the most popular and available materials used for shaft dipping. They can be found in any town, and the only problem is in being sure of the compatability of the lacquer with the lacquer thinner used. If they do not agree, the end result will be a bubbly mess that will peel off the shaft. Keep in mind that, when using the auto lacquers, the finished product will have a bright, shiny lustre to it. To eliminate this, lightly buff or rub the shaft with steel wool to dull that gloss, still retain the color and have an excellent hunting shaft.

Some hunters have had success using latex base materials instead of lacquer. However, many of the latex paints are

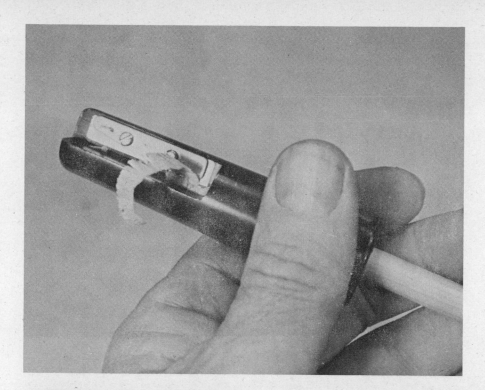

As broadhead end now is flat, a five-degree taper must be put on the cedar shaft, using a simple tapering tool.

When cutting cedar shaft, remember to allow for taper length. The shaft below was cut for 29 inches, but ends up 28 inches because of taper. Allow an extra inch during the cutting.

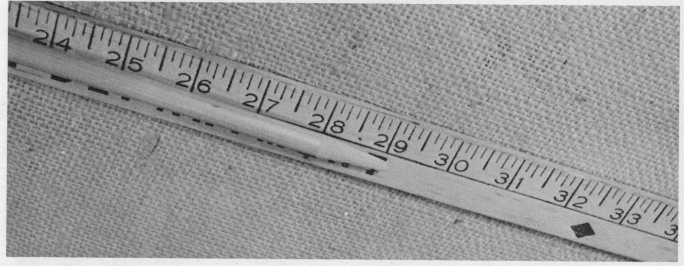

water soluable and will wash off in a rain. Others that are washable would work, but getting a smooth, even coating that does not peel is a problem. Added weight of the heavier type paint is another factor to consider if already on the high end in weight.

The simplest method for any color paint combination is to test it to see how it works. Try dipping a few shafts, fletch them and use them in rabbit and small game hunting to see how well they hold up under these conditions. Use the weekend outings for testing new ideas and materials before dipping the entire supply of shafts.

Another point to consider when selecting a dip procedure is whether that paint will hold the feathers to the shaft. Some paint-cement systems just will not hold, no matter what appears to look good. One combination of the bright dayglow paint material for easy sighting of shafts in high grass proved that the shafts could be found all right, but a feather flew from the shaft on each shot. The cement just did not hold the fletch to the shaft. The paint lifted off

when the arrow was shot and even though they could easily be spotted, the system did not work. This could be a real problem if all shafts had been treated in this manner.

The fiberglass shafts often need no dipping. They have the color impregnated in the resin when they are made. When waxing the final arrow makes it shine, use of steel wool to buff the shaft will diminish the reflections and give a system that will work much better. Wood and the aluminum shafts that have not been anodized must be dipped to eliminate the shiny problem. Fiberglass shafts that have been lightly buffed will often pass the hunting reflection test.

There is one final touch that may be added to the arrow. After dipping a proven color and pigment, add a crest to the shaft. This is usually done just below the area where the fletch is to go and is done with high quality lacquers, using a cresting lathe.

The idea of the crest is as old as archery. How can a bowman tell whose arrow is in the animal or which one hit

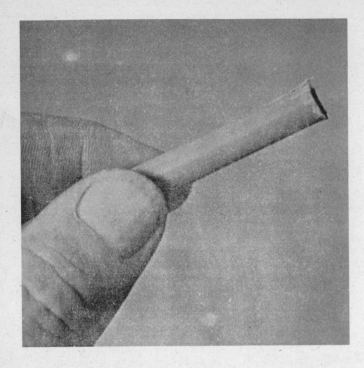

When cutting fiberglass shafts using the miter box setup, be sure to turn the shaft to avoid ending up with slivers like this. Score the entire outer surface and the cut will be clean and square — and shootable!

the bullseye, unless there's some type of identifying mark on the shaft? If all archers shot different shafts, different colors or a different fletch, it would be simple, but they don't. The crest has been used for centuries to mark the arrow and tell anyone finding it whose it is. Some states require that hunters write their names and addresses on the shaft when hunting since it would be impossible to register all crests used and keep them classified. Many hunters go out of state, so the problem is magnified. Cresting isn't necessary, but makes for a neater, cleaner and more impressive shaft.

After selecting the base color, that which will be the full length of the crested area, apply it by rotating the shaft in the lathe and allowing the lacquer to flow onto the shaft evenly. A large brush can be used here to speed up the process. This is allowed to dry, then the next band is placed on the crest area over the top of the base color. For example, it might have a buff green shaft dip color with a red base crest. With the second color selection, possibly yellow, make a half-inch band, then a one-inch band and finish with another half-inch band. This gives balance to the system. After the yellow band is dry, add what are called hairline colors for a touchup. This could be white or even black, if preferred. The hairline is applied at the end of each color, both top and bottom, framing each color. The finished product will have the red base color edged top and bottom with white hairlines, the yellow mid-bands also edged with white and the finished shaft will look more professional.

Cresting can become an art in itself. The colors can be added to the shaft before the fletch is applied and placed in the area where the fletch will go over it. The time it takes to crest an arrow is offset by the appearance of the finished product when compared to plain dipping. It really sets the arrow off.

There is another system used by some archers who prefer not to crest or full-length dip their arrows. This is called shaftment dipping. The upper section of the arrow, where the fletch goes, is termed the shaftment. If the bowman wants to shoot fiberglass arrows, but feels the lacquer will give him a better glue base for holding the fletch to the shaft, he might prefer to dip just the upper section of the shaft in his chosen color and material. This is faster than full-length, requires less material and can be used with any lacquer solvent cement, such as Duco.

If he has the time, inclination and patience, the bowman's arrows can become highly distinctive with the innovation he devises to make them stand out from the run of the mill. The first dipping and cresting may be crude and a little sloppy but, like anything else, it takes time to perfect the system. A dipped arrow will not shoot any better, but it might fletch easier. The crested arrow will not only fletch easier, but will be more distinctive.

To the bowman who makes his own arrows, distinction is the key word. It's very probable that he will never see another arrow exactly like the one he creates. He has the choice of shaft material; the full-length, shaftment only dipping, plain coloring; and no limit to the color combinations he might use for his crest. He can completely bypass the paint and crest systems and fletch directly to the wood, fiberglass and aluminum shaft materials. Woods should be dipped for protection from moisture, but fiberglass and aluminum need nothing in that respect. Many hunters prefer to spend little time on their hunting shafts, fletch directly to the material with no dipping or cresting, and find they are satisfied. They might make a set of hunting-target arrows for group shooting where they can display their techniques, but hunt with the bare shaft.

There is a point where the bowman should stop and think before adding a bright vermillion dip to his shaft. When he goes into the hunt camp for game animals, he wants to attract as little attention to himself as possible. This is the reason for camouflage. Bright arrows that look great among friends will reflect light and show up in the field very easily. A well-camoed hunter often can be spotted merely by the color of the fletch on his arrows. Add to that a bright shaft color and it's a game-spooking situation. Think camouflage, follow through, and leave the gadgets for the target ranges or for home testing.

When selecting arrows, be certain they offer the right bow-draw weight combination. There are charts for checking this, but judge how the arrow flies to be certain. If unable to determine which shaft material to use, try a few of each. Make them simple or elaborate, but make them right.

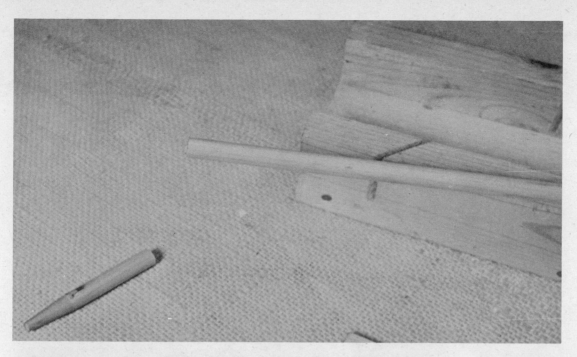

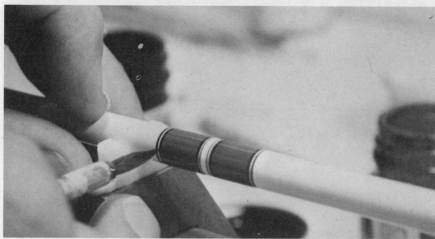

Above: Go slowly when cutting the wooden shaftment with hacksaw to avoid splinters. Left: Cresting the arrow requires a steady hand, and the shaft should be turned while brush tip contacts surface. It is the individual identifying mark.

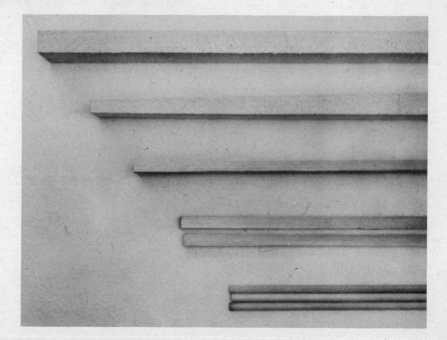

Represented are five steps in the manufacture of cedar shafts. From top, board is tapered on nock end; board is compressed in a press; compressed board is ripped into squares; and squares are then rounded in a doweling machine.

CHAPTER 9

Tips on ARROW POINTS

The Type Of Game Hunted, Terrain And Other Factors Are Crucial In Selecting The Correct Arrowhead

HAVING SELECTED THE bow and arrow of your choice, there is still one factor to consider. The tip that you put on the arrow will determine the success you have in the field. Even though you may have the best bow and arrow combination available — properly matched and tuned — the wrong selection of arrow point can ruin the careful planning so far accomplished.

The first hunting undertaken by the novice bowhunter usually is in the local fields, for small game such as rabbits and squirrels. These give him the needed practice over unspecified distances, so essential when later shooting for bigger game. It also teaches the methods that suit him best for aiming and hitting what he aims at.

The small game heads are many and varied, but perhaps the more popular style is the field point. This is of mild steel with a tapered point that will penetrate pine boards and the soft bodies of small game with ease when shot from a hunting bow. It also can double as a practice head to be used when shooting at bales or dirt banks.

If planning to use the popular weight 125-grain broadheads, then also pick the 125-grain field points. There are a number of makes and varieties on the market, some better than others for minor reasons, but the weight is the more critical feature. They are available in both lighter and heavier weights, although there are few that are heavier than 125 grains.

The reasoning behind the 125-grain field point is that it has the same tip weight on the arrow as the broadhead substituted when deer hunting. The trajectories of the arrows are similar, and the practice obtained with the field point will aid in converting to the deer season. The lighter heads give a shallower trajectory while the heavier ones make it higher.

The field points most commonly used are those with the tapered ferrule, the inside of the point the arrow fits into. There are field points available with the straight wall, that are used with the cedar shafts cut square. The tapered ferrule works better with the fiberglass and aluminum shafts, since they are all designed with this type ferrule in mind. An advantage of the field point is that it can be removed easily. Substituting a sharpened broadhead, the bowman is ready for deer hunting using the same arrow he practiced with; provided it is in good shape.

About the only disadvantage of the field point is that it

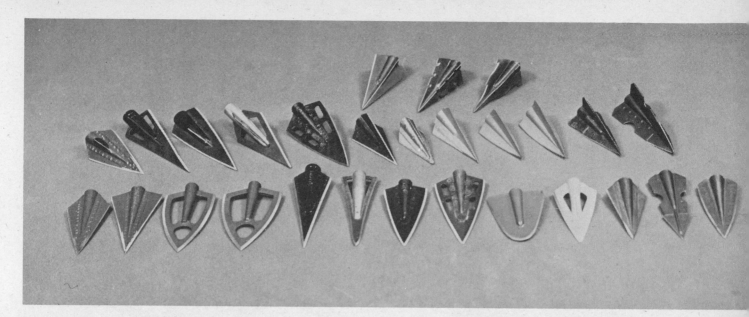

Broadheads available to the bowhunter are varied in design and construction, as demonstrated by the models shown in these two photographs. Bottom row in top photo are double-edged tips, center row shows two-edge blades with bleeder inserts and three-blade heads, and top row shows four-bladed models. Same are shown below, along with a stone arrowhead at extreme left, and a six-bladed broadhead shown in the center. No matter the design chosen, keep the broadhead sharp!

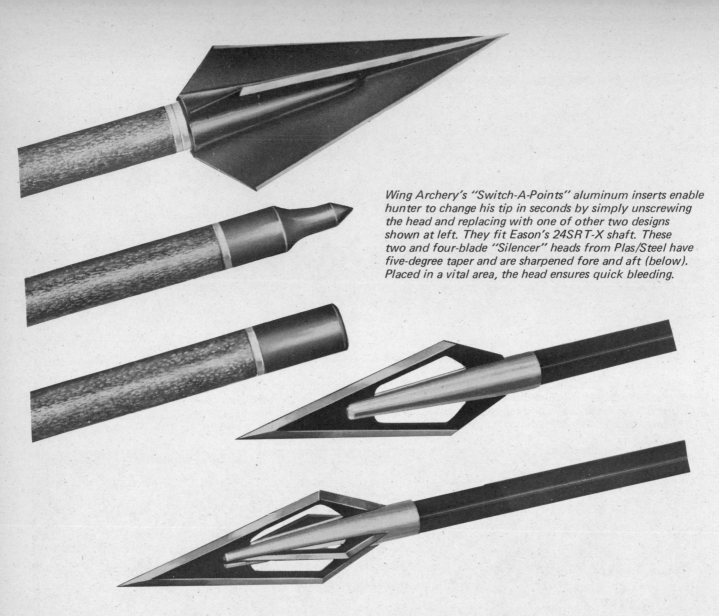

Wing Archery's "Switch-A-Points" aluminum inserts enable hunter to change his tip in seconds by simply unscrewing the head and replacing with one of other two designs shown at left. They fit Eason's 24SRT-X shaft. These two and four-blade "Silencer" heads from Plas/Steel have five-degree taper and are sharpened fore and aft (below). Placed in a vital area, the head ensures quick bleeding.

will dig under grass and into weeds, burying the arrow and making it difficult to find. The archer will lose a few with the field points, but that is one of the hazards of the sport.

When using blunt-tipped arrows, many small game addicts prefer the lighter and cheaper .38 brass cartridges found on pistol ranges. The bowman often can pick up some that the marksmen do not want and usually they will be glad to have someone take them. The .38 brass works well on the 11/32 cedar shafts as a highly effective, blunt-tipped, small-game arrow. The bluntness of the brass also will prevent the skipping of the arrow on impact, helps prevent burrowing under the grass and makes a good game tip. The big disadvantage is that they weigh only 60 grains.

There is a simple procedure that will add weight to the brass and bring it up to the desired 125 grains. Take a hot plate, a small six-inch iron skillet and some solder. Place the brass into the skillet, measure and weigh enough solder to equal the 125-grain weight. Wrap the solder into a coil, insert it into the hot brass and it will melt, run to the base or head and make a tip weigh the same as the broadheads being shot. True, the blunt tip will give some different flight characteristics, but not enough to matter. It makes an excellent small-game practice head that will last for quite a while, and the cost is right.

Another system used by many archers for field practice is the rubber or nylon tip. These are large diameter blunts that slip over the end of the shaft and offer the same weight as the field points. They take impact very well, so arrow

When after small game, field points often are used and three styles are shown below. At left is 125-grain, in center is parallel-wall 60-grainer, and right is 125-grain model dubbed the "Converta-Point." All do the job.

Blunts have proven capable of downing game like squirrels, or others with thin skins. From left are Sweetland's 125-grain, Converta-Point, Copperhead "Shocker," caliber .38 pistol case and 9mm cartridge case. The .38 case neatly slips over the end of an 11/32 shaft, and the 9mm specimen has worked well on cedar shafts. Experiment to find which you like the best.

breakage is greatly diminished. The skipping and burrowing are nil, making the arrows easier to find. They strike the target with force and are an effective small-game tip.

The makers of one of the better broadheads, Zwickee Archery, also manufacture a very slick, small-game head. They call it the Judo point. Made of steel with spring wires protruding from the sides in four directions, it is excellent against rabbits and small game. It costs a little more than the field point, weighs the same and will last for many months and years of hunting. It's almost impossible to lose an arrow, as the wires dig in on a miss and will not slide.

Every region of the country seems to have an innovation in small-game tips. Some utilize the .38 brass, others have found that the 9mm brass also works, and a still different system is encountered in Arizona. These hunters take sections of copper refrigeration tubing that fit over the outside diameter of the wooden shafts, cut them to a length to give them 125 grains and slip them over the tips of the arrow shaft. They leave them a little longer than normal and as the shafts hit rocks, the shaft tip breaks off, shoves the copper back and they continue shooting till the arrow breaks or becomes too short.

Wing shooting often is attempted with the bow and is successful. There are a variety of heads on the market designed to give the archer a simulated spread not unlike that obtained with a shotgun. These heads have wires sticking out the sides, some of them cut at four inches or so, others wrapped back into the head to form loops. Those who have used them say they will down a fast flying pheasant on the first hit. They extend the area of the arrow from the small diameter of the shaft itself to the span of the wires.

The archer can make similar heads if he desires. One simple method is to drill holes through a field point or a .38 brass head, run piano wire, stainless or any other stiff wire through these holes, cut them the desired length and solder them on the inside. The innovations for small game and bird heads are endless.

After some field work with the small-game heads, the archer looks toward the hunting season, perhaps his first with the bow and arrow. Now he must make another decision. The heads he has been shooting will not work on deer. The state laws require a minimum two-bladed head, razor sharp, and they usually specify that the head be large enough to exceed a hole of 7/8 inches.

There are more broadheads — the term used for these hunting heads — on the market than there are field points. The selection continues to grow as new ones come on the market and some of the older ones phase out. The choice of broadheads comes down to experience and the novice bowman has none at this point. The next best thing is to talk to those who have hunted and used these steel tips.

There are some basic classifications of broadheads. They have two-bladed, three-bladed, four-bladed, two blades with bleeders, two and three blades with razor inserts and some newer models on the market that have a main body resembling the field point with slots for inserting razor blades. The styles, shapes and designs become interesting and at the same time confusing, so let's look at each.

The two-blade head is perhaps the oldest style. The American Indians made them from flint, obsidian and other hard rocks by chipping the points. These were replaced with iron when it became available, and we still use a type of iron today. This type head ranges from the aboriginal types of the Stone Age to modern steels.

The first item to consider with any head is the ferrule. This is the section that slips onto the tapered tip of the arrow shaft. The ferrule is produced in several sizes to fit the variety of shaft sizes, but will be found in 11/32, 21/64, and 5/16 inches as a rule. Be certain of the size of the shaft

Bowhunter Dennis Ballard screws a two-edged broadhead into a Converta-Point-equipped shaft, this one of cedar. The advantages of the Converta-Point outfit are many, including not carrying many differently tipped arrows into the field.

before buying several dozen and finding out that they won't fit. Most woods used in hunting take the 11/32, as do some of the larger size fiberglass shafts. The aluminum shafts usually take the 5/16-inch. A compromise attempted by many manufacturers to fit all types with accuracy is the 21/64-inch. It fits snug on the 11/32 and still fits properly on the 5/16-inch shafts.

Some ferrules are machined in one piece, making them stronger and more resistant to breakage on impact. Some are laminated and, depending on the maker, they can be just as strong but will sometimes separate on heavy impact. They remain on the arrow but telescope into the shaft. Regardless of the type, the ferrule must be true in roundness and design. If it is out of round or off-center, the broadhead will not mount properly and the arrow will not fly true.

The two-blade heads have certain advantages. They are easy to sharpen and can be made of harder steel. Some have laminated ferrules, some solid. The size of these two-bladed heads can vary from the 125-grain standard to as light as 110 grains and as high as 200 grains. Be sure of their weight before buying them. Test them. Depending on the design, the weight of the bow and other factors, the heavier heads can be extremely deadly. If using a light bow, under or up to fifty pounds in draw weight, then stay with the lighter heads. A sixty-pounder will handle almost anything on the market today.

The archer will find some two-bladed heads with slots or cuts in the blade on the inside areas. These are cutouts made by the company to lighten the head, to give them the larger cutting area from a large blade, but still achieve the weight requirements. There are some heads with cutouts that will whistle in flight from the bow. Many hunters who use whistling heads claim there is no problem in spooking the game. Sometimes it may be eliminated, but with others it is just a feature of design.

Regardless of design, ferrule type or whistling, the main reason for placing that head on the arrow is to cut arteries in the deer. To do this, the head must be razor sharp. To obtain a good edge and hold it, the steel in the head must be hard enough to sharpen yet soft enough to withstand impact on bone. Bone isn't too much of a problem on deer, since the broadheads usually will cut right through it.

The steel used in most broadheads is tool steel. Stainless steel is too hard and brittle for this purpose and breaks easily. Tool steel can be made to specifications that meet the archer's demands. The usual method of testing steel hardness is the Rockwell C scale. A system used by metallurgists to test the hardness of any steel, it does not differentiate between the types of steel, but the hardness of each. The higher the Rockwell reading, the harder the steel. The lower the reading, the softer the steel. Steel is hardened in a furnace and it can be carefully controlled to any degree. The softer heads, around 45C, will be easy to sharpen; the edge will be soft and can be rolled while sharpening, but it will not last. The tip of the head often will curl right back on impact.

A head that scaled out at 50C may be the ideal hardness. However, the tempering of steel to obtain hardness usually causes some brittleness as well, a defect manufacturers are careful to avoid. A 50C head would be hard enough to take and hold that keen edge required, yet not be too hard for impact. Some heads tried up to 52C were great for sharpness but shattered when shot into a soft pine board. The biggest problem in the archery field is the penetration test. Numerous tests have been made on arrow heads by shooting them into styrofoam, plywood, soft pine and other materials, but nothing equals the test of penetration, with arrow against bone, hide and body cavities of game animals. They must be tested in the field.

Most manufacturers will be glad to relate the hardness of the steel in their heads if asked. It might be below 50C, but be of a better or different type of steel and still retain all the qualities the hunter needs. Regardless of the price, the design and the material, it must be sharp to do any good in the hunting field.

One of author's favorite heads is this two-blade, non-planing specimen. It is designed to slide around bone and get to the vital areas, instead of bouncing off.

For individuals who prefer using rubber materials on the ends of their shafts, try the HTM black design (below). The other large one is from Saunders and works. In center is Zwickey Judo point, also good.

While just a small sampling of the small-game heads to be found on the market today, these give some idea of what's available. Give them a try on small game.

If shooting at flying birds sounds challenging, pick up a couple of these Snaro bird heads. They look weird, but are capable of downing a bird in flight by the design.

If there is one two-bladed head that has downed more game than any other it would probably be the Bear Razorhead. Why this head? Availability is the key here. They can be purchased in just about any sporting goods store, discount store and archery shop. They have provisions for a bleeder insert, but fly and kill very well as a two-blade head. They weigh in at about 110 grains without the inserts.

One of the better heads on the market, and perhaps the toughest, is the Black Diamond. These are made in several sizes, with bleeders and a large size they call the Delta. The steel is good, it takes and holds an edge and they are extremely rugged. Slammed into a rock, the head probably will not survive — the ferrule may well delaminate — but that is about all that will destroy them. They make an excellent choice for field shooting if using broadheads on rabbits. The large, lop-eared jackrabbits require a broadhead to bring them down and the Black Diamond will not only do the job, but survive to get another and another.

Some new designs have appeared in recent years, such as the Browning Serpentine, a twisted edged, two-blade head. Some heads have been made with plastic ferrules and hold a stiletto type, narrow, needle-tipped steel edge. However, they cannot be heat mounted as the ferrule will not take much impact and often the steel is too thin and will not sharpen easily. If looking for some one-shot arrows for running varmints they might be a good choice, but the tips on some will bend over if dropped from waist high into pine.

A new style, but hard to obtain, is the Rounder. This head has a rounded point rather than the usual needle tip. The steel is good, the ferrule true, they take and hold an edge and stand up well against impact. The biggest problem is in finding them, and availability is something to consider.

Occasionally, some old style heads will appear in hunt camps that are open at the back or feature a barbed head. This type head is illegal in many states, if not most, since it is felt the head will not work out of a wounded, but lost animal. Usually required is a rounded or slanted back edge rather than the barbed back edge. The Indians used the

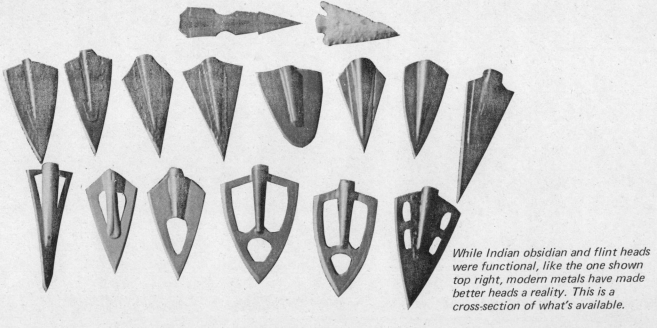

While Indian obsidian and flint heads were functional, like the one shown top right, modern metals have made better heads a reality. This is a cross-section of what's available.

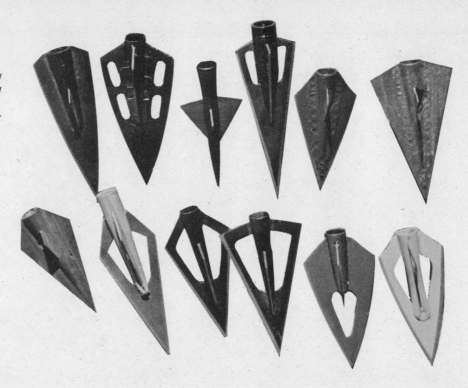

These heads are basically two-bladed in design, with bleeder inserts added to open a larger hole in animal hide. Some are hard to find today, but may still be on some dealers' shelves.

There often is a problem with sharpening three-bladed broadheads, because they sometimes are of three separate pieces. This calls for a steel soft enough to laminate or weld, yet hard enough to attain razor-sharp cutting edge necessary.

Four-bladed heads with full-length cutting surfaces are rare. At left is Catclaw head, with six cutting surfaces. Three models on right are from Copperhead, designated the Magnum, Ripper and Slicer. The Magnum really cuts on passing.

barbed style since they needed game for survival. We hunt it for sport. The best bet for today's bowman, should he happen onto one of these antiques, is to turn it over to a collector. They try to obtain the many varieties on the market and will be glad to take them.

The next style to consider is the two-blade head with the bleeder. This can be found in several styles. One style used with the Bear Razorhead is a small insert of hard steel that will sharpen, inserted at the back of the ferrule but below the shaft tip. The tips of some shafts must be cut to use these inserts, but they give the added cutting edges, promote bleeding and also help to prevent the hole from closing while the deer moves.

Another system, as used by Black Diamond and similar styles, is to cut a section in the ferrule, bend it back and sharpen. It gives the same effect; a bleeder to open the hole made by the main blade and makes a larger hole for better bleeding. They are of the same material as the head and are made so that they cannot fall or be pushed out.

An innovation used on the Little Shaver is the insertion of razor blades at the back cutting edges of the main blade.

The two blade sections are laminated and the pockets that hold the razor inserts are formed when the blade is made. The hunter merely inserts an injector blade and then has a razor edge that cannot be duplicated by the stone and steel sharpening method.

The three-blade head is the next style to consider. These usually are made by taking three pieces of steel, forging them on dies and spot welding the sections together to form the three-sided edges characteristic of this method. The majority of these heads are laminated and will have two laminations meeting at the edge for sharpening. The type steel used cannot be as hard or they will not form. They do cut a big hole in game and that is one plus factor. They usually won't sharpen as well as some two-bladed heads, but they often fly truer and straighter than the two-bladed style. One of the three-bladed heads on the market is the Hi Precision, Bodkins MA-3.

The style and type materials will differ in these heads, but those hunters who have taken them into the field and have scored, continue to use them. Archery is a very individualistic sport and that is one reason it is as great as it is. Everyone is entitled to his own ideas and opinions. The

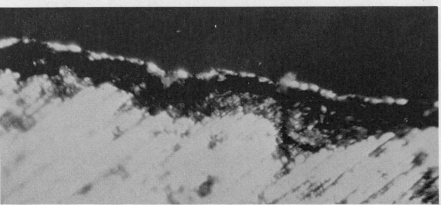

Highly magnified, this is the edge of a standard factory-produced broadhead, after it has been knocked about for a time. Such edges often are taken into the field, however; not a good idea.

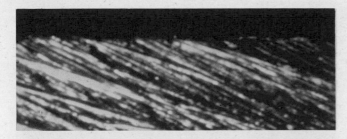

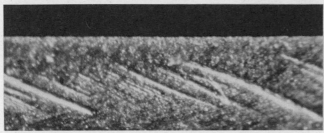

Top: This is edge of broadhead, after being filed with a mill file. Note channels formed by file teeth. It's not shaving sharp, like one (above), the latter having been honed. Some file marks are visible, but away from edge.

determining factor is success of one type or another — trophies for target and meat for the hunter.

There are a few of the razor insert styles on the market. These would include the Little Shaver in three-blade style, the 003 Wasp, which has no main blades but looks similar to a field point with the inserts placed at the back of the head. This has become a recent rage in the broadhead market, requiring the insertion of two, usually three and even four razor blades or commercial blades of razor sharpness. If an archer misses his target, he can retrieve the arrow and insert new blades for any that have become lost or broken.

With the exception of the Black Copperheads, the few four-bladed heads on the market have the similar laminations of the three-bladed. The heads are all full-length four-bladed, but are offered in a variety of blade styles. One features the usual four full-length blades, fitted to a very good ferrule. These are called Slicers. Serrating the edges on the same type blade/ferrule combination makes a very wicked head called the Ripper. As if that were not enough, they make a slash serration with forward sloping edges and name this the Magnum. The success of these heads has been attested to by many well-known archers.

The four-blade heads are very limited. The insert style, such as the Shakespeare Wasp, is one found on the market, but although the four blades will certainly cut a hole, the design and manufacture of the multibladed heads becomes complicated; the steel is formed and that limits hardness and thickness. The end result often is a softer head. The insert styles like the Wasp get around the forming problem by slashing the bullet-like or field point style to insert the cutting edges. With this design the bowman gets a hard, tough point and the sharpest edges.

Some archers find they just cannot shoot a two-bladed broadhead, regardless of the make. When they turn the arrow loose, it planes and makes all sorts of weird patterns in the air. This may be due to several reasons. Usually, it's possible to rule out the broadhead design. More likely it is a mismounted broadhead, one that isn't on true, that causes the erratic flight. An inadequate spine in the arrow can be a factor if the head is too heavy. The buying instructions from arrow manufacturers recommend buying the next heaviest shaft or higher spine if shooting broadheads. This is due to the tip weight and the partial guidance the broadhead wants to put on the arrow.

A good addition to the hunting coat pocket is this Cutmaster, from Bear Archery. After a miss, touching-up the cutting surfaces will insure a sharp head, should the arrow be used again. The Cutmaster is compact and worth packing.

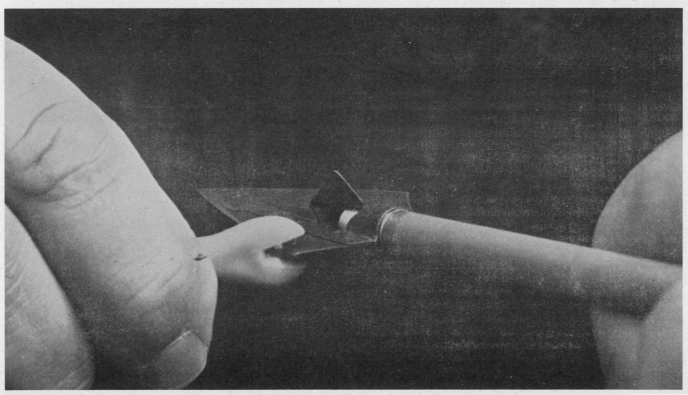

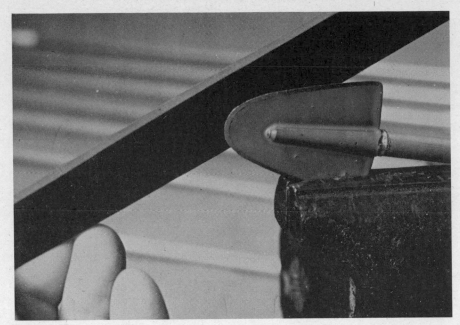

In sharpening this non-planing head, file is pushed forward to make a ragged edge that will grab arteries in a telling hit on game, aid in bleeding.

When the edge is filed back to obtain slimmer edge on blade, process is continued by honing with medium stone.

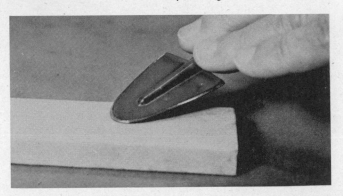

Another reason the arrow may plane is the type of fletch used. A straight fletch will not hold many broadheads but will direct a field point. Broadhead arrows are usually fletched with a spiral or helical twist to offset the planing and guiding of the broadhead. Combine a straight fletch with a crooked broadhead on a light arrow and the arrow might fly like a boomerang.

The blades of the broadhead want to act as a steering system and if they fight the fletch the arrow flies erratically. For many archers the two-bladed head presents the only planing problem. The three-blade and four-blade heads have the third and fourth vane on their steel head that acts as a stabilizer. Thus, the wind does not catch in the same manner and the heads fly straighter on shafts that might be mismounted. The multiple blades in front do some steering to offset the possible planing and the end result is an arrow that gets to the target. If having problems with the two-blade, try a three-blade head. It's possible to eliminate the problem by switching to the multiple blades.

The object of putting that piece of steel on the tip of the arrow is to penetrate the game and kill it. After penetration, the hole made by the head should leave a blood trail easy to follow. The two-blade head often will obtain the greatest penetration since the blades can slide around and between bones. The bleeder blades often will rip off going between ribs and can hold the arrow back. These are exceptions rather than the rule, but it has happened. The two-blade makes the smallest hole in comparison to the other heads. Again, a two-blade of one design will make a different-sized hole than another. One particular head makes a hole approximately three fingers in width.

The three, four and two with bleeder heads open the hide and tissues more, allowing the blood to escape and giving an easy blood trail for tracking. This again is relative to the hit. A hit in the upper lung area will leave little blood trail regardless of the head, as the blood drains into the body cavity instead of out and makes tracking very difficult. This is not a fault of the head, but rather the placement of the hit; and that can be a big factor regardless of the type of steel or how sharp the head may be.

The type head selected should be sharpened to the maximum degree. If the head will not take and hold an edge, discard it for one that will. The edge desired and not too difficult to obtain is basically a razor type edge. Here we find two schools of thought. The first feels the jagged edge left by a file and minor honing will grab and cut just as well — the jagged edges will not close and the blood trail is better. The other school feels the razor edge is best, since it will cut anything and a blood vein or artery is a rubbery, tough material to cut. If the head isn't sharp, the artery will slide around it easily. Deer have been killed successfully with both styles of sharpening. It is very difficult to maintain that razor edge in the field, especially after shooting and missing with an arrow. At this point the file system works, and many hunters agree that they use it in the field to keep the head killing sharp.

The method used in archery to kill game is not to knock it down, or blow it up with projectiles as in rifle hunting, but to slide a razor-edged instrument into a vital area such as the lungs, heart or liver, or to slice an artery and allow the animal to hemorrhage or bleed out. If hunting properly, a deer may be fatally shot but do nothing more than flinch, continue feeding and drop over dead a few minutes later. If a man accidentally cuts himself with a sharp object, but doesn't know it, he might bleed quite a bit before he realizes it. That is the same idea, bleeding, but to completion. There is no shock or knockdown power with a bow and arrow combination. The only shots that will drop a deer in its tracks would be one directly to the head that either penetrated the brain or at least knocked the deer senseless until the hunter could move in and finish it off.

When buying broadheads off the shelf, do not be surprised to find that they are not sharp. They may appear to be sharp, but they aren't ready to take into the field.

Broadheads manufactured in the major plants in this country are frequently tested for the Rockwell scale hardness of the steel. Chuck Buck sets equipment for a test (above). Quality control is exercised continuously.

In testing, the broadhead is positioned on a flat surface and the lever held by left hand is lowered. The scale is located on the gauge and gives the accurate measurement.

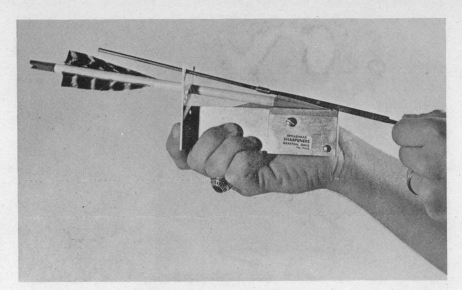

Loray's broadhead sharpener takes some of the work out of sharpening heads, by positioning blades at proper angle. This saves work!

They must be reworked and honed down. Two methods are used. The first is to take the head and put it into a vise, use a file and move the edge back and make it more slanted, or slanted back toward the ferrule. This gives a thinner and sharper edge. The edge left after filing both sides will be jagged, but some archers feel this is the edge they want. The filed edge won't shave hair, but it will cut easily and as deeply as the pressure applied.

The second method is to take the same head after filing, move to a sharpening stone and hone the edges. The archer might stop after using the first stone, or he could go on to a finer grit stone and even to jeweler's rouge and a leather stropping. The edge will shave hair and hide, and cut like a razor which it basically is at this point. To maintain that edge in the field is next to impossible, and a filed edge will usually replace it after the first shot. The steel in some heads makes it impossible to obtain this edge. They are too soft, and the edge just rolls over. It doesn't take long to obtain this shaving edge, and the archer can start with it and feel assured he has done all he can to obtain the maximum.

There is a third method that falls in-between the two above and includes a basic filing system to slant the edge back, then use of a sharpening steel to further align the edge. The file will leave rough, jagged, tooth-like projections all along the edge of the steel. The sharpening steel will align these edges and put them into a system that cuts better, takes little time and is easy to use. The steels used can be the same used for a carving knife or the smaller models now on the market.

Regardless of the method, start out with the sharpest broadheads available, even if it means having someone else sharpen it. After that first shot with an arrow in the field, it's necessary to touch up the steel again. Dirt or gravel will dull the edge. There are many filing units and all have advantages. The little Bear edger, smaller than a cigarette, will do an excellent field job. Just place it on the edge, apply some pressure and pull it down the edge. It actually lifts off strips of steel and the resulting edge will definitely cut.

Saunders came out with a combination file and edge unit that also is excellent. They have incorporated a file with a dual wheel edger in the handle similar to the kitchen knife sharpener, but with only one wheel on each side. First, file the edge back from the dulled condition, then pull the edge through the overlapped wheels. It is similar to the Bear in that it will align the edges and clean up the jagged file edge. It really works and is compact for travel.

There are a great number of units on the market. Most are small files for field use, small enough to fit into a pack, onto a belt or into the pocket. They will clean up a dulled edge and replace it with a fine-toothed file edge, adequate for a good blood trail and sharp enough to cut arteries. Many of the razor edge advocates will touch up with the file or similar sharpening devices in the field.

When mounting the broadhead, problems can be avoided by mounting it correctly. The usual and most popular method is to heat the head lightly with a torch, apply some Ferr-L-Tite — a hot, melted, sticklike cement — to the shaft ferrule and, with the cement and head both warm or slightly hot, join the two with a twisting motion to assure deep seating and to spread the cement to all areas at the same time. If the head gets too hot, it causes expansion, and the head will continue to lift off the shaft end until it cools. If heated properly, a head that is painted will smoke lightly, but the paint will not even blacken from the heat.

There are two methods of mounting the two-bladed head on the arrow. One is to align it with the blade laying flat along the arrow as you look over it on the arrow shelf. The opposite is to mount it vertically. Some state that the vertically mounted head will act as a rudder, throwing the fletch guidance off, and the result is a planing head and arrow. Others that mount vertically state that placing the

With Loray's kit, the broadhead first gets the treatment with a file, then is followed by touching-up with hone.

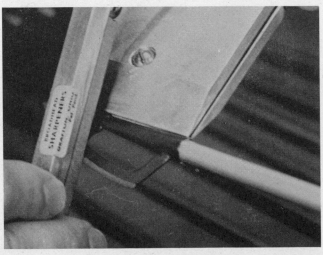

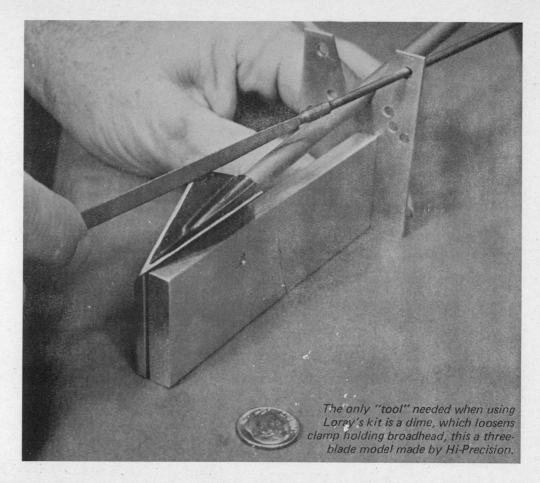

The only "tool" needed when using Loray's kit is a dime, which loosens clamp holding broadhead, this a three-blade model made by Hi-Precision.

Such a small unit as the Loray Broadhead Sharpening Kit can easily be packed in the tackle box when heading afield. It's then a simple matter to sharpen heads when back at camp during the hours when game isn't up and about. Sharp heads are a must, for an arrow kills by bleeding the animal in the case of big game, not by impact shock as does a rifle bullet.

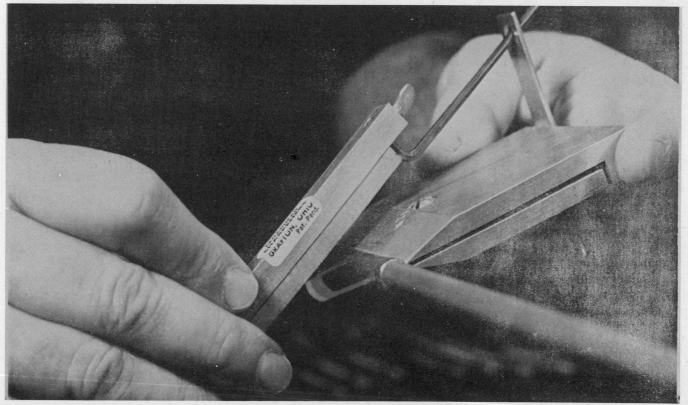

blade on the tip in that manner slows down the oscillation of the arrow, straightens it out from the launching movements of the bow and gets it on its way to the target or deer faster. The archer will have to try both to find out for himself which is best. Two hunters with opposite mounted two-bladed heads can often swap arrows for a check on the horizontal versus vertical systems.

Another reason for vertical mounting is that the blade is less distracting when looking over the bow and arrow system to the target. If using gap or point of aim sighting, try the horizontal; if instinctive, the vertical. The best answer, although evasive, is to try both.

After the cement has set on the broadhead, check the head and shaft for proper alignment. A fast and usually adequate method is to spin the mounted broadhead on a hard surface. If the arrow and broadhead spin like a top with no wobble, they are in alignment. If there is a wobble, reheat the head, set it again and repin until the wobble disappears. This system works, unless the archer should run across a broadhead that is ground off-center at the factory. It will never spin true, even though it is sharp.

Another method that works, regardless of grinding and point problems, is to set up a small vise on a table. Clamp the vise to the edge and set up a board or other method of marking on the opposite edge of the table. Place the broadhead in the vise and be certain of clamping only the blade on the ferrule. Determine exactly where the jaws of the vise are working on the broadhead. Set the jaws tight so that the arrow shaft is solid. Move the board up to the edge of the nock on the arrow and make a mark for the edge or exact center of the nock. Turn the broadhead over in the vise and clamp in exactly the same manner. If the nock mark lines up on the nock in the same manner, the broadhead is dead center on the shaft. If it is off, check the shaft for possible crookedness or realignment of the head on the shaft.

Both the above methods will work. An archer may prefer to use the vise system at home while setting up the field arrows and use the spinning system in the field, since the vise is not one of the tools normally taken into hunt camps. If the arrow wobbles, first check for crooked or

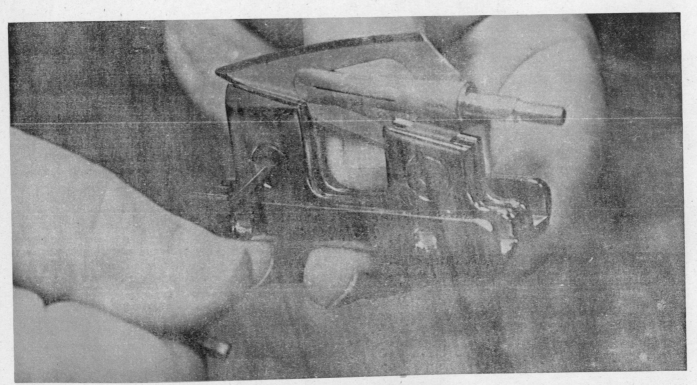

A popular sharpening tool is the Razor Edge, consisting of a clamp and two stones. Allen wrench is used to tighten a two-blade head in clamp.

The good results of the Razor Edge unit are shown on this Bear Razorhead two-blade model. Note the sharp bevel and fine cutting edge. This tip will kill, if it finds the mark!

bent arrows, then for off-center grinding on the head, and finally for realignment on the shaft. The spin is easy, fast and usually accurate.

There may be a rare occasion when the ferrule on the broadhead does not prove true. It can happen, but seldom does. There is nothing that can be done for this situation, but use the head for rabbits and small game. Heads are examined by the makers, but once in a while, some off-center grinding or some ferrule problems will get onto the market. Do not use this as an excuse, but check it out when plagued by erratically flying arrows.

If there is one thing that should be done before going into a hunting camp, it is to test, check and cross-check heads before leaving home. Be sure that the heads are sharp. Check to see that the shafts are straight with no breaks or flaws. Know that the head placed on the shaft will not plane; whether two, three, or four-bladed. If doing the testing at home, and satisfied of continually placing those arrows into a nine-inch pie plate, the hunter's first problems are solved. Be sure the tackle is correctly set up and in top condition. Check broadhead alignment and possible planing. Knowledge of the tackle, what it can and cannot do, is the first step to success. All that remains is to find the deer at the right time, be in the right place and put that arrow into the vital organs.

For the hunter who has checked out his equipment carefully, his efforts will be rewarded at the campsite as well as in the field. Many beginners are heckled unmercifully during their first hunting trip. That is part of the fun; but if they aren't properly prepared, the heckling will place doubts in their mind. If they have prepared their tackle and tested it, they can and will ignore the hecklers.

The archer who shoots a straight arrow, mounted with a razor-edged steel broadhead that is properly aligned, will have most of the hunting problems solved. All that remains is something to shoot at.

Noted bowhunter Doug Kittredge has devised a sharpening tool that has found favor with many archers over the past few years. Simple to use, the tool is pressed down the length of the blade, achieving a fine, sharp edge. Of course, as with other sharpeners, the degree of sharpness the blades attain will be much dependent upon the degree of hardness of the steel, and the quality of that same steel. These factors may differ in heads even produced by the same company, so check out tips when you buy. Don't wait until you're in the hunting camp!

It's safe to assume that, if the broadhead can shave the hair off your arm with little effort, it's sharp enough to do the job when in the field. Naturally, a little bit of caution should be exercised when performing this test so you don't have to miss opening day. The shaving-sharp head shown received the treatment with the Razor Edge unit, getting a total of forty strokes on alternate sides of the stone. There's no substitute for sharpness.

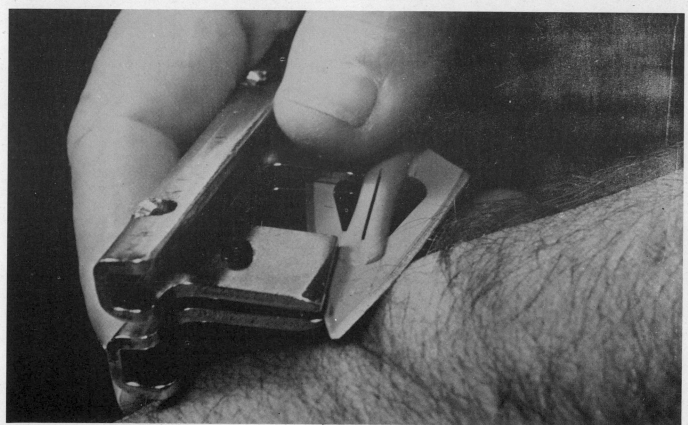

FLETCHING THE ARROW

CHAPTER 10

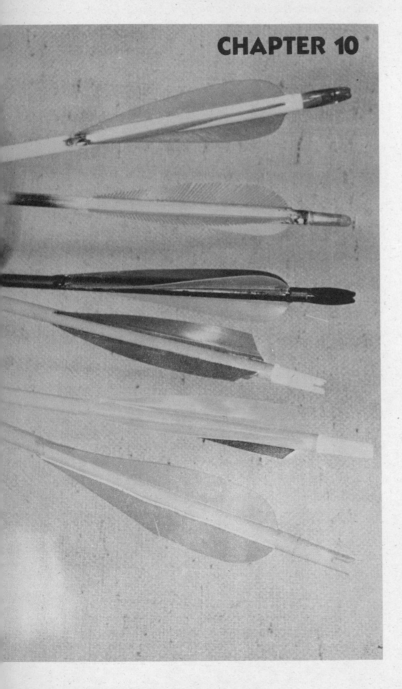

JUST AS THE choice of shaft material and point type are vital to the accuracy of arrow flight, so is the selection and placement of the feathers — the arrow's "guidance system."

For many years, the guiding method most favored has been the turkey feather. These were, in the past, mostly left-wing feathers from the grey barred birds. The farmers trimmed the wings to prevent the birds from flying, usually picking the right wing. Obtaining right wing fletch or feathers for fletching was next to impossible. Today, they no longer trim the wings. However, they raise fewer of the grey barred turkeys, favoring the hybrids in white instead.

There has been some argument over the years as to the better type of fletch materials. The grey barred often were considered the stronger feather, since the white birds, not raised to full maturity, seldom had need for flight. Today, we can obtain both right and left-wing feathers for our choice of fletch, but the grey barred are difficult to come by.

The feathers from the famous Thanksgiving bird are offered in natural colors of either grey or white, as well as dyed colors. The dyed feathers are popular, since their line of flight is easier to follow, the hits quicker to determine and lost arrows more prominent in brush. Most hunters also follow the white fletch with no problem, but may find that they lose the arrow as it moves from sunny to shaded areas. If this is the case, testing of different colors will determine the one that gives the best results. Some bowhunters prefer the bright yellows or oranges. One that is certainly easy to find — and for many to follow — is the bright, pink-dyed white fletch. This one almost appears to glow and can be followed much easier than the whites.

The only way to determine the color that works best is to buy different colors, fletch them up and test them. Better yet, try to follow the different colored fletch used by other archers. This will give a variety of color at no cost.

A number of years ago, the plastic fletch came on the market under the trade name of Plastifletch by Max Hamilton. They greatly improved target accuracy but left little advantage for the bowhunter. The biggest fletch made of plastic still wouldn't guide a broadhead-tipped shaft. When placing a regular shaving edge on the arrow the head took over, causing the arrow to fly erratic. Hamilton went so far as to design a broadhead for hunting in Arizona that would allow use of Plastifletch in the field.

Today there are a number of plastic vanes on the market that will allow use of the standard broadheads. These are of soft materials, in comparison to the stiff plastic used by Plastifletch. The waterproof vanes may be fletched with right or left-wing clamps, straight, spiral or helical. Many hunters have turned to this new material and find they like it very much. Others, who have reservations about it, have tried a few samples for testing and admit they plan to put a half-dozen or so shafts fletched with the plastic vanes in the arrow box for rainy weather.

Some bowhunters, who keep in practice on the straw bales shooting animal rounds during the off seasons, have found the plastic vanes excellent if their shaft passes into the bale itself. In contrast, when a feather-fletched shaft is pushed back, it may ruin the fletch, the feathers become ratty and will not lay down properly. If the feather-fletched shaft is pulled through a bale it compresses the feathers and causes them to lay on the shaft, again giving bad flight.

Beginners in the sport of bowhunting might be wise to test both the turkey feathers and the plastic vanes before deciding on which to stay with. Perhaps a mixed bag would prove best.

Plastic vanes, like these, are the newest things on the market for the bowhunter. As depicted, they come in a dizzying array of shapes and colors, so each hunter can fletch to his own preference. Besides good visibility in the brush, the flexible plastic doesn't break easily.

Whether Of Plastic Or Actual Feathers, The Fletch Truly Is An Arrow's Guidance System.

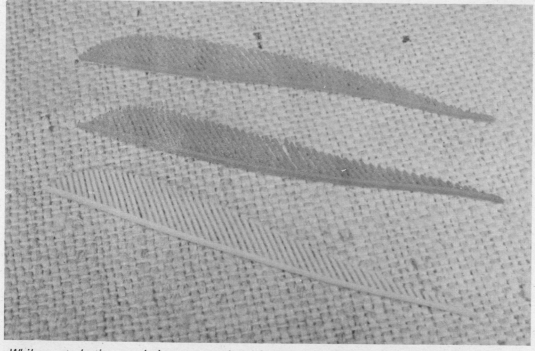

While most plastic vanes imitate conventional feather patterns in construction, there is one style on the market that duplicates the turkey feather. Again, these come in many colors.

Once you have selected your vanes, you need some way of attaching them to the shaftment. These clamps, used in different jigs, are Gebhardt's left-wing helical fletcher (left), Bitzenburger's left-wing helical (center), and Gebhardt's straight clamp (right). All work admirably.

The Bitzenburger Dial-O-Fletch jig operates like its name signifies: dials (knobs) are adjusted to set the angle of the clamp for either straight or helical.

One of the top jigs on the market, this Bitzenburger with left-wing helical clamp in position can be adjusted for many types of fletches. It will last for years.

Once the selection of fletching material has been made, it is time to choose a jig to place the material on the shaft. Here, again, there are many styles and varieties on the market. How much fletching to be done will determine the type of jig purchased. If perfection is desired, try the Bitzenbuger fletcher, long known as the leader in the field It can fletch the shaft with a straight, spiral or helical fletch, but requires a straight and helical clamp.

If planning to fletch only a few shafts from time to time, the accuracy and cost of the Bitzenbuger jig may not be needed. The extremely simple systems will work, but are not very accurate in giving the same fletch twice in a series of twelve. When making up arrows the bowman usually will make them in sets of dozens, or half dozens, unless he is refletching or testing new materials. There are some jigs on the market that allow him to make a three-fletch at one time on one shaft. Each shaft made in that style will come out the same if using only the one jig. They usually are not as adjustable as the other styles, however.

Another factor to consider is how much time is available to spend making the arrows. If he likes to do a batch at a time and then forget it for a while, the archer might find the Gebhardt Multi-Fletcher just right for his needs. They make a single jig or one that allows him to make six arrows at one time, one fletch at a time. With the straight clamp he can make them straight or spiral-fletched. By buying a right or left-wing helical, he also can make that style. The bars on the jig are fully adjustable for right or left-hand fletching.

Let's consider the feather fletch for the first situations. Manufacturers offer fletches with a precut shape, called diecut, as well as the full-length feather with only the base sanded for ease in fletching. The base of the quill section must be ground flat to assure the feather will stay on the shaft, providing a gluing surface and adhesion at the same time.

The diecut feathers have been precut by machine to the desired shape. They have a good taper to the fletch and the shape will be the same all the time. They are available in the popular parabolic shape with rounded tips on the back or the older style of shield cut, the angled cut favored by many in the past and still considered the more accurate of the two styles by many bowhunters. The older shield style has been known to whistle in flight, however. It is a minor problem but prompted many to change to the parabolic. In burning the feathers, the wires of the parabolic are easier to form, as well.

When using the diecut feathers order the shape, length and color desired. Most hunting shafts have a five or 5½-inch fletch on them if three-fletched, while some hunters prefer the four-fletched shafts with four-inch fletch. Diecuts are simple to fletch. Place the feather in the jig clamp, apply glue and place on the shaft. When they are removed all that remains is to add a drop of glue to each end and place them in the arrow box.

Occasionally, the bowman may make a wrap-over helical — one that has lots of twist in it — and find the forward point of the diecut does not have enough feather for gripping. If so, the front section of the fletch will run straight or at odd angles, making a ratty looking arrow.

The full-length feather has advantages, too. In viewing the entire feather, the archer is able to select the area from which he wishes to cut the hunting fletch. What does he look for in feathers other than color? If he holds a feather up to the light, he will see a section along the base that shines more than the upper or outer section does. This is called the oil line. The higher the oil line, usually the better the feather and the stiffer fletch it will make. How can he tell whether the fletch is right or left-wing? Here, again, it is simple. Look at the feather from the side. If it is shiny all the way along the base or quill area and rough on one side, he can easily pick the wing the feather came from. If the rough side is on the right side, with the heavy or base end of the quill pointing away from him, it is a left-wing feather. The opposite is true for the right-wing feather. It is necessary for the bowman to determine whether the fletch is a right or left-wing feather, since he cannot successfully fletch a left-wing feather in a right-wing helical clamp or vice versa.

Pick the preferred area on the full-length fletch and cut this at the base with scissors or a pair of diagonal pliers. Pliers work very well and can handle the heaviest quills. Measure up the feather and cut the full length, say five inches, then place the cut section in a pile until the desired number for the fletching session is filled.

While it is possible to fletch this full-feathered fletch using the clamp, it is easier if the excess feather is cut away with a pair of long scissors; long enough to make the cut in one sweep of the blades. Make the cut about one inch high above the quill base. This makes the fletch handle easier in the clamp and produces a neater fletch.

The shaft should already be prepared with the nock of choice and the color if dipped; or cleaned if a bare shaft of fiberglass or aluminum is being used. If using the lacquer-dipped shaftment or full-length dipped shafts, the choice of cement is simple: use Duco. Duco is a lacquer solvent and will fuse nicely with the lacquer dip on the shaft. Or, you can use one of the other cements, such as Easton's or Fletch-Tite. Just be certain it seals the fletch to the shaft, or it will fall off when the cement dries. For example, do not use Duco on bare aluminum or fiberglass shafts; it just will not hold the fletch regardless of how much is used. If unsure, try fletching one or two shafts to find out — before making up a big batch for the hunting box only to find the feathers have fallen off when it's time to use them.

Some archers like to use two colors when fletching arrows. They will use a yellow for the cock feather and white for the hens or other two fletches. This lets them know which is the fletch that goes outside when they place the arrow on the string. If using speed or indicator nocks, it is possible to tell this without the different colored fletch. Three feathers of the same color, however, do give a brighter image to follow, presenting a circle of color as they spin toward the game.

The Gebhardt Multi-Fletcher jig is loaded with six left-wing helical clamps. The unit's upper and lower arrow slots can be set for left or right-wing helical fletch, or the straight fletch many bowhunters prefer using.

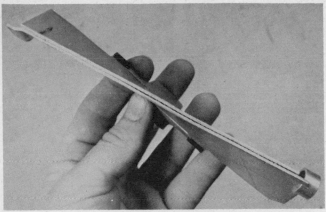

Understandably, with a left-wing helical clamp, like this example from Gebhardt, a bowhunter only can fletch the left-wing helical. Note index mark at upper left for setting the proper arrow nock distance. It saves time!

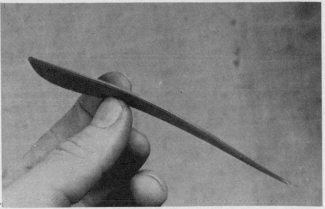

After setting the jig and selecting the proper vane you intend using, break out the cement. Note that this vane from the Ultra Vane Company has a cement trough running its entire length. This aids in sealing vane to shaft.

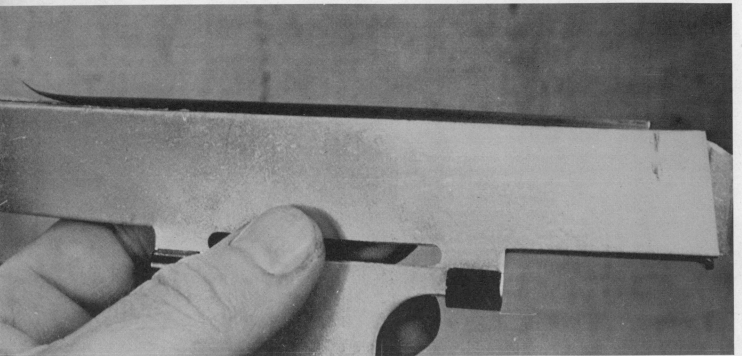

With the vane inserted in the clamp, you'll notice that a small distance between the clamp and the fletch exists, which allows the fletch to tightly fit against the arrow. Tip (left) must be checked when fletching to assure it isn't off shaft.

Regardless of the use of one or two colors, one fletch will be the outside or cock feather. Rotate the index knob on the jig until the cock feather is up or in the right position to place the first fletch on the shaft. Place the fletch in the clamp allowing a distance of at least one-half inch from the base of the nock on the shaft to the back of the fletch, and mark this on the clamp. This will prevent the fingers from getting in the way of the fletch when drawing. Once the clamp is marked, all shafts will have the same distance between the nock and the fletch.

Leave a small section of the feather between the clamp and the quill. This will allow for slight compression of the fletch onto the shaft as you place the fletch. Take the proper cement and run a light bead down the quill of the fletch. Not too much, or it will gob and make runs on the shaft.

All that is needed is a light covering of the quill. This is easily accomplished by holding the cement in one hand, the clamp in the other and easing the cement onto the quill.

Set the clamp into the slots or on the magnet of the jig and ease the fletch onto the shaft. Move slowly and the system will work easily. Moving too fast often causes a smeared, sloppy fletch. Apply a light, down pressure to the clamp to be certain the fletch is seated all along the length of the shaft.

If there is anything tricky about the jig, it would be in getting it adjusted or tuned the first time. The fletch must fit well, not sloping over the ends or running off at odd angles. If using the helical fletch, it must curve slightly around the shaft as the fletch goes on because, if adjusted too far, the forward end will miss the shaft entirely. Try placing a dry fletch in the clamp and a shaft in the jig. Then, either visually sight it into alignment or run a pencil line down the shaft for proper alignment. Once it has been tuned lock it down, or mark it for return to those positions if using the jig for different types of fletching.

When the cemented fletch is placed on the shaft, wait a reasonable time; at least twenty to thirty minutes before removing the shaft and clamps from the jig. Remove the clamp too soon and the fletch will curl around the shaft and often lift off at the ends. The humidity, temperature and type materials used all are factors to consider.

It is then time to decide between the right and left-wing clamps and settings for a spiral fletch. If purchasing the helical clamps, it is necessary to buy either right or left-wing clamps. They cannot be intermixed or used alternately as the straight clamps can. Whether or not it makes any difference to use right or left-wings is an open question, but most archers agree it makes little or no difference in the hunting field. The basic idea is that the right-handed archer should shoot right-wing fletch and vice versa for the left handed archer. The different types of fletch attachment make the arrow clear the bow better, at least in theory. It is unwise to mix arrows, combining right and left-wing or straight, spiral or helical. They should all be of one type. Some archers pay no attention to the cock feather when shooting and often shoot it on the inside, passing the entire fletch over the bow window.

If the diecut fletch is used on the above fletching system, there is nothing left to do but place a drop of glue on either end of each fletch, set them aside to cure and forget them until hunting season. If the full-length style is used with the same fletching system, the shaft becomes an excellent flu-flu arrow. The fletch will be high, square and ugly. To convert it to a hunting arrow, burn the fletch to shape it.

The Gebhardt Multi-Fletcher, used in this case, has been set, the index nocks mounted for the shafts, the fletch set behind each unit, clamps behind them and Fletch-Tite cement waiting at top. All that's needed now is patience.

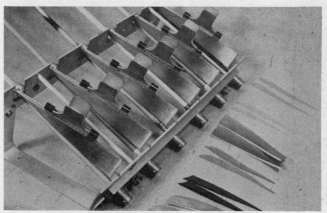

The next step is to apply the fletching cement to the first series of vanes, which now are applied to the shafts. They should be left for curing. See text.

After the final vane has been applied, following the directions outlined in text, you can see how the various fletches should appear when done properly. From left are diecut fletch, shield cut plastic, feather-vaned plastic, end cut from full turkey feather, and last two are the plastic designs in shield and parabolic cuts. The choice is almost unlimited, and there's something for everyone.

This is done with a nichrome wire clamped in a transformer to create a high heat. The nichrome wire is pre-shaped to the desired cut, height and shape, either shield or parabolic. Most hunting fletches are at least one-half inch high and often five-eighths of an inch. Preshape the wire by bending; checking and bending until it meets the style requirements. This can become somewhat frustrating, as the wire changes as it heats. One of the best styles of burner favored by most archers is the Young feather burner. It will last for many years and offers ease of adjustment.

Check the fletch in the burner before heating the wire. It may be necessary to change the nock accepter — a glass nob or similar system of allowing the nocked end of the shaft to rotate. If the distance isn't right, the fletch will be cut too far or not far enough. This is easily spotted when looking down onto the burner-shaft system.

When satisfied with the adjustment, place the plug into the circuit, heat the wire red hot, place the shaft into the locator and start rotating the shaft in the guides, burning the fletch as it rotates. Burn all three fletches, one at a time, but in the same position. It may be smart to do this in the garage or in an open area, since the stench of burning feathers is very unpleasant.

Place that shaft aside and burn the other untreated ones. When they all have been burned, take a small piece of sandpaper or an emery board and clean the burned edges of the feather. These burned sections come off easily and it makes a more professional looking fletch. The tip or forward end of the fletch will have a ridge where the quill thickness rests on the shaft. Shave this down with a sharp knife or razor blade, or sand it down with a small sanding wheel. It is best to slant this and lower the ridge, or it may catch on the hand as it passes. A sharp knife works fine. Place a drop of cement on each end of the three fletches and set them aside to dry.

We have just described the method of three-fletching a shaft for the hunting field. There are various variables and choices to make, but it's possible to start anywhere and adjust with time and experience. The first fletching job will either be discouraging or very pleasing, and often both.

Some hunters prefer the four-fletched hunting arrow. The procedure is the same, except there are two different styles of four-fletch. The three-fletch jigs place the feathers on the shaft at 120-degree increments to give a full circle on completion. The cock feather takes care of bow clearance. If trying the four-fletch system, there are two basic types: the 75-degree/105-degree, and the ninety-degree systems. The ninety-degree styles place a fletch at ninety-degree intervals around the shaft. The other system alternates between the one at 75 degrees, the next at 105 degrees, the next at 75 and the final at 105. This makes a wide, then a narrow area of spacing on the shaft, allowing the fletch to pass the bow window with ease. Some say they find it flies better.

When using the four-fletch system, the archer usually uses a four-inch fletch. What he basically is doing is adding more feather mass to the shaft for guidance. If the area of the three-fletch was measured at five inches, then calculating the area of the four-inch, four-fletch, he would find the area has increased quite a bit. The area on the four-fletch can be decreased by burning them lower, say to one-half-inch high. To increase the area of the three-fletch, five-inch, burn them higher, say five-eighths of an inch. Too much area produces a very slow arrow. Too little area, naturally, gives a faster arrow, but it also may be erratic, since it cannot handle the weight and deflection of the broadhead.

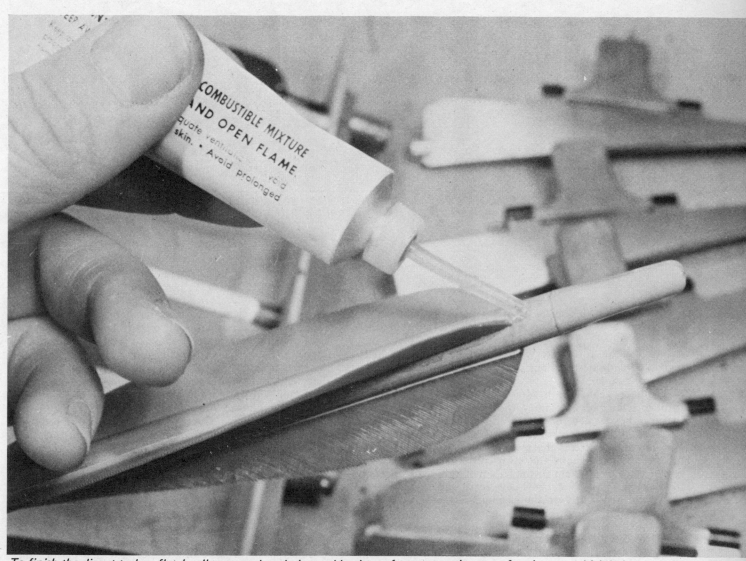

To finish the diecut turkey fletch, all you need to do is to add a drop of cement at the rear of each vane, which helps to hold the fletching sercurely to the arrow when afield. Always carry spare equipment when hunting, or face disaster!

Turkey feathers, because of their size and strong construction, have been used in the fletching of arrows since the first bowyer discovered he needed something to stablize the flight of the shaft in the air. Here are a few examples.

The archer who realizes he has a bad release problem, but is unable to correct the release, also can find aid in the use of a high-cut fletch. He has a tendency to pluck the string, and the arrows fly wild or wobbly on release. The higher fletch will straighten out the shaft faster, but also will slow it down.

Feathers wear out, become matted or, if they pass through game, become ratty from the blood. Sometimes they can be steamed for reuse, but it is better to clean the fletch from the shaft with a knife or other sharp edge, sand the area and refletch. The aluminum and fiberglass shafts can be refletched many times for continued use. The best system is to clean them to the base material, redip or clean the shaft and place an entirely new fletch on it.

We touched lightly on the cleaning of the shaft, but it is important and perhaps should be gone into in more detail. The dipping makes it easier, but colored fiberglass shafts also can be fletched directly, without dip. Clean the fiberglass area for fletching with some alcohol. Rubbing alcohol is easily found and works very well. It will clean off the fibers from the grinding and the oils from the hands at the same time. The fletch will always adhere better.

Cleaning aluminum shafts is a bit more complicated. If they are not clean, the fletch will fall off easily. The method recommended by the Easton plant is to scrub the shaftment — if planning to fletch to the bright aluminum —

with a powder cleaner, such as Ajax. This will clean off the oxides of the metal and the oils of the hands. Do not handle the section after cleaning or it will merely add oil again. Test the cleaned shaft by dipping it in water. If the shaft has been cleaned properly, the water will appear as a film evenly spread over the surface. If the shaft is not clean, the water will show up in droplets on the shaft. Continue scrubbing with the Ajax until the droplets do not form. Cedar shafts are the easiest to clean, requiring only a light sanding. Better yet, dip them to prevent moisture from getting into the wood.

We have used turkey feathers for many years. They are readily available and the cost is reasonable, but they have some problems, too. In rainy weather they get matted down. If shot into an animal, they become matted and useless. And if pulled through a bale when target shooting, they become ruined, regardless of whether pulled forward or backward. But, until recently, they were all we had.

Today we have more of a choice. The new plastic vanes make all these old problems a thing of the past. They will take rain, they pass through game with no problem and can be pulled through a bale either way. If they have any problem it is that they should be shot from a side rest of the bow window and not from the shelf. Many of us have preferred to shoot from the shelf, regardless of how many times we are told it makes the arrow fly erratically. Try it

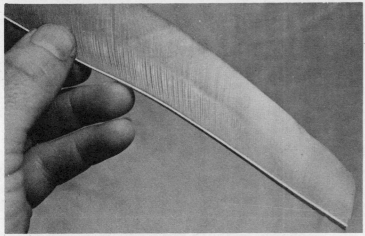

One thing to look for when purchasing good turkey feathers is the oil line. As shown here, it is the glossy section close to the quill base of the feather. This one is good.

This is how your complete set of trimmed turkey feathers should look, cut to five inches in length. They are ready for clamping and fletching to the shaft.

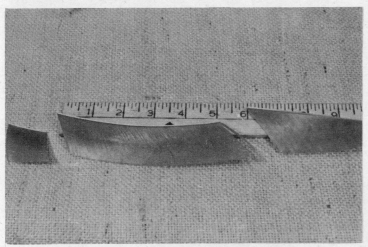

When good feathers have been secured, get a ruler and scissors and cut the feathers into five-inch segments.

With the arrow removed from the jig, glance down the shaft from the nock. If it's a left-wing helical, this is how it should look. If not, you've gone wrong.

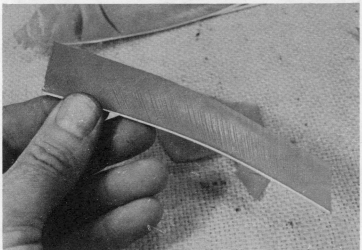

The fletch handles easier in the clamp if you cut the upper end and also along the length of the feather. The width, when cut, should measure more than one-half inch.

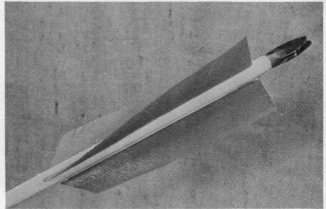

When the fletched shaft is removed from the jig, this is how it will appear. It can be left this way and used as a flu-flu, or can undergo further modification in a burner.

If you've decided to burn the fletch, the Young Feather Trimmer is good and accurate. You must shape the nichrome wire to the desired fletch shape, however.

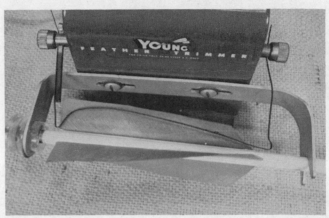

Before heating the cutting wire, you should check to be certain the nock is properly located, or you might mis-trim the fletch. A visual check for clearance is needed.

When the wire is heated, it might be wise to hold your nose — the stench from burning feather is awful. Here, a feather is being trimmed to five-eighths-inch parabolic cut. The burner completes the task in a short time and works well.

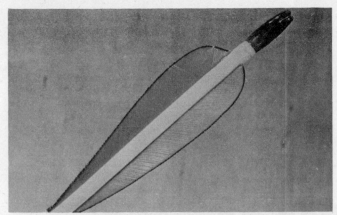

After the burn treatment, the edges of the fletch will be hard. They could be left thusly, but it is neater to clean them up. Also, the bottom of the quill must be trimmed away from the nock to keep it low on the shaft.

Sandpaper of any grit is customarily employed in cleaning the charred edges of the feather. By lightly scraping against the feather, all evidence of burn will disappear. Don't get carried away, or you may jerk feather off!

with the plastics and you will soon learn what an erratic arrow looks like. However, this problem is easily handled by adding an arrow rest that either mounts on the base of the shelf, allowing the fletch to pass the window, or mounts on the window itself. If going to plastics, go to rests as well.

The new vanes are supple, not stiff, pliable and basically soft in texture and feel. They have a wider area for better adherence to the shaft and will mount on the shaft using any jig-clamp system. Some archers have found they obtained better results with a right-wing helical on broadheads than with the left-hand styles, but that is a matter of testing.

There are several styles on the market offering color and length selection as well as a new shape, the French. It is similar to the parabolic, but slightly different. Many hunters are testing these new vanes and finding the color, cut and make that appeals to them. It's a good idea to try this new plastic vane material. It would be excellent to add to the arrow box for that rainy day that used to be spent sitting in the cabin or tent.

There also are some sprays that can be used on the feather fletch to help prevent water matting. If using the spray waterproofing, it should be done before going to the camp. The spray smells and deer will detect it if it is too fresh.

Moths love feathers almost as much as wool, and storing feathers in mothballs, or better yet with some pieces of red cedar — the type used for lining closets — will keep them out. Store feathers in solid containers where water and insects cannot get to them. If they are kept in direct sunlight, the sun, eventually, will bleach any color from them. Plastic shoeboxes, with some cedar sections, in a cabinet would be ideal. Protect the arrow box and the stock feather box from bugs and keep them dry, and they can be used for many years. Fletching is fun, simple and one item that should be included in the archer's equipment inventory.

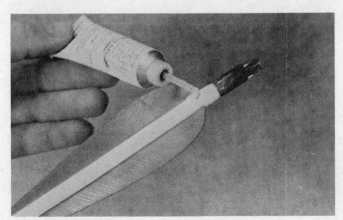

About all that's required before heading out to shoot your new creation — if it hasn't turned out to be the equivalent of an archery Frankenstein — is to place a drop or two of cement at the base of the quill and the upper and lower attachment points. While it can be shot as soon as the cement dries, most cure overnight.

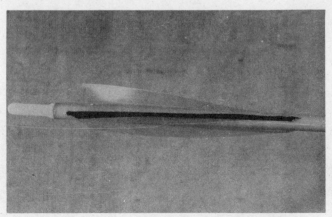

The left-wing helical plastic fletch with shield cut is turned down and around the shaft like this. They are semi-transparent and can be easily lost if not colored.

The Arrow Nock

CHAPTER 11

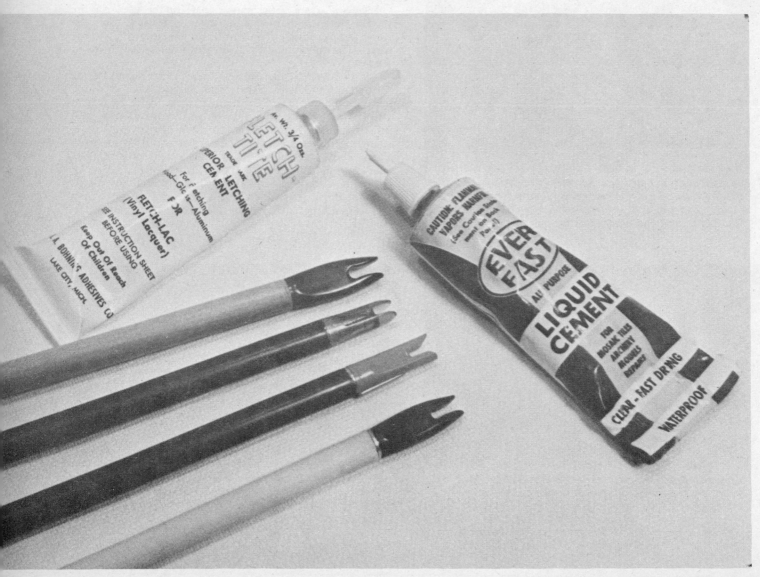

A Seemingly Minor Item Which Plays An Important Role In Assuring True Arrow Flight From Release To Target.

THERE ARE SEVERAL methods of attaching the arrow — for a short time — to the string of the bow. One is the nock, a small section of plastic that fits over the string and guides the shaft of the arrow as it is launched. This may seem a simple unit, but to the archer eager to make his own arrows, it can be one of the more important needs. If this small piece of plastic is placed on the back of the arrow shaft in a haphazard manner, it probably will wobble, causing the arrow to fly erratically.

The interior of the nock plays an equally vital part in flight accuracy. Each nock is calibrated to an internal taper of eleven degrees, designed to fit the taper on the arrow shaft. Should this mould or method of making the taper vary even one degree, the nock will not seat properly and will wobble.

There are numerous styles of nocks from which to choose. One type preferred by many hunters is the butyrate plastic style, a soft but tough plastic that will not break on impact, with a slight ridge running down the edge.

The ridge down the edge of the nock is what archers term a speed nock, and is designed to identify the cock (or lead) feather on the arrow. Most hunters prefer to shoot three-fletch (arrows with three feathers) shafts with the cock feather a different color than the other two. Equalized placement of the three feathers allows the arrow to whip around the sight window unhampered, as discussed earlier.

Occasionally, such as in night shooting or when temporary distraction from the target is undesirable, it is not always possible to make a visual identification of the cock feather. This is when the speed nock comes into play, since

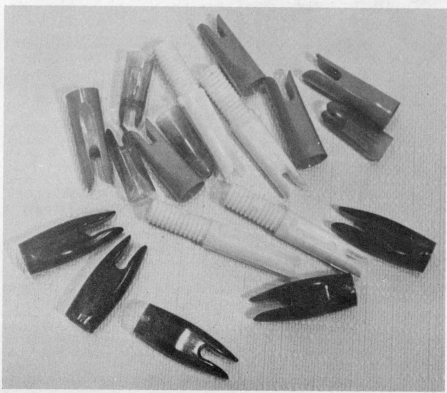

A sample of the nocks available includes Speednocks, Bjorn nocks, Goodyear nocks and Gordon Nockserts.

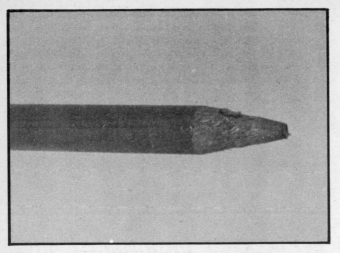

The tip of this cedar shaft has been tapered to the required eleven degree angle. However, the tapering tool had a dull blade, leaving a rough surface not best for installing nock.

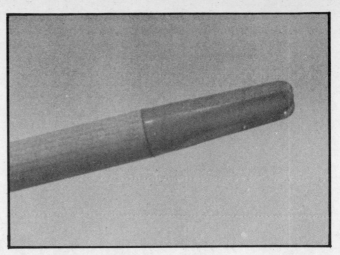

When aligning the nock on a wooden shaft, you should have the grain of the shaft in line with the index nock for the best results. This is the stiffest portion, provides proper spine.

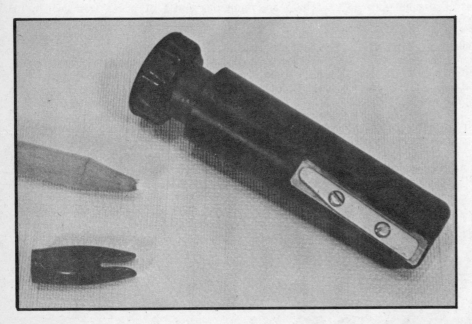

A properly tapered wood shaft with the tapering tool on the right and a Bjorn nock. These now are made in the 11/32 size, to fit over the tapered shaft, held on with cement.

it allows the archer to place the arrow correctly by feel rather than by sight. It is a quick, speedy system and works well on any style of nock.

While there are many styles of nocks to choose from, there are a few whose design makes them preferable. One style of nock that is becoming more popular in the hunting field is the imported Bjorn nock. Composed of a plastic material with a tight fitted section, it features a gap or hole that the string fits around. This style seems to grip the string better than some of the others and allows the arrow to be carried on the bowstring with little fear of its falling off. It has no speed index, but with the aid of a file one could easily be added. The nock is somewhat thinner in the center and presents fewer finger problems. The thinner center section allows the two fingers to get closer together and there is less pinch.

Another style favored by the bowhunter is the butystyrene nock. Although excellent for hunting, these nocks are somewhat more brittle than the Bjorn nock, and may break on impact, making them impracticable for practice or stump shooting.

In recent years, the Gordon Plastics Company has introduced a nock that is moulded along with the nock insert for their fiberglass arrows. They call it a Nocksert. It is moulded of nylon for the various size shafts they produce. It has an advantage in that the archer need not buy a separate nock; with just the unit, he is ready to fletch and shoot. If it should break, it can be replaced in the field, provided it hasn't been epoxied into the tubing.

To replace one that has popped in the field, simply push the broken nock into the tube, insert a new one and continue shooting. They fit tightly and must be literally forced into the shaft. (If the broken nock has been epoxied into the shaft, it can be removed by drilling a hole in the end and pulling it out with a screw threaded into the hole.)

Regardless of the choice of materials, each nock should meet certain standards. First, the taper of the inside of the nock for attaching to the shaft should be true. Second, the nock should have a deep enough taper to allow good leverage on the shaft end. The depth of the nock or notch in the end should be deep enough to allow the string to be seated. The width of the slot in the nock should be wide enough to fit the bow's string size. If it is too loose, the arrow may fall off when being carried on the string or may slip forward on a fast shot. It should fit snug, but not tight. If it fits too tightly, it will hang up on release and arrow flight will be erratic.

If the archer happens to like a particular nock and it is too loose, he can build up the center section of the string where the nock fits with an extra wrap of serving. Just an inch or so will do and the nock can be made to fit.

If it is too tight, it's possible to file or sandpaper the insides of the nock, but this must be done carefully so as not to leave edges that may cut or fray the string. Sanding with medium grit paper will open up a nock with a minimum of passes. Sand and fit until the desired tension is reached, but try to sand evenly so the nock doesn't become lopsided.

Occasionally, the bowhunter finds an arrow that flies wild even though its alignment appears fine. The shaft is straight, but it still flies crazy. If in rolling the arrow on a flat surface the nock wobbles, it isn't straight on the end of the shaft. This may seem minor, but it can and does cause wild-flying arrows.

On handmade arrows, one of the first things to check is the taper of the shaft. It should be even on all sides and the nock should fit snugly without too much flare on the edge. If the nock wants to open or flare at the bottom, the angle of the taper may be off on the shaft. Check the tool or grinding method used for tapering. A variance of just a degree or so may yield a taper that will not allow the nock to seat properly and the arrow's flight is again erratic.

When shooting fiberglass or aluminum shafts, the nocks are either aluminum inserts or swaged tips on the shaft material. This usually is the last thing that can cause a problem, but if there is one, check the taper on the nock. Occasionally it's possible to run across defective nocks. although they are carefully checked before sale.

The main reason for a nock to be off on the end of the shaft is improper placement. When seating the nock for gluing, put it on the end of the shaft, then turn it around a few times to remove any burrs on the inside of the plastic

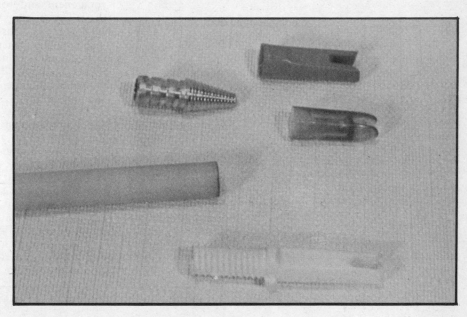

Fiberglass shafts arrive as a hollow tube. You can use the aluminum taper insert at top or the molded nylon Nocksert from F. Gordon Plastics. Other nocks are Goodyear and Speed.

A Bjorn nock has been cemented to the tapered end of this wooden arrow, providing a neat and streamlined appearance.

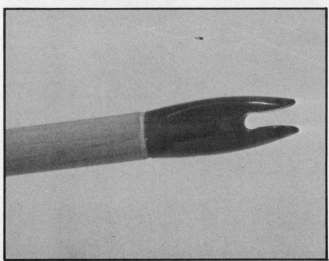

A Nocksert in a fiberglass shaft, showing the index. It's a tight fit and can be used with or without epoxy or cement.

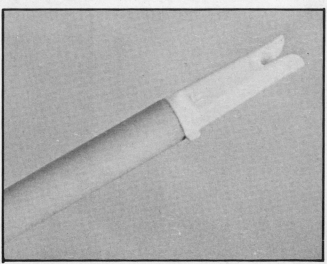

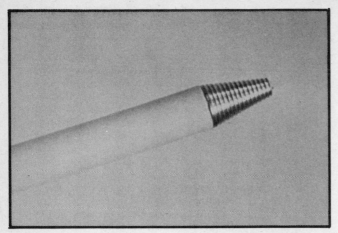

This aluminum insert has been machined to fit inside the hollow fiberglass shaft, being held in place with epoxy and tapered to eleven degrees to accept the epoxied nock.

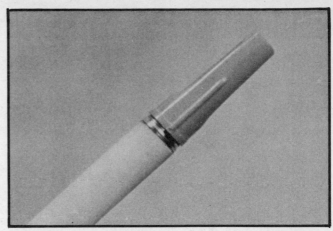

Here, a Speednock has been fitted to an aluminum insert in a fiberglass shaft by means of epoxy, completing an assembly as shown in photo at left with just the insert.

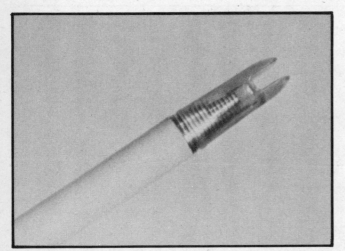

A fiberglass shaft and aluminum insert, as shown at top of page, with Goodyear transparent nock cemented with epoxy.

component and to align it with the tapered end of the shaft. This twisting works to fit the two units and often will keep later problems from occurring.

Before the cement is placed on the shaft, roll the arrow on a flat surface and watch the nock. If it rolls smoothly, it is mounted correctly. If it wobbles or you see an added size to the end, it is crooked. Turn it on the shaft some more and recheck it.

A cresting lathe makes an excellent nock checker. Place the tip of the shaft in the lathe, run the motor and check for wobble. The slowness of the motor allows a positive alignment check and several shafts may be tested in a few minutes.

Add the cement that works best with the shaft material and turn the nock as it's seated. Before the cement hardens, spin, roll or place it on the lathe for a positive check.

The cement used will depend on the shaft material or on the dip material. For any dipped shafts using a lacquer, you can seat nocks with Duco or any other cement. The Duco is a lacquer solvent and makes a tight bond. If there is a bare aluminum insert or taper from the aluminum shaft, do not

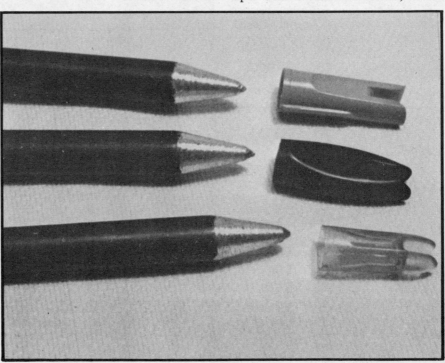

Easton aluminum shafts have been anodized to subdue light reflections for hunting. The tips have been swaged to the 11 degree taper at the factory for perfect fit with the nocks which are, from top, the Speednock, Bjorn and Goodyear.

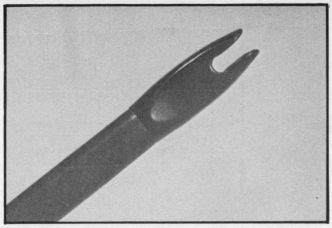

The Bjorn fitted to the aluminum shaft makes a good rig for hunting as the nock will hold onto the string until shot.

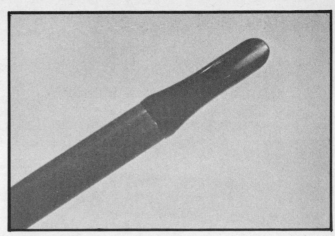

Side view of the Bjorn nock, as in photo at left, shows the narrow profile that keeps fingers closer, prevents soreness.

use the Duco type cement. Duco does not adhere well to aluminum and chances are the nock will fall off in a short time. Instead, use Fletch-Tite, Easton or a similar cement. Applying epoxy to the nocks does have its drawbacks, however. Should it become necessary to replace one, removal becomes complicated and may damage the taper on the insert.

Allow the nocks to dry for several hours before using them. Overnight is always a safe time period. It can be embarrassing to retrieve arrows and find the nocks have fallen off or flown away. They sometimes will pop off on impact or from a ricochet on wood or rocks, but the nock usually will be with the arrow as long as the archer owns it.

Nocks come in many colors, many styles and many sizes. If ordering by mail, be certain of the exact size of the shaft. It might not be a bad idea to save the nock end of broken arrows for mailing with the order to be certain of obtaining the proper size. A nock that is too small won't seat properly and one that is too big will flare out at the base and won't fit right, either. The larger one will work, but it isn't an ideal system.

The best time to check nock alignment is prior to fletch-

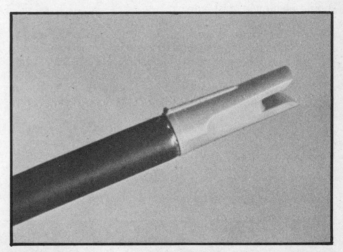

An aluminum shaft with Speednock.

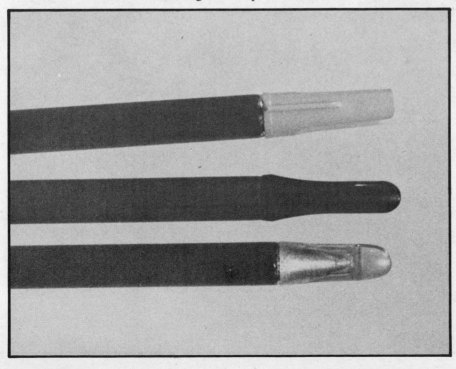

Note that Bjorn nock, center, is slimmer in profile than the others.

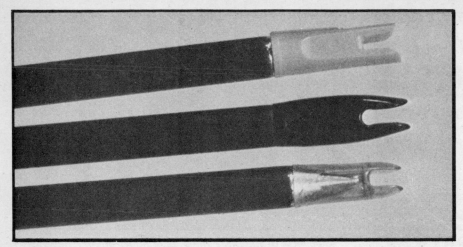

Side view of the same nocks shown on bottom of preceding page. Here you can see the index on the Speednock.

ing the shafts, when the shaft is bare and easier to work with, but it will be necessary to replace nocks from time to time. A few nocks in the tackle box or quiver often are a godsend in the field. On an extended hunt, the bowman should plan on at least a dozen.

Sometimes, if the cement isn't right, the nocks will fall off with temperature changes. To the bowhunter who has traveled several hundred miles to reach his favorite haunt, only to find he has no arrows to shoot when he gets there, extra supplies are a necessity. The cost of the nocks is one of the lowest in the entire archery tackle section. They run from a few cents to about fifteen cents each, a small price considering the cost of the trip and other tackle.

To replace a nock — if and when one is lost, broken or comes apart from a glancing shot — first check the arrow for straightness and in the case of wood, probable splits. If the shaft is crooked, straighten it, or if cracked, throw it away. A cracked shaft can break on release, inflicting serious injury to the hunter.

With fine sandpaper, smooth the taper of the shaft to remove the old cement and clean the nock pieces that might be left. If most of the nock is still on the taper, use a pocket knife to cut up along the taper and the nock will come off easily. This is the point where an epoxied nock would be difficult to remove. Cement works better, if the nock has to be replaced. If the nock is shot off from a glancing arrow, check the taper for damage.

After sanding lightly to clean the area, replace the new nock by turning on the taper, aligning the speed notch marker with the cock feather or, if one isn't used, the string slot with the cock feather. This will help prevent undue wear on the feathers. If the nock is replaced even slightly

Here a Speednock has been fitted to the string, showing depth of its nock and index in position for shooting.

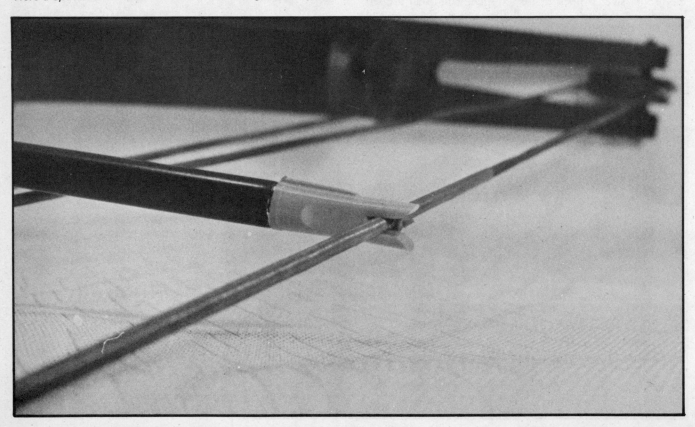

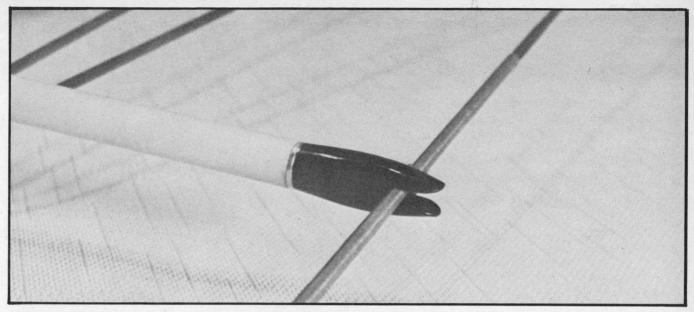

The Bjorn nock snaps lightly over the string and remains in place until shot, making it handy for hunting.

off its original alignment, the feathers will start to fray along the edges from striking the window or shelf of the bow.

Regardless of whether nocking a new set or replacing old nocks, keep them clean on the taper, turn them for proper seating and use the correct cement for the materials involved. If uncertain as to which nock to use, try one style, then another, until you find the one you prefer.

The nock must be tough enough to withstand the impact of the string from dead stop up to and including a two hundred feet-per-second velocity. If it isn't tough enough to take the impact, the arrow won't fly properly. A simple item in the order of things, the nock is quite important, but usually misunderstood by many and not even considered by others.

Archery is an individualized sport. The novice may find the knowledge and direction of a professional invaluable during the fundamental stages. However, many bowmen soon find themselves intrigued by the aspects of making their own equipment. At that point, curiosity takes over. It's fine to experiment with the many items on the market, to design your own feather shapes and color schemes, but never take a new item into the field until it has been carefully checked out, especially a nock.

Buy, test and determine, but keep the nock on right and the arrow will be true in getting from the bow to the game.

The Gordon Nocksert in place on the string. The small knob or indicator can be seen here.

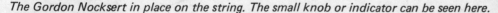

CHAPTER 12

Bowhunting QUIVERS

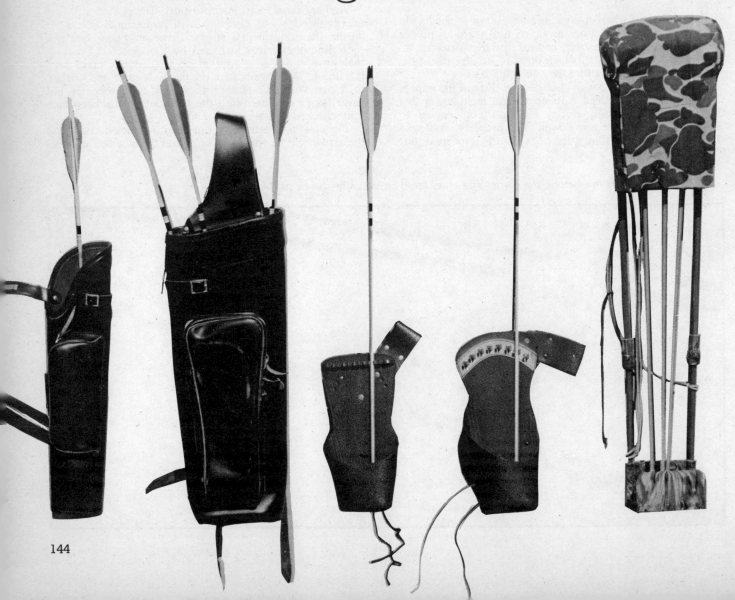

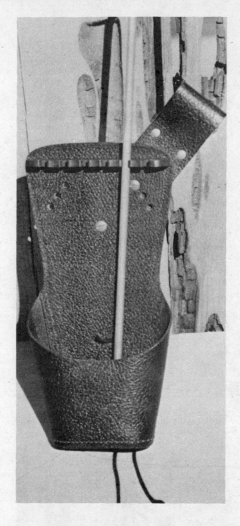
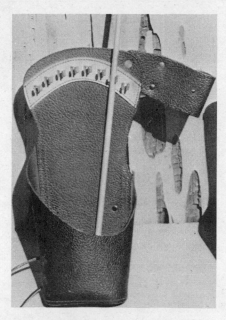

Belt-style hip quivers (at left and above) will work in the field, but care must be exercised when moving through brush, backing or stooping as arrows can be dislodged. Field or target quiver at right could be used for hunting. Any of the three would serve for hunting from stand.

A Look At The Many Types And Styles Available, And Some Helpful Suggestions For Determining The Right One For You!

AFTER SELECTING AND fletching his arrows, the hunter still needs a method of carrying them into the field: enter the quiver.

There are numerous styles of quivers available, depending on the size needed. If planning to make a short hunt for small game, the hunter could place his arrows in his hip pocket. An archer can carry up to six field-tipped arrows in a hip pocket quiver. This is merely a section of leather folded over to prevent the tips from going through clothing.

However, extended hunts and larger game call for larger quivers. One of the oldest styles of quiver in use today is the over-the-shoulder back quiver which can hold up to two dozen arrows. The biggest disadvantage of the back quiver is its open top and the noise it makes as you move. The shafts rattle and can easily spook game. Adding some oats, grass or other such items to the quiver will reduce much of the noise, making the quiver a little more practical.

Another disadvantage with this style is the motion the archer makes when withdrawing the arrow. He must sweep

an arm over the shoulder, withdraw the shaft and swing it back over the shoulder to the bow. From the deer's vantage point, it may appear as if the bowman is waving at him. There is no way to change this withdrawal system.

A further disadvantage is in traveling through brush. If the hunter bends to go under a limb, arrows might easily spill to the ground. If he doesn't spill them, he may hang one up on a limb until he learns to lower the back quiver to miss the limb. The ideal use of the over-the-back quiver is off the shoulder entirely. The back quiver makes an excellent standing quiver, where the arrows become much more accessible and available.

When using razor-sharp broadheads, it also is somewhat disconcerting to place them all together in the back quiver, thereby rattling them around and dulling their edges as they rub together.

Another quiver style that fits on the back, but has better design for the hunter, allows the arrow to be withdrawn from the base of the quiver. This is the St. Charles quiver,

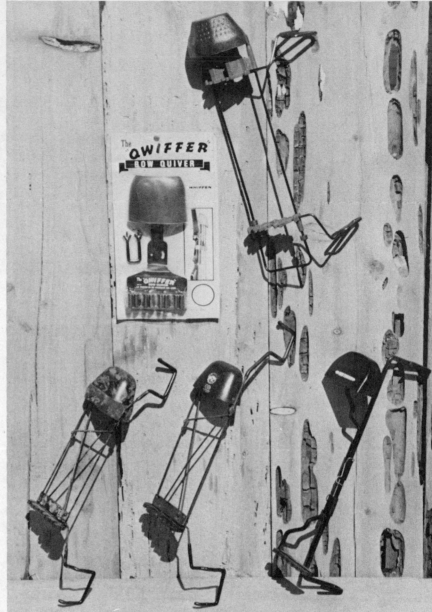

Quiffer quiver (above) attaches to bow by means of small clip and wing nut. Holds four arrows, is light and functional. Quiffer is similar to variety of bow quivers (right) which attach to bow limbs without drilling or alterations. Popular in Southern California is quiver (below) which holds seven, single-bladed arrows; comes in two sections and fits any bow, but requires use of inserts or drilling and tapping for attachment.

named after the gentleman who sold many of them. The top of the quiver is shielded or has a leather or similar material hood that wraps over the top, protecting the shafts, the feathers and negating the glare of shafts from the game. The fletch will not get wet in a rain squall, colors can be used and not affect the game, and there is no waving motion as the bowman withdraws an arrow.

This style is open on one side — often both sides — at the base and the arrow is withdrawn by moving the hand to the base of the quiver, gripping the base of the shaft with the fingers and exerting a slight upward pressure to lift it off the base and slip it out. There are several versions of this style in which one can carry up to eighteen arrows.

To replace an arrow after a miss, reverse the process and push the shaft up into the hood. This sometimes rumples the fletch, however. The broadheads are protected from each other and must be carefully withdrawn to avoid grasping the razor edge and slicing a finger. A little practice with small game heads will perfect the defenses. The hood usually is curved, allowing the hunter to get through and into brushy areas easier since he now has only the large hood section, rather than several dozen shafts, to hang up on limbs. The arrows will not fall out when he stoops over, either.

One of the newer quiver styles in the last few years has been the side quiver. It fits on the belt and along the leg of the archer. This model will carry six to eight arrows. To remove a shaft, reach along the side, pick one by the mid-section and pull it from the clip keeper. The heads are kept separate and sharp, the hand does not come in contact with them and the bowman's motion, as he draws the shaft, is to the side and not over the top.

If there is a disadvantage to the side quiver, it is the big fan effect it gives as the archer walks through the woods. The shafts are spaced apart in keepers, the heads seated in a rubber base. This creates a wide fan at the nock end up to two feet across. Look at a hunter wearing the side quiver and note the waving flag he carries with the quiver. If using a bright fletch, he has a bright colored flag waving with each step. There usually is a tie-down string to hold the quiver to the leg as he walks, but this accentuates the waving. If he doesn't tie the string to the leg, the waving is diminished, but the quiver then flops about.

In brushy country, the side quiver will become an

Some of the many variations available in bow quivers are illustrated in this selection which includes styles that can be attached to the bow by means of screw inserts, use of adapters, or require certain modifications to the bow, such as drilling and/or tapping.

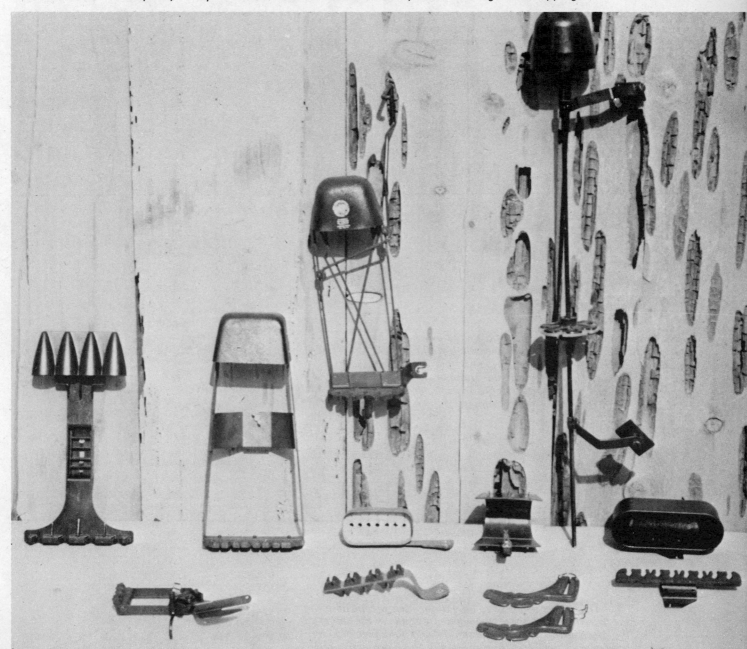

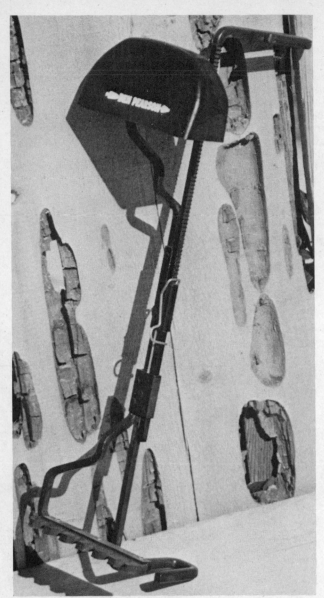

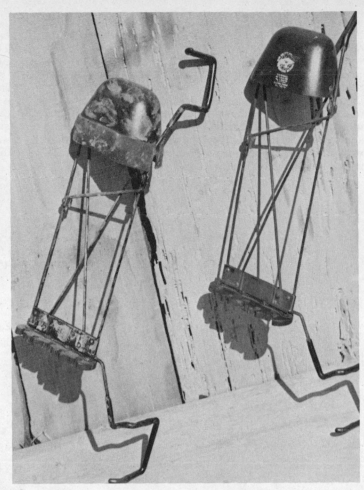

Ben Pearson quiver (above) fits almost any bow simply by sliding the upper and lower arms over the bow limbs and pulling them together until they grip and hold tight. Two styles of Bear bow quivers are shown at upper right. At the left is one designed to fit on short bows; longer bow model is at right. Main difference is in attachment arms.

This quiver attaches to bow using a screw-type base and may be removed by loosening wing nut visible in the center of the brace arm. This particular model will hold a maximum of nine arrows, is light and compact with a good, protective hood.

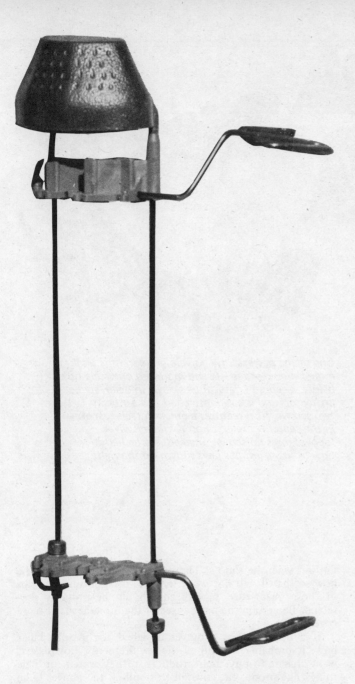

irritant if the hunter has to back up to change paths. When he backs up with the quiver tied down, the shafts often will catch on brush and then the entire quiver will be dumped on the ground. The clips are of light spring steel or rubber and will not hold if he sidesteps or backs into a solid object.

The side quiver is great for small game and for stand hunting. The archer can place the quiver beside him in the stand and the shafts will not rattle, fall down or get in the way. When he needs one, he reaches over and picks it up easily. One model must be rotated to remove an arrow. It has a center section on a pivot and requires the lining up of a shaft with the exit slot to remove the arrow.

Back in the late 1940s, an archer known to all who take to the field for game designed a bow quiver. Fred Bear made them then and still does.

The first model of the bow quiver prior to Bear's was a small leather quiver that held six or eight shafts. The hunter held this small quiver in his bow hand.

The styles of bow quivers have changed over the years, but Bear's have become one of the most popular hunting quivers on the market. Today's designs hold from three to eighteen arrows.

Successful hunters carry no more than eight arrows, some only five. When he first takes to the hunting paths, the archer tends to take with him enough arrows to allow for misses. As technique and ability improve, he drops off the number of shafts and realizes it isn't how many he carries, but how well he places them.

There are several things to expect from a bow quiver. It should hold the arrows needed, whether three or eighteen. It should hold them close to the bow so they will not snag on brush or limbs, yet fit snug in the quiver so they will not

Saunders BQ 7 model grips the arrows at top and bottom, resulting in firm, almost vibration-free quiver. Upper cap protects bowhunter from broadheads. This model may not fit some of newer take-down bows with long risers.

Jennings Compound bow quiver is designed to fit on compound bows. Holds eight arrows under deep hood.

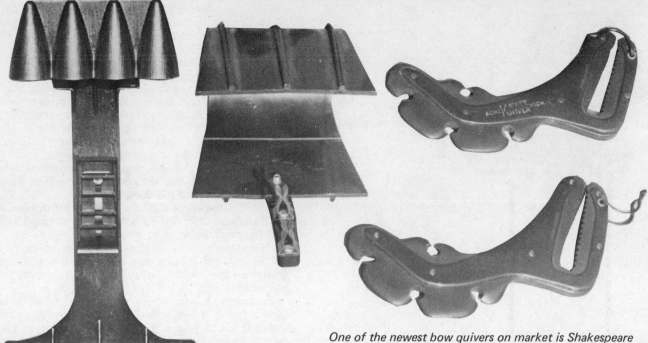

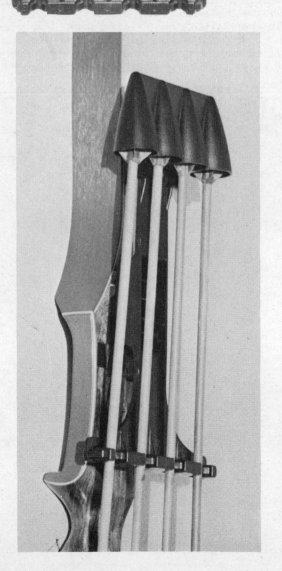

One of the newest bow quivers on market is Shakespeare model shown at far left and mounted on Ocala bow below. Accommodates four arrows in deep, socket protectors and is easily attached to riser using two screws. Also features a quick detach system in the center. Three-section Kwikee Kwiver (above), uses no screws; instead is attached to bow utilizing gripper jaws shown on the right.

fall out when he shoots. The quiver should be tight to the bow so that it will not work loose while shooting. The tips of those razor-edge broadheads should be properly protected. Be certain the back edges of the broadheads also are covered.

If a bowman has a quiver designed for his particular bow, it probably will fill all the requirements. Bowmakers want archers to buy their product, so they watch for little things like proper fit, covered tips and all the above. If he has a bow that has no specially built quiver for it, he will have to purchase one of the adjustable styles. They also should fulfill all of the listed requirements — and most do. He can bend the wire frame of the quiver to make it fit closer to the bow. He cannot do much about the attachment method, but must rely on the maker to engineer it for him.

The advantages of the bow quiver are many. It keeps the arrows with the bow at all times. The hunter can lay his bow down while he drinks from a spring and know he won't walk off and leave his arrows behind, unless he forgets the bow, too. He can move quietly, as there is no rattle. If a shaft works loose, it will make a few tinkling sounds. Shove it back into the base material of the cup found on most styles and it will stop rattling. The quivers are ideal for moving through brushy terrain. The archer can work his bow ahead of him as he finds a hole; the bow and shafts go smoothly ahead and he can move as fast as he likes.

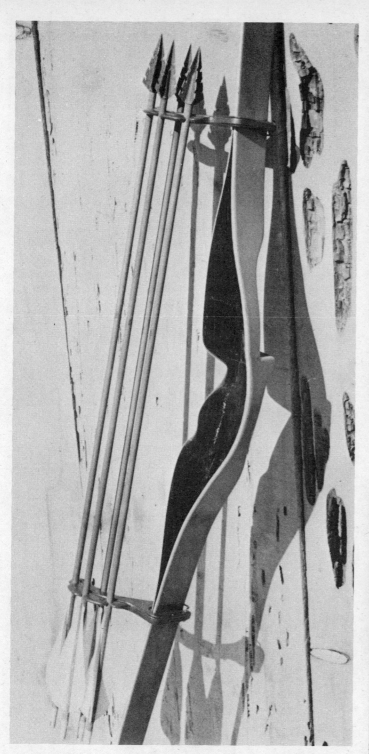

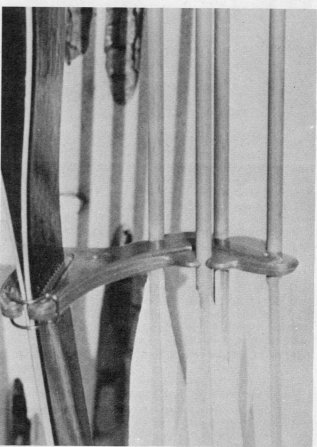

Sight to make any bowhunter shudder (above and upper right) is razor-sharp broadheads being carried in an unprotected position. Trip and fall or slight brush against blades can result in bowhunter becoming a statistic. Lower jaw of Kwikee Kwiver (right), also illustrated on opposite page, never should be used on broadhead end without the proper hooding.

Protective cover designed for use with the Kwikee Kwiver has spring-type clamps which attach to one of the arrows being carried. Never use without hood!

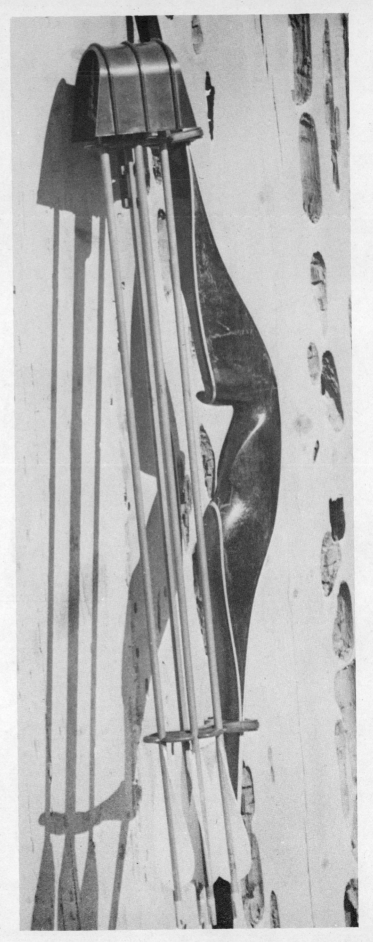

Some archers feel that eight arrows are not enough. If he is serious about hunting, the archer often will spend more time looking, stalking and listening than shooting. He can spend days in the field and never take a shot. On the other hand, if he is throwing arrows at game, hoping to connect with those long shots, he will need all he can carry and probably go back for more. There is a great difference between hunting and placing one arrow in the right place, and just throwing shafts at game hoping to hit. One method is hunting, the other is hoping.

Another factor to consider is the carrying weight of the bow with the bow quiver attached. This can become a burden, if loaded up with fifteen or so arrows adding to the mass weight of the bow. The bow is carried in the left hand of most right-handed archers, and their shoulder will tell them in a few days that it doesn't like the weight factor. A hunting arrow will weigh about 600 grains — 1¼ ounces. Total up the number of shafts and there is an additional pound to that bow weight. Not only does the archer have to carry this while hunting, but when he brings up the bow to shoot he will have the added weight on the left arm. This can affect accuracy.

A few quivers are mounted in front of the bow. The idea is to have the arrows act as a stabilizer. The concept of a

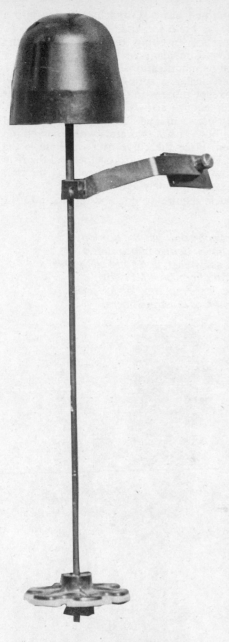

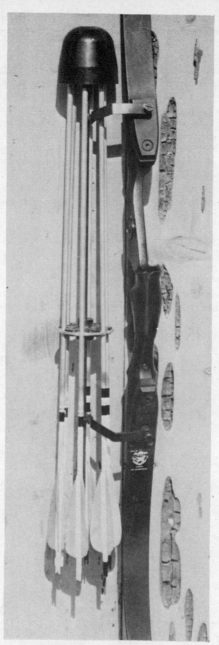

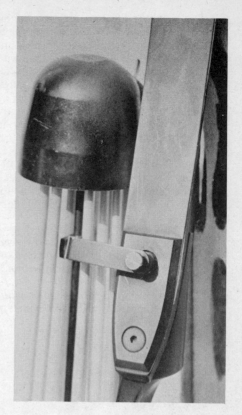

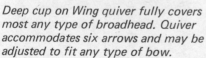

Deep cup on Wing quiver fully covers most any type of broadhead. Quiver accommodates six arrows and may be adjusted to fit any type of bow.

Wing take-down bow has inserts on the upper and lower limbs to accommodate bow quiver. One of author's favorites, quiver fits snug; won't snag on brush.

Close-up views (above and below) show how Wing quiver is attached to Wing Competition II Hunter bow. Arms on quiver are adjustable by bending.

stabilizer in front is fine, but this stabilizing influence will change with each arrow being shot, as the weight is reduced by each arrow removed for shooting.

The majority of bow quivers fit on the bow at the riser section with a spring clamping system. If he can adjust the clamps, the archer should move them back so that the clamps or spring action is on the feathered section of the riser, or as far back as he can fit it. If he places this spring action on the upper and lower limb sections, he can change the bow's shooting characteristics.

Wing Archery designed a bow quiver to fit their products. This holds six arrows in a circular pattern with a rubber-based upper cup that will hold any style broadhead. The archer can bend the arms of the quiver as close to the bow as he likes and it stays there. The quiver is attached to the feathered section of the riser on the back of the bow by two screws that fit into a nut formed into the limb. He can tighten the screw with a coin or a screwdriver.

The old standby in the bow-quiver department is the Bear style. There are several styles, ranging from those that can be taped to the bow and hold four arrows to those that are held by two spring arms fitting over the upper and lower limb sections by the riser. They are available in right and left-hand styles, holding four or eight shafts. By loosening a screw on the side arms of the Bear and adjusting the two lengths, short and long, it will fit most bows.

Some of the newer three-piece, take-down bows have long riser sections. No quiver will fit over them, so Bear came up with a modification that fits the upper spring hook over the upper limb and has a slotted base fitting into a holding screw base on the lower riser section. This can be added to the bow by inserting the adapter into the stabilizer socket found on many of the newer models. It could also be added by modification.

Saunders Archery makes a spring bow quiver that also will fit all bows, except those with the extremely long riser sections. This holds enough arrows for the serious hunter.

Pearson Archery uses a unique clamping system to hold their quiver to the bow. It has two arms with a curved top and bottom section. Place the curve over the limb in the extended position, slide the two arms together and the rigid curves grip the bow to make the quiver solid at the riser section. It holds six arrows snugly and quietly.

Some bow quivers require drilling and tapping into the

Bear bow quiver (left) may be modified to adapt to most any bow. This particular unit has the bolt-on bracket at the bottom, instead of a spring arm, and will fit all the new Bear bows. Center photo shows same quiver mounted on author's magnesium Bear take-down bow. Quickly assembled, quiet and adjustable, it is made to hold eight arrows, but with slight modification can carry ten. An old reliable (at right), the Bear spring arm-style bow quiver has been around for many years. Shown here mounted on a Herter's bow, it is adjustable to fit most bows. Arms should be in feathering of the riser, as illustrated here.

 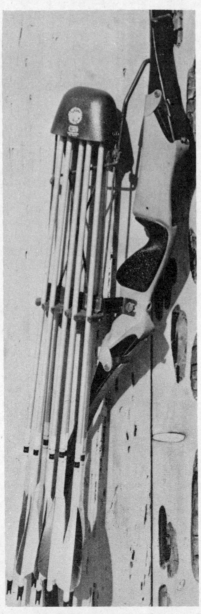 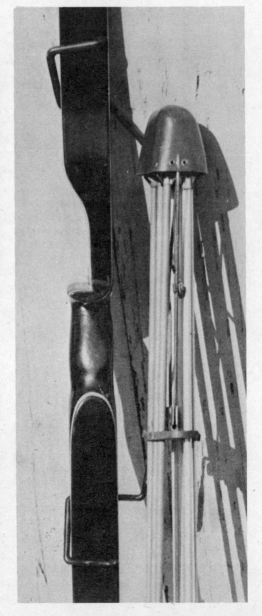

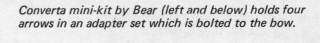

Converta mini-kit by Bear (left and below) holds four arrows in an adapter set which is bolted to the bow.

The "Compleat" bowhunter's kit from Bear (left) includes a set of brush buttons, camo bowsocks, arrow holder, bow tip protector, broadhead sharpener and a quiver, plus vinyl tape necessary for attaching quiver to the bow.

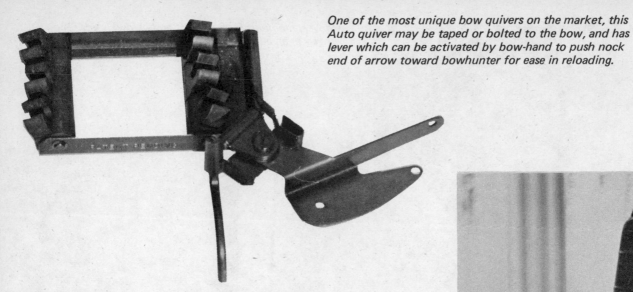

One of the most unique bow quivers on the market, this Auto quiver may be taped or bolted to the bow, and has lever which can be activated by bow-hand to push nock end of arrow toward bowhunter for ease in reloading.

Taped to bow and loaded, Auto quiver carries arrows forward of the bow (above). Left, as thumb pushes against lever, nock end of arrows swing upward. See close-up view directly to right on opposite page.

As quiver nears horizontal position, fingers of bow-hand are used to pull the lever all the way back, moving arrows into right angle position to bowstring. Bowhunter then removes arrow for nocking and quiver falls forward and back into its original position. A unique and novel idea, but there is no way to protect the exposed broadheads and still retain auto-loading sequence for which the quiver was made.

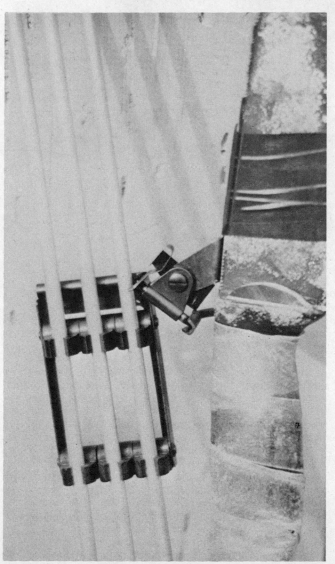

riser, itself. They are solid on the bow, fitting close, but they must be placed properly and the alignment done correctly or there may be unnecessary drill holes. There is no fiberglass on the riser where most bow quivers would be mounted, so there is little danger or problem involved in this mounting procedure. If there is a metal riser on the bow, and a mounted bow quiver is desired, then drill and tap into the metal for a solidly mounted quiver.

There probably is the least motion in withdrawing a shaft from this bow quiver than most other styles. There is less waving motion and, if the shafts have been camouflaged, the reflections will be nil. Rainy weather is an argument against the bow quiver and some archers state the fletch will become wet. That could be true, but they can buy waterproofing for the fletch or place a plastic bag over the feathers if it rains, or try the plastic style fletch that water won't bother.

An archer might find a quiver now and then which will drop an arrow after a few shots. This usually is because of a weakened clamp or damaged rubber base on the quiver. By replacing many of the low-cost parts of the quiver, it will last for many more years.

All quiver types are out there for selection. There are good points and probably some bad ones about any style, depending on who is talking. If asking a back quiver-style hunter, he will run down the bow quiver and vice versa. The back quiver is great for rabbits and squirrels when many arrows are needed, since a hunter is apt to lose and break many in a day's shooting. The side quiver is handy if he goes to a broadhead shot since it will be out of brush and he needs easy access for replacing arrows pulled from the targets.

Many hunters place a bow quiver on the bow and that is all they ever use. They might hunt rabbits with aluminum arrows tipped with a Judo point and use that one arrow for months by keeping track of where they shoot. They pick the shot and do not lose the arrows.

Pick the quiver carefully, modify it if necessary to fit specific needs, and work with it to become accustomed to it. When a second shot at a trophy is offered, the serious archer will never spook it by waving arrows or not being able to find them.

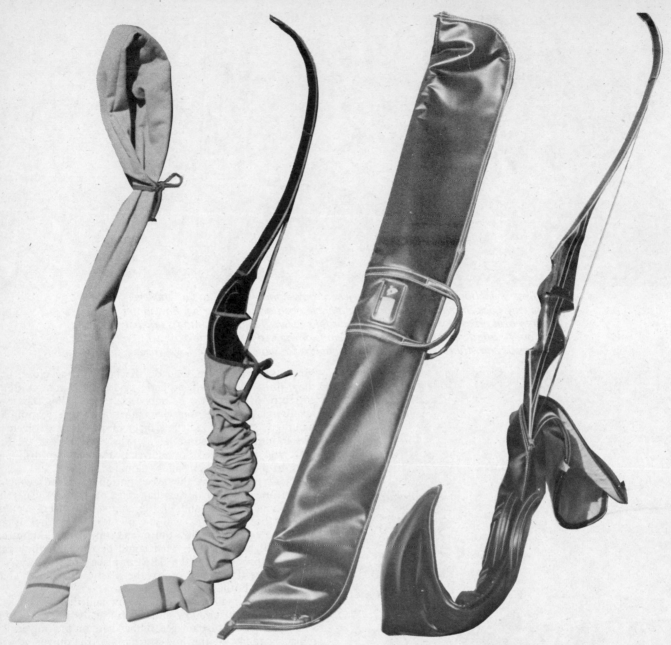

The two most-seen examples of bow protection are pictured above. The sleeve or bowsock protect the bow from dirt and dust, but does little to discourage dings and dents caused by contact with hard-surfaced objects. A little more costly are the vinyl bow cases, which can be padded or lined with a soft material to protect the finish of the bow from dirt and debris, and from contact with rocks or the like. Most of the latter come with an integral carrying handle.

ONE OF THE tasks confronting the bowhunter is that of transporting equipment to the hunting camp. If traveling by car or truck, this usually is of little consequence. If going by air, however, it becomes somewhat of a nightmare trying to get that long bow properly stowed so that it will not be broken.

This is one of the major advantages of the take-down bows. They are easily carried by any conveyance. The packages are small, light and legal, compact enough to be stowed in the closets just off the passenger sections, rather than in the baggage compartment.

The long or single unit bows present another problem. They are unwieldly anywhere. If traveling by car, there must be sufficient room to lay them out full-length — with no weight on them which possibly could damage the limbs. Station wagons are a happy solution and a pickup truck

with a camper better yet. Many bowhunters have adapted one of the rifleman's units, the rifle rack, to carry bows in vehicles. These racks can be attached to the windows, frame or other sections of a car and keep the bow out of the way during transit. A simple and convenient method, the racks are available in most sporting goods stores.

Some bowhunters make long cases of wood for their bows, but most traveling hunters now have adopted the take-down bows. Many of these bows offer an optional case when purchased. Some cases are of soft material and protect the bow against minor blows, but do very little against hard knocks. To protect against the latter, it may be necessary to buy a custom-styled hard case or handmade one. The bowman who owns or has access to a bench or radial arm saw can whip out a case in an afternoon with little or no problem. It can be an elaborate affair or a basic

CHAPTER 13

Protective Containers Solve The Problems
of Storage And Transportation And
Keep Supplies And Accessories Organized.

BOW CASES AND TACKLE BOXES

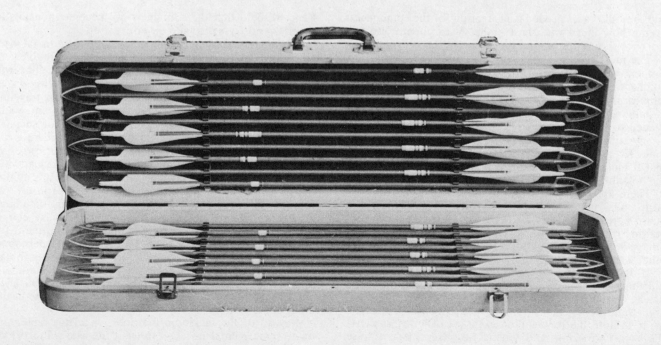

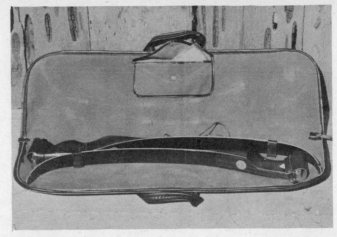

The take-down bow started a revolution in the bow case market, resulting in shorter, more compact cases for transportation ease. This Ben Pearson case is furnished with the bow and, despite apparent size, can be filled with numerous accessories.

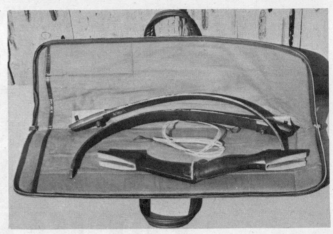

AMF/Wing Archery supplies this multi-compartmented case with their Competition II Hunter take-down bow. It contains the riser, a set of limbs, extra strings and paraffin for the Slide Loc limb system. It's lightweight and durable in design.

one, but all that is needed is protection for the components of the bow in transit. Hard or heavy cardboard also will work for short trips or emergencies.

The most recent take-down bows make the transit problem extremely simple. The boxes in which the bows are purchased will serve as a case for about one trip. A box of long cardboard also will work. Not many of these bows are as long as the arrows they shoot, so something also is needed to transport the arrows. Arrow boxes can be made in any style and shape and to hold any quantity, in a short time. Keep in mind while planning or laying out the box that it must be long enough to hold the arrow tipped with the broadhead.

There are some cases on the market that will work for both units, the bow and the arrows. The only deciding factor here is how many arrows are considered enough for a hunting trip. Some hunters feel two dozen to be sufficient; others have to store enough for themselves and possibly other members of the family or perhaps a hunting buddy.

If hunting with the same group, you might consider splitting the projects. One person can make the arrow boxes, another the bow cases, or combine them into one unit using the ingenuity of the group. The bow case can be made to hold the bow and an extra set of limbs, as well as the extra bowstrings and serving for field emergency use.

Keep in mind that the containers can become monsters in themselves if trying to take the entire shop.

When Groves Archery came out with their metal riser take-down bow, they knew the transport troubles of archers. They made an optional case available that will carry the riser, two sets of limbs and about two dozen arrows in the top compartment. This is ideal for traveling on planes, since the entire unit can be locked and withstands much abuse. Sometimes the extra cost of such an item is well worth the few dollars when considering the time, effort and materials involved in making your own.

Before buying a case or making one, determine just what will be needed. Which bow will be used and, if it is a take-down, will it accommodate extra sets of limbs in case of breakage in the camp? If so, plan on making the case large enough to include an extra. Also consider what else is carried in the bow case. There should be a compartment for bowstrings, enough for a spare in the field and perhaps a backup set for the extra limbs. A section of serving thread for nocking points, or the small Nocksert made by Saunders, should be considered. If the take-down requires an allen wrench or similar tool, there should be two of these in the event one is lost.

Lay all of the tackle on the floor, or a large table, and make some mental notes as to what the case's dimensions should be. If unable to do this, make a pattern from cardboard boxes and then try to actually place everything in it. The unit often will prove to be much smaller than originally thought. When satisfied with the design, use the pattern for marking and cutting the wood for the final case. With the modern glues and epoxy cements available, it is possible to make a case that will withstand almost anything. Again, do not get carried away and make a case that takes two men to carry. The case must be loaded inside the transportation vehicle and stored in a safe position, so keep this in mind and forget the two-by-fours and inch-thick planks. Try using a light wood, door paneling or masonite.

After the exterior is completed, add the refinements for inside storage. Foam rubber comes in many sizes and sheets of it can be purchased at a minimal cost. This makes a great cushion for limbs and also prevents the different sections from banging together. The interior can be padded, cut and shaped to accept the bows and limbs.

The arrow box may become more of a problem. When designing the bow case, it is surprising to see how much longer it must be to accept arrows, too. If the bow has a long riser and limb system, the upper section of the case can be adapted to hold a few dozen arrows. If the bowman has an extra-long draw, he might prefer to store the arrows in the case without the broadheads attached. They always can be put on in camp during the first day or evening before the season opens — but take care not to leave them behind.

If planning on making an arrow case as an extra project, it really is simpler than the bow case. All that is needed is a box — either of present manufacture or of individual design — long enough to hold the shafts tipped with broadheads. The razor edges of the heads should be protected from banging together by a clamp system which immobilizes the entire shaft. There are arrow clips — small metal clips designed for use with arrows and obtained in archery shops or mail order houses — that work very well. The clips may scratch the paint on the shaftment, but this can be prevented by placing the clips below the dip or cresting.

After determining the length, decide on the number of arrows needed for a two-week deer hunt in some remote

Groves Archery's case is purely delightful, provided with their take-down hunter. The hard case has cut foam rubber to fit two sets of limbs, riser, wrench for limb attachment, room for two dozen arrows, spare strings, bow quiver, inserts for arrows — all that's required for a hunt.

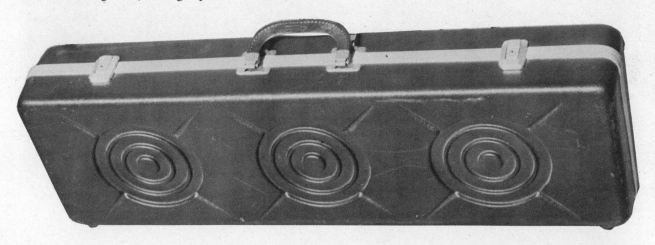

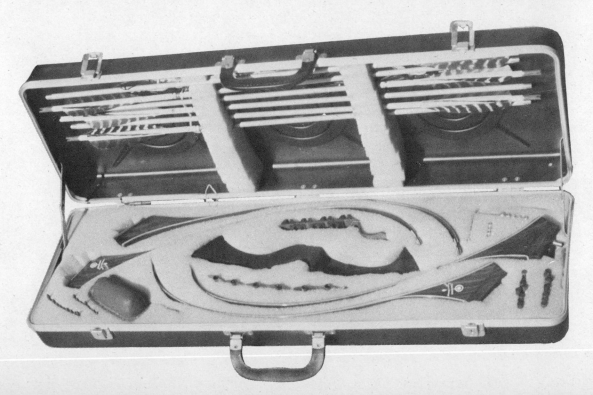

One of Bear Archery's more popular cases for take-down bows is the soft, vinyl-covered model shown in the two photographs above. It will carry two or more risers, two sets of limbs, spare strings and other tackle. Zipper closure keeps out dirt.

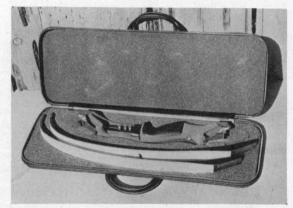

Capable of taking plenty of punishment from careless baggage handlers is the Bear hard-covered bow case pictured above. It is not as large as the vinyl-covered model, but it will transport one riser and limbs. Padding is thick foam rubber.

Another fine example of portability with protection is from Herter's, Incorporated, which is supplied with their take-down bow. Foam rubber on top and bottom ensure little or no damage to take-down riser and two sets of limbs packed inside.

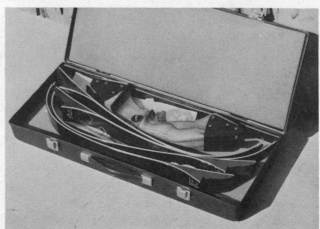

camp. A careful hunter can get by with fewer arrows than one who takes those long, hopeful shots and loses arrows. When placing the shots, the arrows should nearly always be retrievable; unless the grass is high or they dig under leaf mold.

There are several methods of holding arrows in position. We mentioned the clips and they are excellent. There also is a foam rubber system, which consists of cementing strips of the material in the finished box and slitting the rubber to accept the shafts. Alternate the fletch from one end to the other and more arrows will fit into a small space.

Wooden slats can be added to separate and hold the arrows apart; spaced with blocks of wood, they are held down by a spring-loaded slat on top.

If shooting an arrow of one spine, only those arrows are needed and storing is little or no problem. When two different spines are used to accommodate two archers with different bow weights, problems do arise. When my wife and I started hunting together, she shot a bow ten pounds lighter than I did. We both thought we needed at least two dozen arrows in the field. We found we actually never used one dozen, but for those first few trips we wanted a

security blanket. I made up an arrow box — still in use today — that will carry almost eight dozen broadhead-tipped shafts of any length, spine and color. At first, it was a nuisance. Since then, I have been very glad I made it.

It consists of a box long enough to hold tipped shafts with a six-inch top that holds extra cement, bowsocks, nocks, strings and extra broadheads. The interior section lifts for selecting arrows. They may be drawn from the top as well. The interior section was made from strips of masonite, with holes drilled to accept the shafts and cut to allow my two-bladed broadheads to slip in-between for inserting or removing. We could load it up with enough arrows for myself and the wife, and some culls for practice and small game if we had any in the area.

This box reposes in the rafters of the garage and is always loaded with a full rack of fletched shafts, some with razor-edged broadheads, but some not tipped. If anyone calls and says, "Let's go hunting," I can drag the box down and either take it along or just select the shafts I want for the trip. This gives us enough finished hunting arrows for any occasion. If I have time, I sort through and pull out some of the older ones that have been used in previous hunts

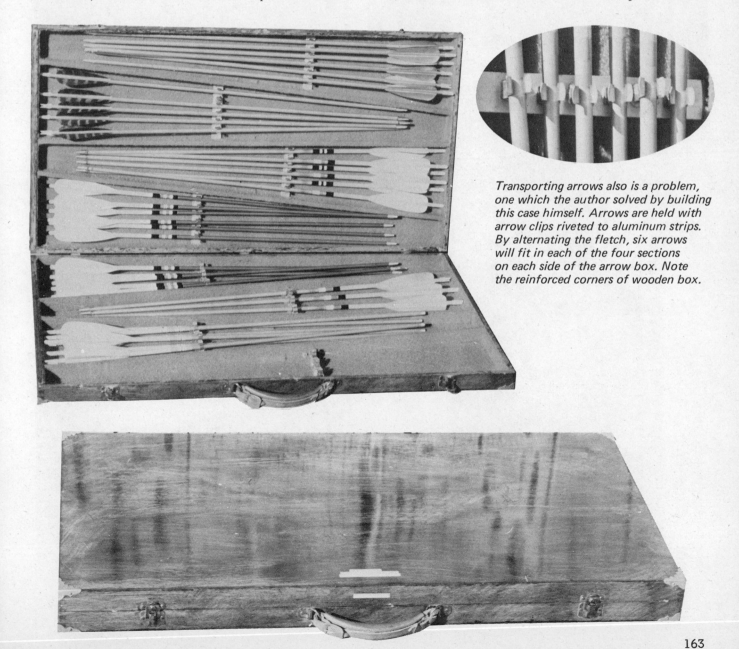

Transporting arrows also is a problem, one which the author solved by building this case himself. Arrows are held with arrow clips riveted to aluminum strips. By alternating the fletch, six arrows will fit in each of the four sections on each side of the arrow box. Note the reinforced corners of wooden box.

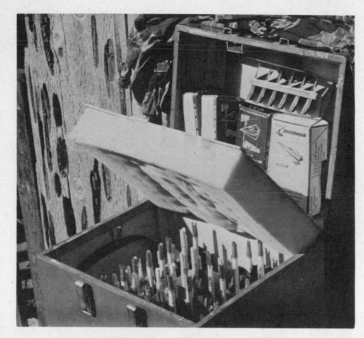

If four dozen arrows aren't enough, a homemade case like this can be made, which holds eight dozen, tipped with two-blade broadheads (below left). Foam rubber applies pressure on arrows to prevent rattle and allows space for packing (left). The insert that holds the arrows lifts out to disclose the angled aluminum sides and slotted double section for holding the arrows (below).

and replace them with new ones that seem to be coming off the fletching jig at regular intervals. This gives me all the small-game arrows required for local hunting, and more than needed of the first-class tipped shafts for hunting trips anytime, anywhere.

The box wasn't a problem to build, but it was a problem filling it. Eight dozen arrows is far more than needed unless planning to carry arrows for the entire camp — and it has been used for just that. Hunters often have borrowed shafts when they have run short, the fletch has become wet or for any other reasonable purpose. The top of the box has a padded section of foam rubber that applies a slight pressure on the nocks of the arrows when it is closed. This prevents them from rattling around.

One of the best arrow cases found in many years was one made for show displays of a product. The salesman had stopped going to trade shows and had several of these cases collecting dust. They were purchased for a small fee — considering their basic cost — and will hold four dozen fletched, tipped arrows with ease. This box could be used for air travel. It is light, can be strapped and is solid enough to walk on. To convert this to an arrow box, a set of the Saunders arrow clips and some aluminum strip metal were purchased. The clips were fastened to the metal strips with screws — they are adjustable by tightening or loosening the screw for a firmer grip on the arrow — and these strips ground on each edge to fit into the frame inside the cases. By staggering the clips, I can get six arrows in each of the box's eight compartments. To top off the elegance, the cases had been flocked with a bright red material when they were made. It produced a truly distinctive arrow case and is very functional.

Another system, favored by many, is to keep arrows in

A close-up of slotted double section shows the ease with which arrows can be removed or replaced (right). A thick hunk of leather was placed on the bottom of the case, to keep the tips dry and sharp (below).

Noted bowhunter Charlie Farmer made the case shown on these two pages, which is easily transported (above). Looking at front shows it comes in three sections (left).

one case, bows in another and carry a tool kit with all the extras needed such as string, nocks, cement, broadheads, inserts and all the gadgets archers seem to collect and feel are necessary. The idea of separate items is to keep all the eggs out of one basket. In this way, should the arrow box become ruined or lost, only the shafts would be lost and not the entire archery shop.

While making up a tool kit, plan on including some field arrows for practice. It is not always possible to find a bank or bale to shoot broadheads into, and the field points will help loosen up the muscles in the morning. Some Judo points would be an ideal addition for helping fill the camp pot with small game. Rabbits usually are in season during most of the big-game seasons and do not require a razor-edged broadhead.

One item that should be in all kits is a bow stringer. These come in many shapes, but most are of the string and pouch style and take up little room. Many archers carry one in the tackle box or bow case, and another in their hunting gear in case they need to change strings in the field. They do not take up space and are well worth carrying.

Plan the arrow and bow cases with care; then, build one from scratch, modify existing ones or purchase one ready-made. The choice is somewhat limited, but only by imagination. Keep the tackle protected and you will enjoy the trip and the hunt much more.

Broadheads in Farmer's case are held by clamps, and the case is long enough to accommodate hunting heads (above).

Half of Farmer's case holds his riser and two sets of limbs, padded snugly in foam rubber (above). There also is space for his quiver and other accessories. The opposite side of the case features space for his broadhead-tipped arrows (below).

CHAPTER 14

A Place to Rest Your Arrow

**Arrow Rests Are Designed Primarily
For Increased Accuracy In Target Archery:
An Advantage Recognized By Expert Bowhunters**

IN BYGONE YEARS, the only arrow rest used was
the hand. The arrow lay over the hand's upper section and
the bowman shot over it with the old self bows. They had
no sight window as we have today, but with the advent of
the sight window cut into the riser came a series of arrow
rests — some good, some bad and some strictly for emergencies.

There are many arrow rests on the market, most
designed for target archers. However, hunters need accuracy
as well, so do not sluff off on the rest just because it says
for target archery. The best method — as in any project — is
to try it first, then make a decision.

The simplest rest to use is straight off the window ledge
or shelf of the bow. It also is the method of least value. The
arrow remains in contact with the wood of the window and
accuracy falls into the "sometimes" category. It is possible
to shoot from the bare shelf, but the arrow will slap or skip
from the shelf, causing erratic and wild shooting of each
shaft. With the newer bows this style of shelf-shooting is
impossible, since the shelves are radiused and have no angle
that will hold the arrow while drawing.

*Durable in any weather, plastic Shakespeare rest (left) has
sideplate, cushioned rubber base and is cemented to bow.
Long-lasting, bristle brush rest by Herter's, Incorporated
(below), is made for drilling and cementing to bow window.*

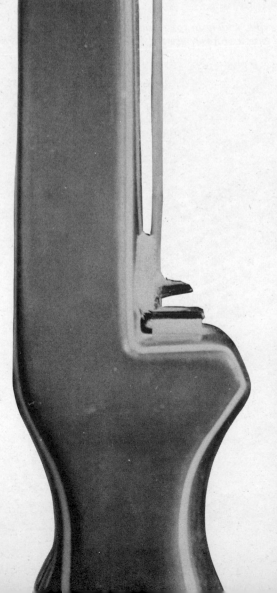

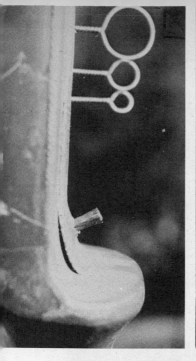
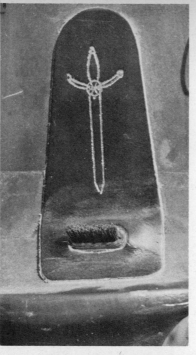

Wide brush rest (above), also cemented to bow window, has wide leather plate for arrow to move against. Clear plastic finger rest at right prevents arrow from getting under rest, and comes with self-sticking adhesive for application to bow.

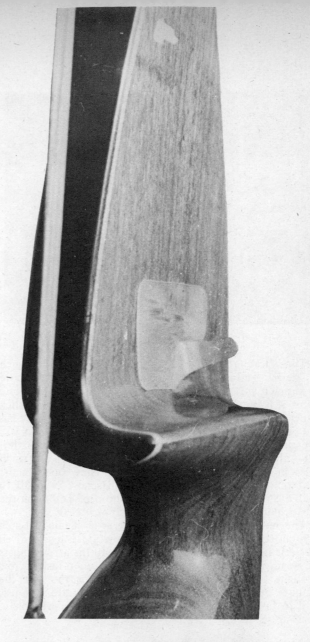

The second system involves a piece of carpet, mohair or other soft material which is cemented to the shelf for the arrow to ride over when shot. The carpet pile acts as an absorber of the action and the arrow will shoot fairly well. Many manufacturers use the mohair rest, since most archers change whatever they put on the bow, anyway. The cushioning effect helps the degree of accuracy, yet it still isn't the ideal solution.

What the archer is trying to achieve is to have a soft but stable platform to draw and fire the arrow over when shooting. Why not just use the commercial rests offered on the market? Many hunters do, but the target archer has all the time he needs to place the arrow, draw and fire at a stationary target. In contrast, the hunter has very little time, and with his attention diverted to the moving game animal, may nock the arrow and place it at full draw only to note that he has the arrow below the arrow rest he found worked great for him in practice.

The arrow rest should be designed to prevent the arrow from dropping while nocking. With this style the hunter never need look at the shaft, but simply slap it on the bow, draw and shoot. If the arrow does get below the rest, the nocking point will be far off scale, the arrow probably will skip on release and a hit is a pretty unsure bet.

Aside from an arrow rest on the bow, the hunter also needs something on the side of the window to prevent just what was mentioned above: arrow slap. A section of plastic tape will work in an emergency, but better yet, some light leather glued to the side of the window will last for years and give the bow protection as well as prevent noise.

If shooting from the bare shelf with a bare window, the arrow will slap the window area with enough noise to spook a rabbit. By adding the carpet or mohair, along with some leather on the side window, the archer can draw and shoot that same bunny without him knowing what hit him. A hunter needs at least two factors working for him in the hunting field: quiet and speed. The idea of remaining as quiet as possible is simple hunting knowledge and technique. The speed factor shouldn't be needed if hunting properly, but if necessary, he should be able to place an arrow on the rest without making a rattle.

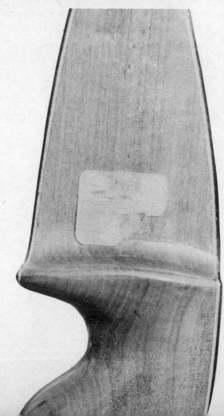

Extremely low, homemade rest might rip fletch.

One of the older styles of arrow rest material still used is the feather rest. These are made from sections of feather cemented together to form a section of feather area to place the arrow on. They have the vanes of the feather pointing in one direction and the rest should be mounted with the vanes forward. When drawing the arrow back, these feather rests will chatter — it's unavoidable. During the earlier years I used these quite a bit, until I noted rabbits moving on my draw. They could hear the arrow chattering across the feather rest.

The feather rest will work, but it gets wet and soggy in the rain and will take a groove over a period of time. The carpet or mohair rest also becomes soggy when wet and the arrow will drag on draw and on shooting, affecting accuracy. The ideal rest would be one that allows the arrow to move over the sight window area with no noise, has a surface impervious to weather and remains slick in any weather conditions. It also should last a lifetime.

Those are pretty stiff requirements, but there is just such a material: Teflon. This space-age material has all the above requirements. It is soft enough to remain silent on draw and firing, it is impervious to any weather and will remain slick in below-zero weather or in the heat of the desert. It has one problem: gluing it to the riser. The Teflon material will not stick with contact cement, or any other for that matter. The only method that has proved successful is to drill small holes in the ends of the rest, drill matching holes in the shelf of the bow and either use small screws or brads to hold the rest to the bow. Place a section of Teflon on the sight window and it is there until the bow breaks.

The rest, if handmade, should be at least one-half-inch high above the shelf of the bow window. It has been proven that this height will allow the feathers of the arrow to pass the window more smoothly, making a cleaner, faster arrow in flight and to the target. If the shelf is too low, the feathers will tend to fray along the edges. Teflon often is hard to find in blocks or chunks, but should be available in hardware or specialty stores.

Feather rests — for target archery and practice — possess several disadvantages to bowhunters: noisy when arrow is pulled against them, wear out quickly and become soggy

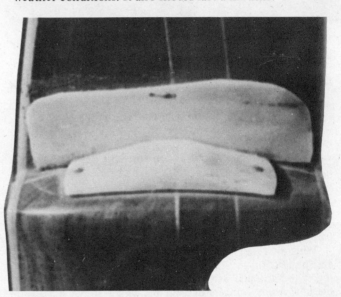

Homemade Teflon rest with high shelf allows clean passage of fletch. Cemented and pinned, Teflon is impervious to weather.

Saunders Archery came out with an ideal system, using the Teflon material on a hunting rest they dubbed the Hush rest. They placed the Teflon on a spring rest that also absorbs some of the pressures of shooting. The window has a soft material for shock and noise. The Saunders rest has worked very well for many seasons, and has the advantage of availability plus it will not allow the arrow to get below the rest.

If another style is preferred, Shakespeare has one made of plastic that sits on the arrow shelf, has a tough, slick window plate material and the same bristly material on the arrow rest. These fit onto the window and shelf with self-adhesive backing. Just pull the paper tape and apply the rest to the bow. They work well and, again, provide the answers the hunter needs to his arrow rest problems.

For some hunters, a higher rest is required than that the shelf styles provide. If so, move to the window shelf rests. These are available in many styles and shapes. Probably the best known in the above style is the Hoyt Pro rest. This has a leather base backed with a self-adhesive strip that allows easy placement on the window. The rest, itself, is a fingerlike system often of a plastic type material that will allow the arrow a clean, swift passage over the rest. This style can be mounted as high on the sight window as desired. If a low rest is needed, trip the base section and move it low.

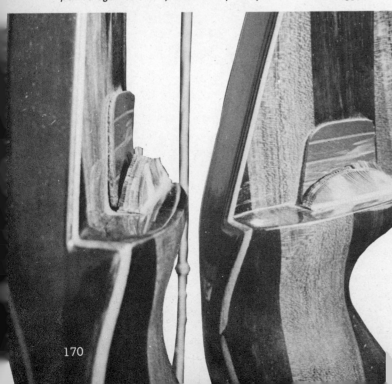

If there is a disadvantage to the Hoyt rest, it lies in the fact that the arrow can drop below the rest. This may prove a problem unless a system of nocking and checking the arrow on the rest without looking is devised. The hunter always can look at the arrow on the rest, but it is much simpler to place it and shoot without worrying where the shaft is. Nocking the shaft high on the window and then sliding it down to the rest also will work, but is noisy and takes time.

There are many exotic types of rests on the market. Some swing away on release, allowing the arrow to move over the window with little friction. Be careful in selecting a hunting arrow rest and be certain that it will withstand some rough usage. In choosing the plastic or wire finger-style window rest, the hunter should consider how long the finger will last. How can he shoot the bow if the finger breaks off? Does he have a strong down pressure on the arrow when drawing due to his style of shooting? Will this down pressure affect the arrow rest over a period of time or break it? These are some of the questions he needs to answer before deciding on one particular style. The best way to find out is to pick a particular rest, mount it on the bow and shoot it during small game hunting and target shooting to find the good and bad points of that rest. What works for one archer will not always work for another.

In observing a champion target archer's bow, a hunter may note a rest with a side adjustment. This is called a plunger. It has spring tension that will absorb some of the shock and pressure of the arrow on drawing and firing. A combination of plunger and flexible shelf or window rest would yield the ultimate in arrow rests. And, if it were durable, slick, and easy to use and mount, it would be ideal for the bowhunter.

Fred Bear, who has spent many years in the hunting field and knows firsthand the hunter's needs, has supplied just such a combination. When the Bear Archery Company came out with its metal take-down riser, they also incorporated the hunter's dream-rest into that riser. The base section allows proper placement of the arrow on the rest — a spring type shelf rest. The rest can be bent a bit higher if more clearance is needed.

There is a sideplate on the riser that looks similar to the material on the rest. A small allen wrench also is supplied. It fits into a small hole on the side of the bow, allowing adjustment of the sideplate in or out to give more center shot or less, along with added tension. This gives not only a clean shooting area over the shelf and along the window, but full adjustment for fine tuning of the bow. During tests, in all types of weather and while carp shooting, the rests have shown no tendency to come off or become sticky. Unfortunately, the rest is found only on the Bear bows.

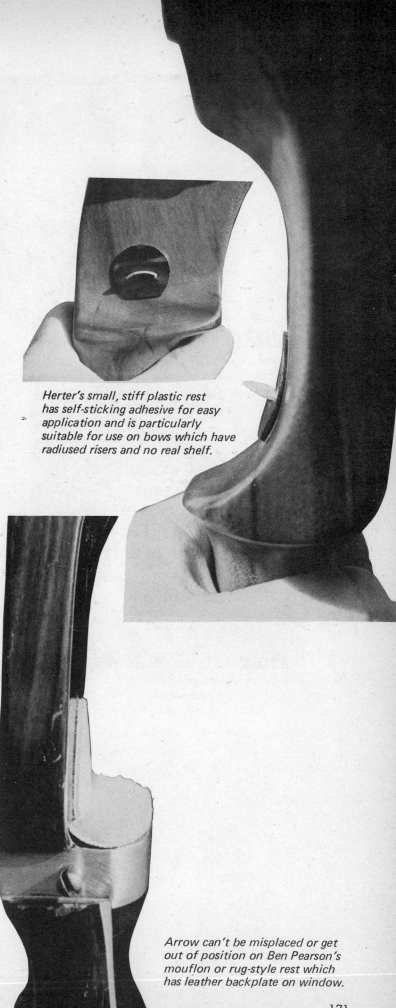

Herter's small, stiff plastic rest has self-sticking adhesive for easy application and is particularly suitable for use on bows which have radiused risers and no real shelf.

Arrow can't be misplaced or get out of position on Ben Pearson's mouflon or rug-style rest which has leather backplate on window.

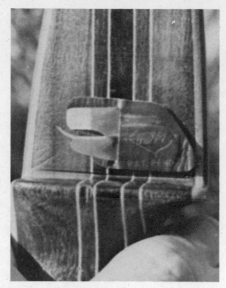

Padded sideplate on Wing's pile-like rest assists in absorbing arrow whip.

Hoyt Pro rest is preferred by many bowhunters and target archers, too. Plastic finger and cushioned sideplate stay slick, clean in any weather.

Adjustable sideplate is feature of Bear rest. Allen wrench is used to adjust for fine tuning to shooter's individual style. Photo at lower right shows amount of adjustment available.

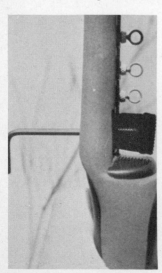
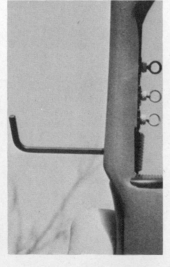

There is no reason the bowman cannot incorporate some of the rests and plungers used in the target field to his hunting bow. Most rests are simple to apply. The plungers can be purchased from a number of outlets and installed in the side window of the bow. This does require some drilling, so be certain of how to do it before plunging ahead. One thing about the plungers is that they will determine the placement of the arrow rest, since they must be in alignment with the plunger in order for them to operate properly. When selecting a plunger, get one that has the Teflon or similar slick material buttons that go against the arrow and be sure it is adjustable for tension. You might like it set up stiff or protruding quite a ways into the sight window, or perhaps have it recessed until it barely contacts the shaft on draw.

It would be nice if we could state, for perfect arrow placement in a game animal each time, all that is needed is to buy brand X rest. This just cannot be done, since we all have different problems and different shooting styles.

All an archer can do is be aware of the problems he may be facing. He may want a simple rest that will allow him to nock the arrow and come to draw without necessarily having to look at the arrow on the bow. It should be made of a material that will remain slick in hot, cold, wet and dry weather. He should be able to mount it to the bow easily and replace it in a similar manner. The sideplate should absorb the noise factor and, better yet, some of the pressures on draw and release. The plunger system is ideal in this situation.

Look over what is available on the market and try a few rests and window plates. While many have become addicted to the Hoyt system, others have found it unfavorable to their style of shooting. Find this out for yourself, before traveling many miles to a hunt camp.

Regardless of the system chosen, it should be open to revision in the field if need be. Carry a few extra rests and sideplates, just to be on the safe side.

Having found a material that seems to be ideal for an arrow rest, the wise hunter will try it at home. The Teflon plastics are an excellent choice, if offered in chunks large enough to mount on the shelf. Delrin is another of the space plastics that is available. It is harder than Teflon, still very slick in composition and available in sheets or blocks. Try various materials and ideas, and hopefully you will find a rest that works ideally for you and will last forever.

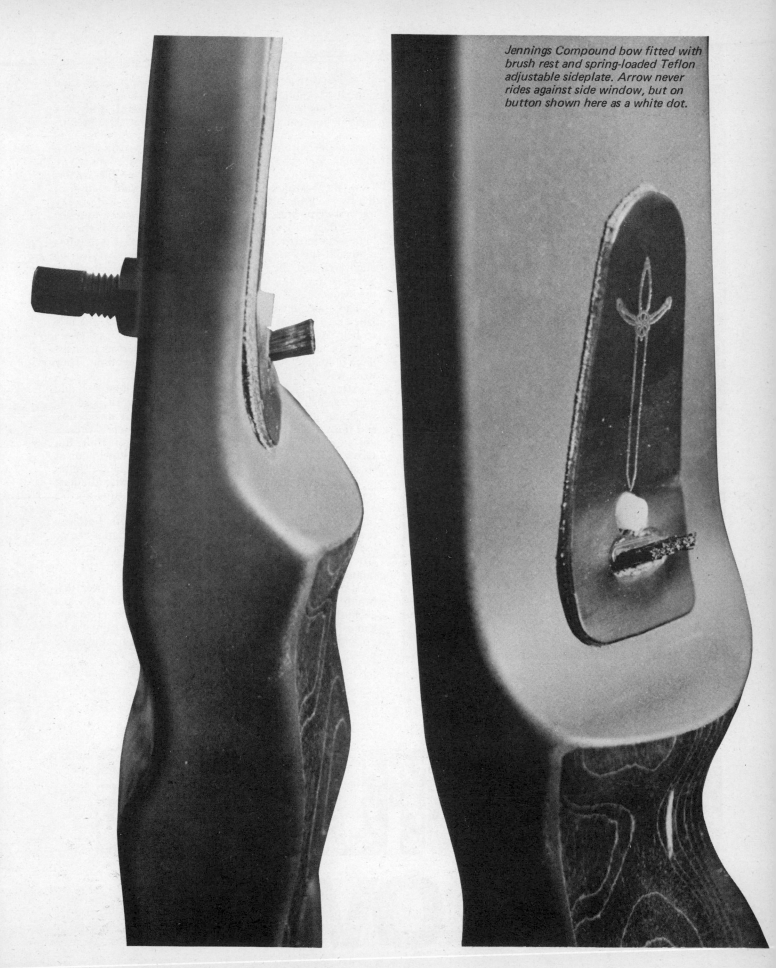

Jennings Compound bow fitted with brush rest and spring-loaded Teflon adjustable sideplate. Arrow never rides against side window, but on button shown here as a white dot.

CHAPTER 15

THERE IS ONE phase of bowhunting preparation that all bowhunters go through, often with some degree of dislike. This is when they must take that bright, shiny new hunting bow and cover its reflective surface with some type of camouflage. For many hunters this is just too much, and they prefer to buy commercially made bowsocks that slip over the upper and lower limbs to prevent reflections.

Bowsocks will do the job, but they have problems, too. First, the bowsock also must cover the forward section of the riser — on bright days the sun's rays may reflect off any uncovered portion of the riser. Game are smart, and the least reflection may spook them just as much as if the full limb were uncovered. A solution used by some bowhunters is to split the sock and draw it down onto the riser, leaving uncovered just the section above the grip. Some plastic or electrical tape will hold the sock in the proper position at the handle.

The upper and lower limb sections of the sock should be tapered to prevent the sock from being too heavy, and also to help keep it on the bow limbs. Many bowsocks have a series of elastic strips sewn into them at intervals to assist them in holding tighter to the limbs and riser sections. They work well until the rains come pouring down.

After placing the bowsocks on his bow, a hunter should notice a slight decrease in the cast of the bow. He is adding weight to the entire length of the limbs, including the tips, and the speed of the bow will be affected. He may feel it is not enough to bother with, and in most cases it isn't. But those same bowsocks, wet and soggy from a downpour or steady drizzle, will slow the bow speed considerably. Unless he is aware of this, he will have no opportunity to adjust for the decreased speed and his chances of hitting a game animal are slight.

The bowman can make his own bowsocks if he has a sewing machine. Any lightweight, mottled material can be used to break the reflections of the bow. The socks can be flared to fit over the riser sections, or tailored to a favorite hunter if desired. The possibilities are endless.

If the bowman does not object to painting over that beautiful finish, he can paint the reflective surfaces and avoid the weight of wet bowsocks. The most common problem associated with painting a bow is finding a paint that is not glossy. What is needed is a flat base color for the entire bow.

CAMOUFLAGING THE BOW

Covering The Various Types Of Paints And Tapes Available, Plus Commercial And Homemade Bowsocks

After carefully removing all wax from the bow, apply the base coat — outdoors or in a well-ventilated area.

One color that has worked well for many hunters is the flat, black lacquer found in spray-can form. Not many colors are sold in the flat base, thus the recommendation of black. Try to find colors that are found in nature for good camouflaging. Green is ideal, as is brown or gray. Gray, the priming coat used on automobiles, can be used as a base paint. Primers are made in a flat, base paint and can either be sprayed on with a spray gun or put on with a brush.

The simplest method of camouflaging the entire bow is to remove the arrow rest and arrow sideplate, if possible, or just tape them with some masking tape to prevent their being painted, too. If the bow has a sight, remove or cover it. The decals and markings on the bow can be taped, if desired to retain them, or simply painted over. Most bows can be identified by the shape and design more so than by the decals.

Before painting, place the bow on a bench and use rubbing alcohol to remove any finish waxes on the bow. One cleaning with the alcohol should remove the majority of the waxes. Suspend the bow from a nail or rod. A rubber band slipped into the upper or lower string nock will hold the bow easily and give mobility to the bow while spraying. Make a few swipes with the flat, black spray can on some cardboard or scrap material to be certain the oils and ether are mixed. Turning to the bow, stand about ten inches from the surface and spray the limbs. Standing too close will cause the paint to run. Do not try to cover all the surface completely with the one coat. Make the first coat a light one, allow it to dry, then spray the entire bow again. Add a third coat if necessary. This will prevent runs in the paint and a sloppy-looking job overall.

Spray the riser and handle, too. The only part of the bow that will not be painted is the one tiny strip where the rubber band held the upper limb, although it can be painted later, as well. If runs do appear while painting, do not worry about them. They won't look good, but they won't hurt anything, either.

Allow the paint to dry for several hours. While it is setting, pick the colors to be used for the desired mottling effect. Green and brown are good choices to splotch the base coat. These colors may be glossy or even semi-glossy, since they will be used in small units and will not create reflections.

The technique of applying the mottling effect can be achieved by several methods. One is to take a piece of corduroy material with the ridges in it. Fold a piece of the

Opposite page: Leaf pattern is applied by placing leafy twig on bow limb and spraying lightly, holding paint can ten inches from surface. Finished product resembles leaf outlined against solid patches of paint. Application of second color to solid background provides mottling effect.

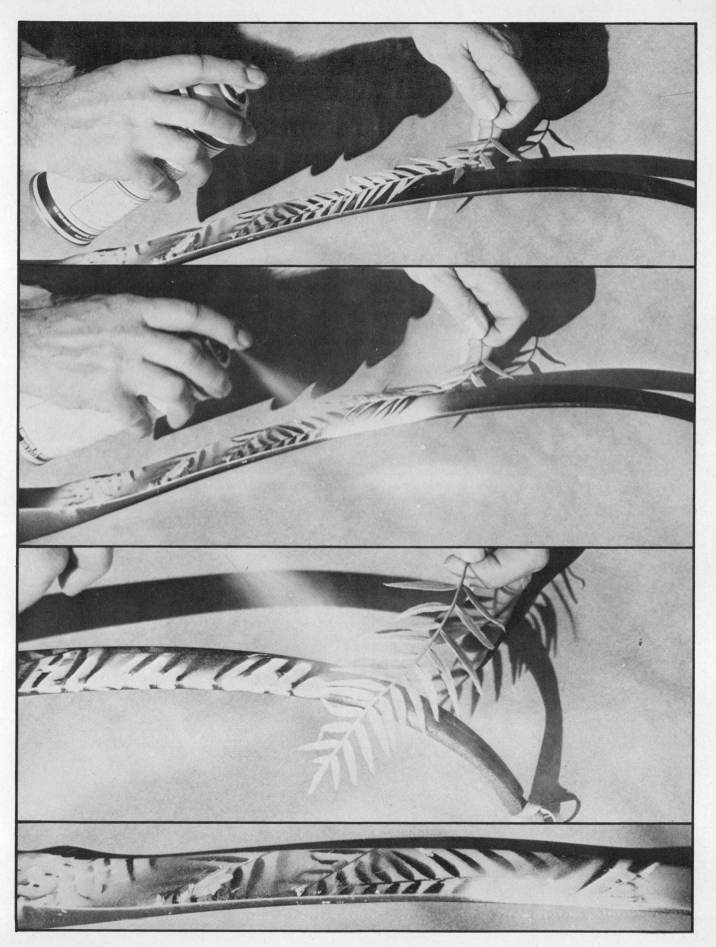

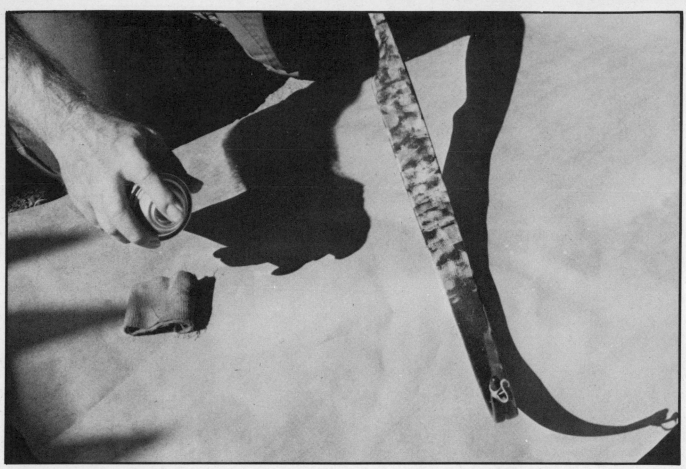

Another method of achieving a mottled effect is to daub a piece of corduroy material into paint previously sprayed onto piece of heavy paper or plastic, and then lightly apply paint-soaked corduroy to bow's surface at random.

Ribbed pattern of the corduroy material leaves a checkered impression which, by itself, is fairly effective camouflage.

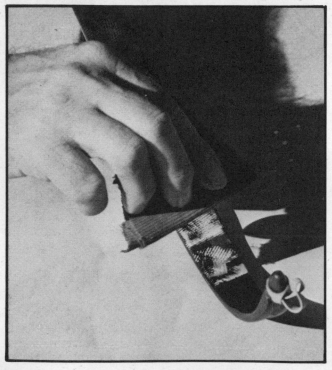

material into a small pad. Place a smear of the green paint on a piece of cardboard or a coffee can plastic lid. Daub the material in the paint to get some on the surface. Dabbing the material to the limb section of the bow with a light pressure will leave a ribbed blob of green paint. Only a small section is done at a time, and the size of the pad will be the determining factor. Dip and rub the paint on the material, then dab it on the limb and riser at random until finished with that one color.

Do not get carried away and cover the black with the green, it will be too much. When the green dabs have dried, follow the same pattern, possibly alternating the slant of the ribs or lines with brown paint. Use the same technique until reaching the desired effect, then stop and allow to dry.

Take the bow into the sun to see if there are any shiny sections that might shine through the paint job. If there are, dab them with the green or brown paint.

Some hunters will state that black does not appear in nature, so they do not like it for a base color; however, burned-over areas have plenty of black in them. The base color is determined by personal choice and availability of paints.

Another method that many hunters have found successful for mottling the paint on the bow is to use open-pored sea sponges. These often can be found in the auto departments of department stores where they are sold as car-wash sponges. The open pores give a unique mottling to the bow and the technique is the same as with the corduroy. Use a section of the sponge in brown paint, daubing the paint onto the sponge, then onto the bow. The paint will go on in

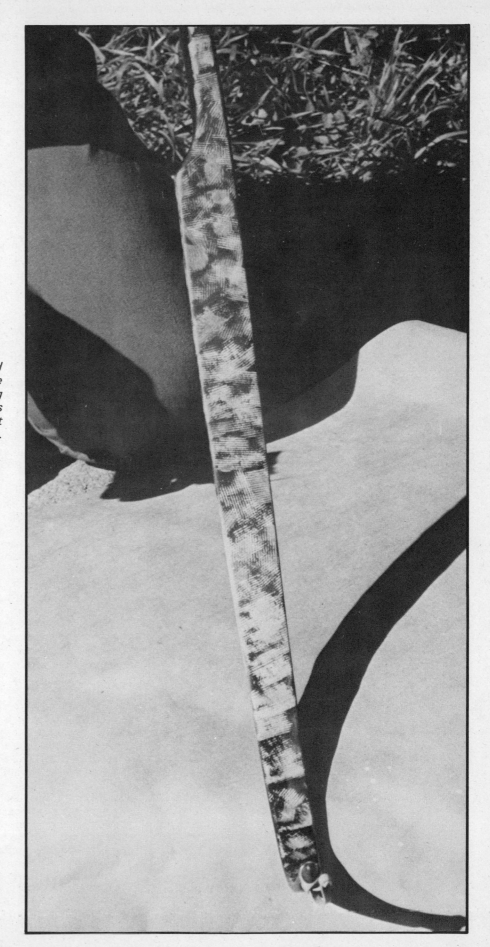

Single color applied with ribbed material results in appearance similar to this bow. Applying a second color in same manner as the first is recommended to get best possible camouflage effect.

Using the ragged end of a piece of sponge rubber to daub on paint provides still another variation in camouflage pattern.

flat colors that give the desired effect. These latex paints do build up in layers rapidly if care is not taken, and the weight can become excessive. Colors are endless with the new mixing systems now available. These paints usually are applied with a small brush, they clean up with water and will last during rains, as well. Using the cheaper brands might mean runoff in a rain, leaving a shiny bow again.

One of the reasons many hunters prefer not to paint the bow is to retain the beauty of the finish. However, it is unlikely the finish would be harmed. The limbs, and the entire bow in many cases, are coated with several layers of quality epoxy finish. That is what gives it the gloss and durability. Even removing the paint with paint remover shouldn't harm the finish. Do not use the super-strong types, but paint thinner in many cases will remove the spray-on lacquers. A bit of waxing and some polishing and the bow finish will be right back where it was when the bow was purchased.

The latex paints might prove more difficult. They should strip off, but may need some light scraping. Never sandpaper a bow and, if scraping, do it tenderly. The latex is trickier to remove and, for that reason, many hunters prefer to stay with the spray lacquers.

Many of the three-piece take-down bows have the riser section already mottled with some type of non-reflective surface. All that is needed with this type of bow is to camouflage the limbs. If the upper and lower limbs need to be identified for proper placement on the riser, code them with a dab of red on either limb where it wouldn't show on the inner section. The Bear take-down bow has this problem solved, since they have a locator pin that prevents the limbs from being interchanged.

If a take-down bow has two sets of limbs, one of fifty-plus and another of maybe sixty-five pounds, try using different base colors for the two sets to keep them in proper sequence. The fifties could be black, the sixties a gray or some similar method. Failure to mark them could result in some weird matings of limbs and riser.

If neither the painting nor the socks are the answer to a camouflage situation, there is yet another method — tape. Saunders Archery produces a camouflage tape that easily adheres to the bow. To remove it, just peel it off. This can be the ideal answer to a short hunt or in an emergency.

Not many hunters use the step-through or push-pull stringing methods anymore. Most archers have advanced to bowstringers that not only are safer for the archer, but better for the bow. Sliding the string in the push-pull method will sooner or later remove some of the camouflage paint. Using this method will peel some of the tape, as well. The tape along the edges of the limbs and the upper section may be peeled off easily with the pressures applied.

There are enough problems in the field when going for deer, so take that extra time and camouflage the bow completely, or use the bowsocks. Painting is perhaps the most successful method, and one that most bowhunters prefer. The type of paint and color selections are endless. Competition among hunting groups for the wildest camouflage job can become very challenging, and the methods and finished products are extremely good.

A sometime hunter who likes to wander through the woods and over the hills, and maybe shoot at a deer, may not need to camouflage the bow he carries. But a serious bowhunter will want to remove the shine from his bow and put as much effort into the complete tackle system as he does into the final hunting itself. We have enough handicaps as part-time hunters after full-time game without the added problem of reflection. Camouflaging the bow improves our chances in the bowhunting of game.

globs now, instead of ridges, and the effect will be different but effective.

Still another method is to take three different colors in spray can dispensers. Spray the black for the base. The brown can be added by holding the can farther away from the bow and allowing only splotches or swipes of the spray to cross the bow at intervals. Do the same with the green. The end effect will look smoother, without any ridges, blobs or dabs.

When painting the bow, do not get too much paint on the limbs. Here, again, it is a minor factor, but if the bow is loaded down with paint it will slow the return action of the limbs. With this factor in mind, consider some of the newer non-ruboff latex house paints. They come in many basic,

When using the sponge approach, paint may be applied in heavy or light splotches, just so long as the outline is completely broken. A second color may be applied between, or even over, the first coat, leaving a result that will blend with any bush. White paint, not normally used in camouflaging bows, was used in these photos for purposes of illustration and contrast only.

Chapter 16

Fashions for the Field

Proper Bowhunting Apparel Won't Qualify You For The Best-Dressed List, But Is A Necessity If You Want To Dress-Out Game.

BOWHUNTERS HAVE FAR different clothing problems than do rifle hunters. Riflemen usually are required to wear a specified number of square inches of bright colored material for protection; however, bowhunters have few such restrictions regarding color. Bowhunting accidents are few, and when they do occur it usually is a personal problem, such as falling on an arrow.

The clothing choice of bowhunters is as varied as the type of tackle they carry into the field. Many prefer to wear Levi trousers and a wool plaid shirt. The Levis may be tough, but they also can be noisy when rubbed together while walking. The wool plaid shirt can be an excellent choice, since wool is one of the quietest materials available. It is warm, will shed water up to a point and will still retain warmth even when wet. The color should be a dark one, with the plaid pattern breaking up the solid color.

Why do bowhunters need a special camouflage material or the equivalent? They need to be as quiet and as inconspicuous as possible. They must move in close to game, the closer the better, and to do so they must blend with the terrain, both in color and pattern.

Tiger stripe, designed for military use in Vietnam, is favorite of many hunters. Gets better with washings.

One of author's favorites is this homemade brushed cotton or flannel shirt. Can get warm, but is quiet.

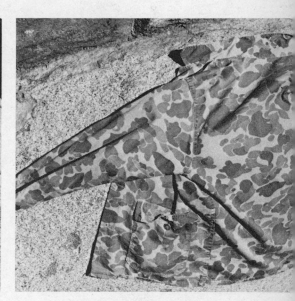

Standard-type camo found in sporting goods and surplus stores is similar to pattern on this shirt or jacket.

Opposite page: Proper pattern of camouflaged clothing must be selected to fit type of terrain to be hunted. Note how tiger stripe at top stands out against bush, while flannel shirt just below blends almost perfectly.

Another military pattern of camouflage, this one made in rip stop material. A good camouflage pattern, but material is too noisy.

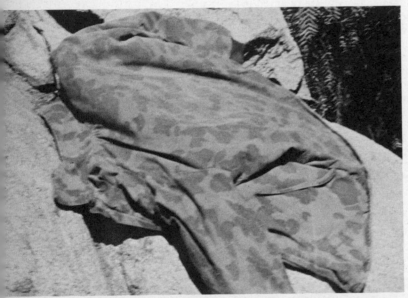

This particular mottled pattern of camouflage is quite popular and is found often on matched, fully quilted jacket and pants outfits. Turn the same jacket inside-out (below) and you have a bright orange reversible garment suitable for two-season hunting in cold weather.

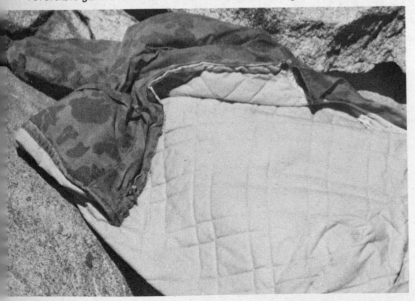

There are several manufacturers who cater to the bowhunter with special clothing. This usually is a basic brown material with a mottled patchwork affair printed on the material in darker browns and greens. Hunters should avoid a solid color when bowhunting. It is more or less considered fact that deer are color-blind, they see only in shades of gray. They do not see color as we do, but will detect brightness. A solid-colored shirt will attract the eye of a deer and, in turn, will probably spook him. The mottled, camouflaged clothing gets around the solid-color problem well, and has proven to be successful.

Camouflaged clothing, both pants and shirts, often can be purchased in military surplus stores. Using clothing designed for the duck hunter may be fine, provided the material isn't too heavy or noisy in movement.

The choice of color is not too important. One company came out with a red-colored camouflaged outfit that had mottled green and brown splotches on it. This could easily be seen by another hunter, but the deer did not see the color and merely passed it off as another bush.

Having selected a color, take a closer look at the material. It should be very tough. Rip stop is an exellent material for toughness, but the material makes all kinds of noise in movement through brush, and tree limbs seem to grab at the material. Clothing manufacturers make items that appeal to the eye, often without knowledge of the problems of the bowhunter. What is great for military purposes in color and toughness might pass for color with the bowhunter, but not for noise factor. A bowman generally is moving through brush continually while hunting, unless he is a stand hunter, and must take the noise factor into consideration.

Up until now no one has made a camouflaged outfit from wool. This would be an ideal choice for many reasons, but it would present problems if hunting during the fall or late summer when the temperatures make wool clothing much too hot for movement. For winter hunting it would be ideal.

There have been attempts at using a cotton flannel that has been mottled for camouflage purposes. It proved very good for color and was quiet in brushy areas. However, most cotton flannel is not very rugged and a hunter might get only one hunt or one season's hunting from a shirt or jacket made of flannel. And, while it is warm, it will not shed water when rained on.

Having become aware of the problems of the various materials, consider the way a shirt or jacket is made. Most are made for the rifle or shotgun hunter. They have large, blossoming jackets that are fine for the shotgunner, but will possibly get in the way of a bowstring when at full draw. If the bowstring slaps the jacket on release, it not only will spook the deer with noise, but the arrow probably will not come anywhere near the game. Check the fit of the clothing for this problem. It should be snug, but still allow movement for the bow arm and, if it has a series of good-looking pockets in the area where a drawn bow would be held, see if they can be removed without ruining the jacket.

The sleeve of the bow arm should not be too baggy. If the sleeve is large the hunter will have to secure it with some plastic tape or even sew it tighter. Many bowhunters wear the arm guard not for protection of the arm, but to prevent the bowstring from slapping the ballooning sleeve. The guard wraps the sleeve into a tight section that will not tangle with the bowstring on release.

It may sound as if there is no product on the market that will fill all the peculiar requirements presented by the bowhunter. Actually, it is merely a matter of pick and choose. By trying on available jackets in the store, and then adding a few needle and thread modifications, almost any jacket will work. Watch out for pockets often found on the left side of jackets or shirts. These pockets make an excellent snag for the bowstring. As mentioned earlier, it is possible to remove simple pockets or obstructions after buying the jacket.

The ideal shooting camouflage shirt would be one made of a soft, quiet material, tailored to the hunter so that he could shoot from any position without worrying about snagging on a pocket or ballooning jacket. The sleeve should fit trim against the bow arm to prevent string slap on that arm. If the sleeve fits properly, there may be no need for an arm guard. As strange as it may seem, there is just such a material available, but not on the open market. Leather will fulfill all of the above requirements, but it costs far more than most bowhunters want to pay for a hunting garment. Leather has disadvantages, too. Leather absorbs water, becoming extremely heavy and stretching. The only proper way to dry it is to wear it until it dries, or it will shrink beyond salvage.

Trousers are an easier problem to overcome. They can be purchased in the same pattern and material as the jacket to make a complete outfit, or can be of any type of dark-colored material. They should be quiet when moving, since pant cuffs and the lower leg sections will rub together while walking. Levis are tough and many hunters wear them, but if stalking close to game, the rustle made by the trousers can be enough to give an archer's location away to a sharp-eared deer.

A good choice would be a pair of green or dark-colored wool trousers. They are warm, very quiet and tough at the same time. In warm weather another material may be preferred, but on chilly days the wool outfit is hard to beat.

Hats for bowhunters are needed items. Light-colored hair will show as a beacon even though the hunter is fully camouflaged in jacket and pants. The hat is a must if wearing glasses. The brim of the hat should extend over the glasses most of the time to prevent reflections of the lenses from giving away the hunter's location. It protects the head and neck from sunburn as well as helping to keep the head warm on chilly hunts.

The hat should be dark or mottled in appearance. Choose between the ball cap or front-visor style and the full-brimmed hats. Keep in mind that the brim should allow a full draw without getting in the way of the string. A hunter cannot shoot properly if he is hampered at full draw by the hat brim fouling the string or preventing it from coming to his anchor point.

There are a variety of hats on the market that the bowhunter will find adequate. The Jones' style was designed for bowhunters and works well. It has a small brim that can be rolled up all around if desired. It often has a lining inside to keep the head warm in cold weather. Some have flaps that will come down for ear protection in very cold conditions. After a few years, the foam insulation may be falling out, but it won't hurt the hat. Merely keep it for warmer hunting weather.

Some bowhunters prefer the bigger brimmed hats such as those referred to as the Aussie style. This has a wide brim similar to the western or cowboy hats, but has one side of the brim snapped up against the crown. This was part of the Australian soldier's uniform and the style has been named after that hat. The right side has the full width of the brim extended. This is fine if an archer shoots left-handed, but for a right-handed archer the brim snap must change to the right side. Wearing the hat backwards produces the same results.

Kay Zeller is an attraction, whether in street attire or hunting garb, but exposed skin is distracting (below); animals can see it.

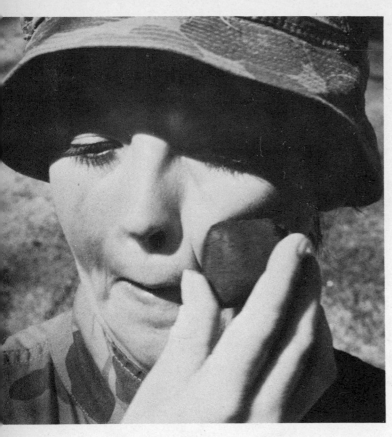

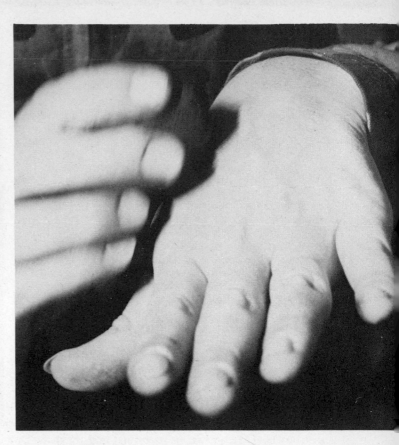

Charcoal briquettes, or burnt embers from a campfire, are useful in dulling the whiteness of the face and hands, if one is interested in foregoing the expense of purchasing commercial makeup. But remember: Use it liberally.

If, however, you want the best possible camouflage job, you'll use the commercially available camo stick that has brown makeup base on one end, green on other. Be sure it's minus insect repellent, or any kind of scent.

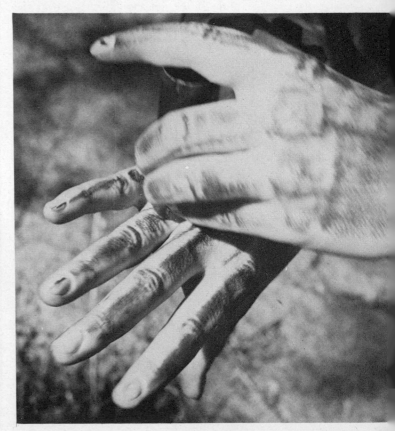

186

By using the charcoal and buttoning up a bit, Kay's image is less noticeable, but she'd still be visible to animals. Commercial makeup (below) hides face and hands better, but hands need additional touchup and her position should be farther back in the shadows of the surrounding foliage.

Some hunters prefer no hat at all. They may take a dark handkerchief and place this along the brow. Minimuffs, such as those worn by skiers, can be used to keep the ears warm with any style hat. The minimuff is a knitted, circular piece of wool that will fit over the head and cover the ears leaving the top of the head clear. They can be used with the regular summer hat, if preferred.

The baseball or visor caps also are popular. They protect the eyes from glare and from glass reflections, if wearing glasses. Any old ball cap of solid color can be used by simply sewing or gluing patches on to mottle and camouflage the appearance. Watch that long visor so that it doesn't interfere with shooting technique.

During the cold winter months, there are chances in some states to venture forth in the snow and cold to pursue the sport of bowhunting. The camouflage changes in snow. All that is needed is a set of white coveralls or an old sheet with modifications or some white trousers and an old white shirt. Don thermal underwear and as much clothing as needed to keep warm under the whites while blending with the environment. Some hunters continue to use their regular mottled camouflage and try to stay in timbered areas or in brush. Warmth is more of a factor now, so keep that in mind. It is possible to overdress and become too warm while moving, but become chilled when standing still.

Warm white hats are hard to find for snow hunting, so take one of the wool stocking caps or a watch cap, cover the top with some old sheet material and have the warmth of the wool cap and the camouflage at the same time.

We have discussed the clothing and hats hunters wear, but a hunter still must move into the timber regardless of the weather. A choice of footwear will be different for bowhunting, too. The big, heavy-soled hiking boots used when backpacking just won't work in the bow system. They get the hunter from point A to point B with ease, but when hunting they sound like a semi-truck moving through the timber. Sense of feel is lost under the foot of a heavy-soled boot.

Most of the bowhunting seasons are in August and early September. These months are still warm, so foot comfort is of little consequence. Wearing the lace-style hunting boots is fine, but try to find them with a light sole. It may be necessary to resole them more often than the heavy Vibram or lugged-soled boots.

Some hunters prefer the simple tennis shoe for bowhunting. It is light, comfortable and will allow as much quiet as possible. Rocks and small limbs are felt much easier than with the bigger-soled boots. Most tennis shoes have canvas sides and uppers, so in wet weather both the shoes and feet are apt to get soaked. However, the shoes dry fast once out of the grass and wet brush.

The American Indians used moccasins made of leather for hunting. Today, the moccasin is still a good choice if the feet are strong and tough enough to take rocks, twigs and some occasional cactus. They are light and allow the hunter to literally "feel" the path beneath the feet when he wears them. Some hunters have tried them, only to limp back to camp with sore feet and a miserable hunt remaining.

When properly camouflaged and situated off the skyline and in shadows, the bowhunter is ready for the final task of making the killing shot.

Although backed up against rocks and brush, alert animal could still spot bowhunter positioned in bright sunlight.

A cardinal rule in bowhunting is: Stay off the skyline. Even the best job of camouflage won't work in this case.

Terrain will determine footgear to a certain extent. If moving through rough, rocky areas with cactus in the open spots, it might be wise to wear the lace-style boots. If moving through pine or aspen thickets with little or no rocky areas and few cactus patches, tennis shoes would work very well.

Each bowhunter must determine the type of footgear that will suit him or her the best. Most of them will pick a boot or shoe style and wear it much of the time; unless in very wet or snowy areas, when they'll switch to the full rubber, insulated boot, if it is possible to move quietly in them. Keeping warm has a direct bearing on the success of an archer's hunt. Unless he is comfortable, he cannot perform at his peak.

Regardless of the final choice of footgear, be certain to break it in around the house, on short trips and small game hunts before going off on a long trip with shoes or boots that will cripple you after a few hours in the field. Break boots in properly, and coat them with waterproofing to keep out early dew and rain. Be wise and carry an extra pair of boots to wear if the first pair becomes too wet to use. A light pair of shoes, slippers or moccasins to wear around camp will allow airing out of the hunting boot and give the feet a welcome change.

At this point, the beginning bowhunter will be ready to take to the field. He has a full camouflaged bow, the arrows are camouflaged to prevent reflections, his hat is on and his boots are quiet and fit properly. But he still has one more step to take. His face and hands will shine like a beacon

In shadows, but bowhunter is positioned so that outline of body can be clearly seen against sun-splashed rock.

190

Completely surrounded by shadows, camouflaged bowhunter blends in nicely, although white nock is highly visible.

You can't camouflage the whites of the eyes; but it does help, however, to keep your hat brim pulled down so the eyes are at least partly shaded.

once he steps out of the shade. Even in the shade it is fairly easy to spot a bowhunter without camouflage on the face. The hands and face can be camouflaged very easily by using any of several methods.

If there is a single, simple camouflage method, it would be to use the charcoal from the campfire; or carry a few briquettes of barbecue charcoal for camouflage purposes. Take the charcoal and rub it onto the face, covering the forehead, cheeks, chin, nose and neck. Take the same material and coat the backs of the hands. This is simple, easy to clean up and will prevent the reflective surfaces of the skin from ruining a nearly complete camouflage job.

While browsing through the surplus store, pick up a tube of the camouflage paint or grease. This usually will be of two colors, black and green or brown and green. It is a pasty type of goo that smears over the forehead, cheeks, chin, neck, nose and hands. Quite often it also will have some mosquito repellent in it for added benefit. Be certain the smell of the camouflage paste isn't too strong or it will betray your well-camouflaged presence to deer by its smell.

Bear Archery, again, has come to the bowhunter's aid with two tubes of easy-on-easy-off camouflage paint or makeup. It isn't as hard to apply as the military types and will come off with soap and water. The paint should be easily removed from the face and hands or it will become more of a bother than an aid.

Occasionally a bowhunter rigged with a full camouflage outfit will go one step farther. He will take twigs from the pines and place them in his hat, shoulder areas and anywhere he thinks it might look good to a deer. He may not need the twigs, but he may have unconsciously done himself more good than he realizes. He has masked the human odor with that of the pine.

Odor can give a hunter away as rapidly as sight. It isn't a bad idea to take a camouflaged outfit into the woods, find some evergreens and rub the clothing over the needles to saturate the cloth with the smell of pine. This will mask the human odor. It is also possible to buy a sage and pine scent that produces the same effect.

Some bowhunters become adamant about odors or scents. The novice hunter may walk into a camp and find no camouflaged clothing in sight. The purists refuse to wear the hunting gear in camp, leaving it out in the timber instead, where it will not absorb the smell of cooking bacon, campfire smoke and other odd smells that appear in hunting camps. This may seem a bit extreme, but it does seem successful. Whether it is due to good hunting skill or the nonodorous clothing might be difficult to tell.

During one fall hunting season, a group came into our area, set up a monstrous camp, hung their camouflaged gear out in the timber and practiced all the prescribed methods of good bowhunting techniques. The next morning they came by camp to ask directions and they had twigs in their hats, and the fully camouflaged faces. But, to top it off, they had shaved early and liberally doused themselves with aftershave lotion. Not only did the shaving lotion make them noticeable, but it was of a variety that almost made the eyes water. We joked about this after they left, knowing more than they did, of course.

Later that morning we were told the two hunters came back to the camp area looking for help to drag in their bucks. They had wandered off into the timber — not knowing exactly where they were and doused with the aftershave lotion — and they had connected with two very respectable bucks. If they had stayed downwind they could have done it, but we still believe those bucks were lured in just to find out what smelled like that.

Examples of Buck knives suitable for use by bowhunters. Larger blades at left double as survival tools. Note knife customized with cholla cactus handle. Buck's top-of-the-line Akonua and Kalinga are at right.

THE KNIFE CARRIED by a bowhunter serves several more functions than the knife carried into the field by a rifle hunter. If a rifleman becomes lost, breaks a leg or is otherwise incapacitated, he perhaps can obtain help by firing his rifle into the air as a distress signal. The bowhunter, in similar dire circumstances, most probably would not attract much attention by firing a series of arrows into the air.

Bowhunters, then, select a knife that can be used for many tasks. The knife chosen must, first of all, be sharp and possess an edge-holding quality that will last for more than just a single animal-skinning operation. Additionally, it should be tough enough to handle the pelvic bone structure of a deer or similar-sized animal, and be capable of doubling as a survival knife, should that need ever arise.

In general, there are two basic styles of knives that most bowhunters eventually choose between; if they elect to carry only one knife. Leading the list is the ever-popular sheath knife that can be attached and carried on the belt. Sheath knives have been the choice of hunters for centuries,

and rightfully so. They stand up extremely well to the tasks of skinning, field dressing of game and — if chosen properly — to the various utility functions which might be required of them in actual survival situations. Another reason for their popularity is that they may be purchased in a wide variety of styles and designs to meet practically every specific demand, plus general purpose uses.

The other choice, which is rapidly gaining favor not only among bowhunters but with rifle hunters as well, is the folding knife. We're not speaking of the well-known folding pocket knife — although some of the "old guard" still prefer to carry that style and a good one will do an excellent, if limited, job — we're referring to a newer style of folding knife designed specifically for the rigors of the hunt. Sometimes referred to as folding hunters, they are too large to fit into the pocket and they, too, are carried on the belt in a sheath made expressly for that purpose.

Perhaps the main advantages of the folding knife are realized in the areas of weight and safety: it usually is lighter than the sheath knife, and there's no way of becoming

Chapter 17

Some Practical Aspects Concerning Size, Length And Shape, Plus A Look At Field-Sharpening Techniques

KNIVES FOR BOWHUNTERS

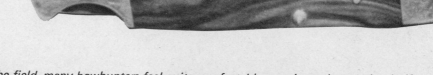

Folding Hunter by Buck has a single blade that locks in open position to prevent closing on the hand when in use. Compact, but too large for the pocket, comes with leather sheath.

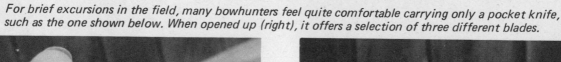

For brief excursions in the field, many bowhunters feel quite comfortable carrying only a pocket knife, such as the one shown below. When opened up (right), it offers a selection of three different blades.

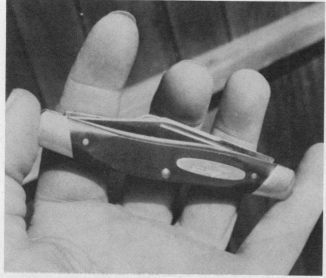

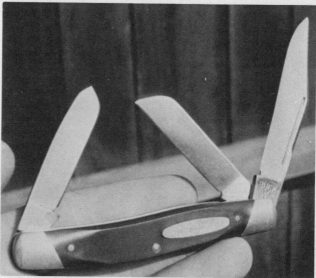

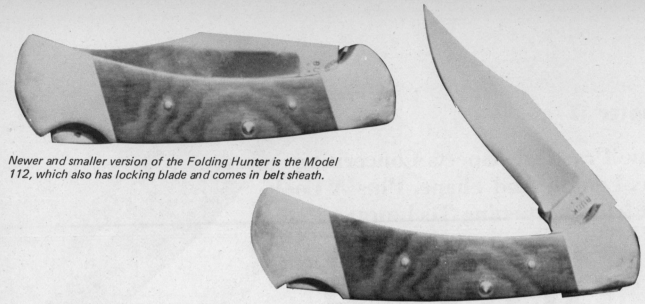

Newer and smaller version of the Folding Hunter is the Model 112, which also has locking blade and comes in belt sheath.

Several other folding knives, both pocket and lock-blade styles, made by Buck for hunting and camping.

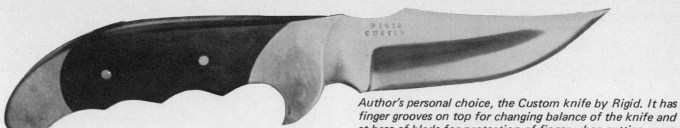

Author's personal choice, the Custom knife by Rigid. It has finger grooves on top for changing balance of the knife and at base of blade for protection of finger when gutting game.

accidentally stabbed by the knife while it's sheathed or closed. Nevertheless, the blade of such a knife is big and strong enough to handle just about any of the tasks a hunter might require of it while in the field.

The most practical difference between these knives and the pocket types, however, lies in the fact that they are equipped with locking blades. Each is designed so that it automatically locks the main or cutting blade in place when in the open position. This precludes the possibility of the blade suddenly snapping shut over unprotected fingers while preoccupied in field dressing game or performing an otherwise routine camp chore.

At present, there are a half-dozen or more good folding hunter knives commercially available; plus innumerable others being custom-made by professional knifemakers to individual specifications. Those available commercially offer a variety of blade styles, shapes and sizes. Although it is universally understood that no one blade can perform with ultimate results all the jobs ranging from skinning and field dressing to caping a trophy, most knowledgeable

sportsmen feel that the folding hunter probably comes closer to meeting the requirements than the larger sheath knives; at least in these respects.

If considering the purchase of a folding knife, keep these ideals in mind: It should incorporate a blade that positively locks in the open position; its edge-holding quality should withstand the normal uses in the field; and, its size and weight should be such that it can be carried on the belt, in the pocket or in the backpack. The blade needn't be excessively large since it is used primarily for field dressing, a task that can be accomplished with almost any size blade. Breaking the pelvic bone on a deer is fairly easy and once the joint is separated, and any blade can open it from that point.

The advantage of the smaller blade is in its efficiency for caping in the field. Most deer hunters do nothing in the field except the field dressing or gutting of the game. The hide or skin is left on until the deer is back in camp and the hide can be taken off while the deer is raised from the ground to prevent dirt from getting in the meat. However,

Photograph below illustrates position of fingers in knife grooves when opening up body cavity of game.

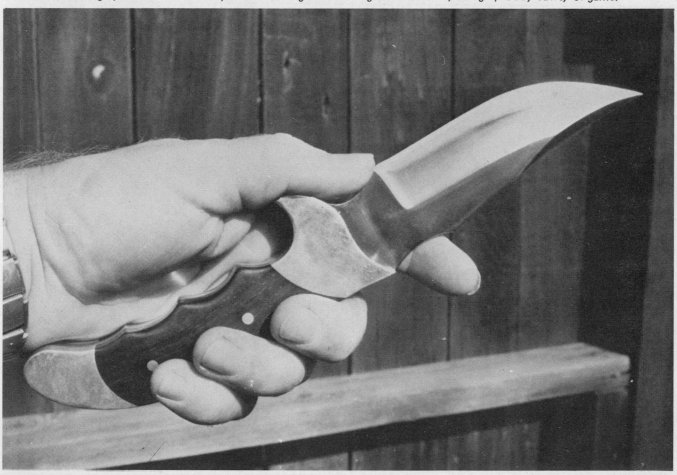

Customized handles were made by the author and fitted to the two Rigid knives displayed above the un-modified Rigid Custom. Choice of handle materials ranges from cactus to bone to composites.

if the weather is extremely hot the hide should be pulled as soon as possible, even in the field, if need be.

The bowhunter kills his game by bleeding. That bleeding is done with a razor-edged steel blade. Many hunters are extremely fussy about the steel in their broadheads and forget this same material when selecting a hunting knife. In actuality, the knife should be of a better grade of steel than the broadhead. Unlike the knife, the steel of the arrow blade must be hard enough to take an edge, but soft enough to take impact on hitting. There is no need for softness in the hunting knife. The steel in knives and broadheads is measured for hardness by the Rockwell testing machine. Usually running at 50 or less on the Rockwell C scale for broadheads, it should register about 58 C for the hunting blade. The harder steel will take and hold an edge much better, lasting through several skinning operations.

When purchasing a hunting knife, a bowman should first be certain the blade has an edge-holding quality that will allow it to take the edge required and retain it. While it is possible to carry a stone in the field for touching up the edge of the knife, and many hunters do carry such a sharpener, it may not always be practical.

Today, it isn't unusual to find a bowhunter carrying two knives on his belt. One may be a moderate-sized sheath knife used for utility purposes, such as cutting and making blinds in likely looking crossings. The other may be a folding, hunter style that is used only for working on the game after it is down.

How sharp the knife blade need be is a matter of personal preference. Many hunters prefer honing their blades to a razor edge to facilitate ease in skinning the game. Occasionally, hunters will attempt to sharpen just the upper front section of the blade, the chamfer, to a razor edge for gutting purposes. Keep in mind, however, that the sharpening of both edges the full extent of the blade is not only illegal in most states, but weakens the blade drastically.

Blade design also is becoming a matter of personal selection. Often the hunter may find exactly what he wants among the selection of commercial blades on the market. If not, there are numerous reputable knifemakers who will custom-build a hunting knife to individual specifications.

A sweeping curve on the tip of the hunting knife makes skinning somewhat easier. However, a stiletto-tipped blade, one that comes to a needle point, is not necessary — since the knife seldom is used for sticking purposes, but rather as a cutting instrument. A blade shape that allows ease in opening an animal's body cavity, with sufficient curve to aid in skinning, is an ideal hunting blade. Recommended blade length should be from three to five inches long.

There are many sharpening devices available for use when it becomes necessary and practical to rehone the

Preference of most bowhunters is to carry two knives; a sheath-type knife for heavy cutting and a folding-type for cleaning and preparation of game.

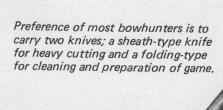
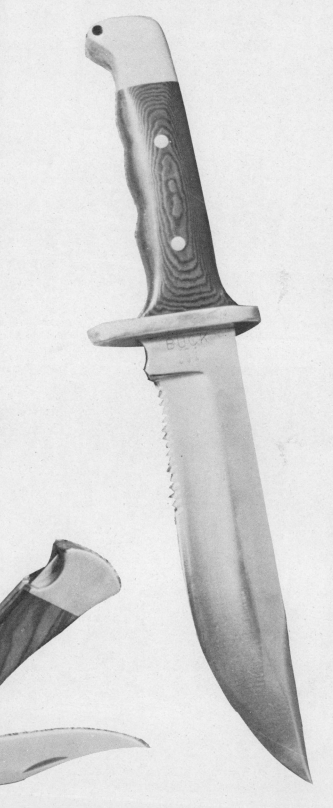

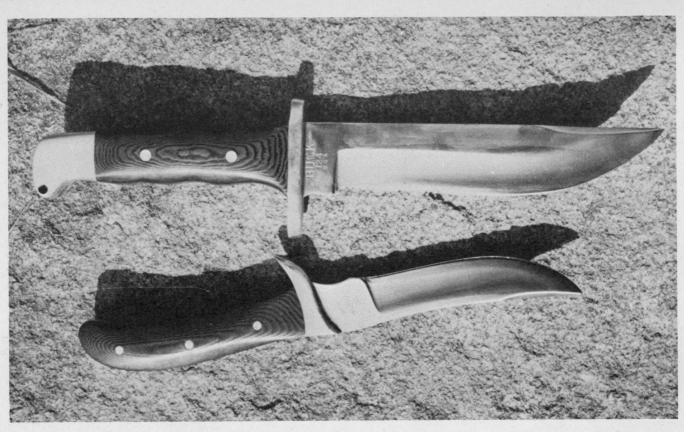

Buck Frontiersman (top in both photos) is displayed with Buck's Kalinga (above) and Akonua models (below). Although quite similar in appearance, each blade is designed to fulfill a specific function or purpose.

hunting blade. One that has been around for some time — and is considered excellent by many bowmen — is the Razor Edge unit. When using this unit, the knife is held in a clamp system that gives the blade the same angle on the stone each time, avoiding the pitfalls of a dubbed edge or shallow angle.

A relatively new system on the market is the Buck Honemaster sharpener. This unit also clamps onto the knife blade and gives the same sharpening edge to the knife with each stroke. The Honemaster slips on the blade and tightens with a knurled wheel locking system.

There are two main factors to consider in obtaining a well-honed knife blade. One, already mentioned, is the introduction of the stone to the blade at the proper angle to prevent inconsistent honing. The other is the quality of the stone itself. The stones most popular among seasoned hunters are the Arkansas stones, found in two grades, medium and hard. The medium stone is often called the Washita stone, and the harder by the name of Arkansas. Both are natural stones found in that part of the country and each makes an excellent abrasive for honing.

Although the idea of survival is perhaps often over-emphasized, it should be a factor to consider in knife selection. To the hunter caught in a storm in the high country, a little shelter could mean the difference between loss of life due to exposure and survival. For this reason, it might be wise to carry a pocket knife or folding knife of some type as a backup for use in emergencies.

Good knives are an asset to any type of hunting and good hunters are aware of this. They are always searching for that blade system, shape, sharpness and other characteristics that will give them the ultimate hunting knife. And while they may not always agree on just which is the "perfect" knife, they're certain to agree on one point: The knife is a must.

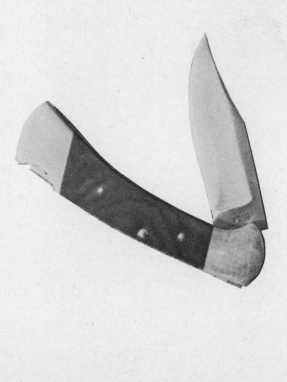

Another good combination for handling almost any situation: again, the Buck Frontiersman, but in this instance it's paired with the folding-type Model 112.

Small-game hunting gets bowhunters out in the open and is a great opportunity to check technique, equipment and accuracy.

200

Chapter 18

SMALL GAME BOWHUNTING

An Excellent Training Activity For Beginners, Small Game Hunting Offers Challenges With Its Eye-Sharpening Aspects.

THROUGHOUT THE EARLIER chapters, discussions centered around the stalking and killing of large game, such as moose, elk, bear and deer. And there was a good reason for this. To the average bowhunter, and this is especially true of the novice, it is the lure of a trophy head hanging on the den or living-room wall that draws them to the field. In this light, it might seem as if smaller game have no place in the scheme of things. Yet, the hunting of small game can be one of the most important phases of a hunter's career — his practice periods. Nothing substitutes for practice, and small-game hunting is one of the best forms of practice. There are no targets to place, no designated ranges, and the similarity in conditions is comparable to that of big-game hunting.

Aside from the practice small-game hunting offers, there is an added advantage: there is hardly a time of year during which some type of small game is not in season. In contrast, hunting seasons for larger game animals are highly restricted by state game departments, lasting only a matter of days, or at most several months.

The type of equipment used in small-game hunting will vary with the game. The choice of broadheads, for instance, is somewhat more limited than it would be for big game, calling for a rugged head that can withstand repeated impact, since the degree of accuracy against small game is drastically reduced because of the target being smaller. The broadheads must be able to withstand those misses. While it won't remain sharp after being shot into the ground or a clump of bushes, it should remain true. For this reason,

perhaps two of the better broadheads to use in small-game hunting would be the Black Diamond series or the popular Bear Razorhead.

Hunting for small game means a high degree of arrow loss, making it an excellent time to use those old shafts that have been gathering dust in the closet. When a hunter returns from a fall hunt, he oftentimes finds himself with several shafts which he would hesitate shooting at larger game next season, for fear of losing a trophy due to poor arrow performance. Some may have ratty fletches, others possess slight end dents or nicks; yet they are still safe to shoot. If tipped with old broadheads, blunts or field tips, they serve as excellent small-game shafts.

If using new equipment, the wise bowman will look to the cheaper arrows for hunting small game. Cedar or fiberglass shafts are particularly good, as well as inexpensive. If an aluminum shaft is to be used, try the Judo point; an excellent choice since it will dig into the grass or brush — rather than sliding under it — making it much easier to spot.

There are many varieties of points for hunting. Most of the small game being hunted is thin-skinned and the point on the arrow can be almost anything. One that has proven to be highly effective is the combination of Port Orford cedar shafts tipped with .38 blunts. They are about the least expensive shaft system available and are excellent against rabbits, squirrels, prairie dogs and numerous other small animals. When going after the larger small game, such as raccoon or nutria, switch to the broadheads. One word of advice: When going after that thin-skinned, loping jack-rabbit, take a good sharp broadhead, since the jackrabbit is probably the hardest of the small-game animals to stop. He is tough, fast and requires a good solid hit to down.

Field points also work on small game nicely. If they have any drawback, it would be their tendency to dig under the grass, making the arrow difficult to locate. However, if the terrain being hunted is open, they can be used with little problem. Keep in mind that the terrain, as well as the animal being hunted, will help to determine the best type of arrowhead to shoot.

The list of small game is almost endless. Perhaps the most commonly hunted is an animal found throughout the United States — the rabbit, be it the cottontail or jackrabbit. Hunting this elusive, cautious quarry is quite a challenge. When a hunter goes after a rabbit, he is facing an effective target range of only about three inches in diameter for a kill, against an animal generally surrounded by instant cover if frightened. As previously mentioned, when hunting for rabbit, the bowman usually will go to a blunt or broadhead, with the broadhead preferred. This gives him the same arrow weight and head as used when hunting large game.

Different areas of the country offer varying types of small game. In the East, one of the most popular animals is the woodchuck or groundhog. Many hunters feel that if they can successfully stalk and shoot an old chuck, they will have little difficulty scoring on the larger game animals, and they may be right. Woodchucks live in the open within easy reach of the protection of their holes. An extremely

Unlike the terrain found in the archery lane, bowhunting shots often must be made from angles and slopes. Do your practicing and you'll score on big-game hunts.

202

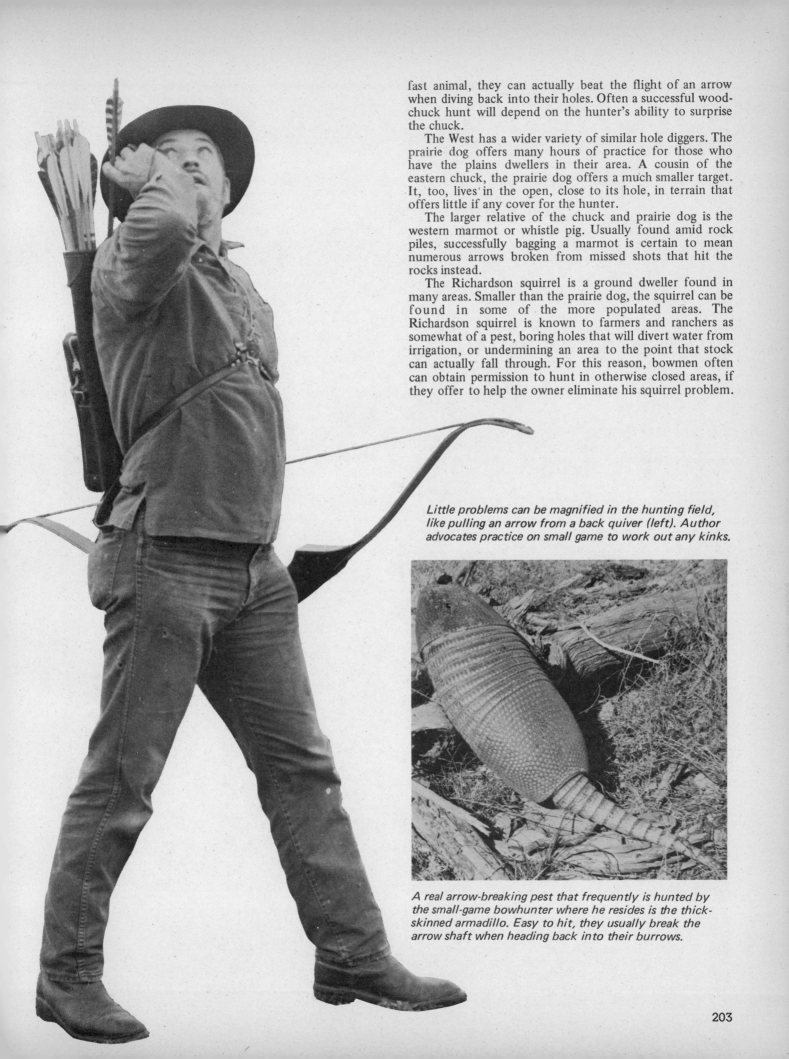

fast animal, they can actually beat the flight of an arrow when diving back into their holes. Often a successful woodchuck hunt will depend on the hunter's ability to surprise the chuck.

The West has a wider variety of similar hole diggers. The prairie dog offers many hours of practice for those who have the plains dwellers in their area. A cousin of the eastern chuck, the prairie dog offers a much smaller target. It, too, lives in the open, close to its hole, in terrain that offers little if any cover for the hunter.

The larger relative of the chuck and prairie dog is the western marmot or whistle pig. Usually found amid rock piles, successfully bagging a marmot is certain to mean numerous arrows broken from missed shots that hit the rocks instead.

The Richardson squirrel is a ground dweller found in many areas. Smaller than the prairie dog, the squirrel can be found in some of the more populated areas. The Richardson squirrel is known to farmers and ranchers as somewhat of a pest, boring holes that will divert water from irrigation, or undermining an area to the point that stock can actually fall through. For this reason, bowmen often can obtain permission to hunt in otherwise closed areas, if they offer to help the owner eliminate his squirrel problem.

Little problems can be magnified in the hunting field, like pulling an arrow from a back quiver (left). Author advocates practice on small game to work out any kinks.

A real arrow-breaking pest that frequently is hunted by the small-game bowhunter where he resides is the thick-skinned armadillo. Easy to hit, they usually break the arrow shaft when heading back into their burrows.

Bewhiskered Bob Learn negotiates one of the hazards found in hunting fields: fences. You must watch the angle at which you bend, to avoid having arrows spill from back quiver all over the ground, spooking game.

Many small-game shots will come in dense cover or with solid rock acting as a backstop for arrows. Taking these shots truly develops the shooting eye, because missing often results in scenes like the one above right: broken arrows!

For their size, ground squirrels and prairie dogs offer a big challenge to archer, because of their quickness.

They may find they have become addicted to the fun and challenge that small-game hunting offers. But there are advantages. First and foremost is that the small-game hunter can hunt year-round. There always is some small-game animal that is in season and many of the rodents and other nonprotected species can be hunted anytime. It offers as big a challenge as the hunter allows it to.

For those who do go on to larger game, there is the reality that successful small-game hunting usually means success in the big-game field. A hunter who has practiced throughout the year with the same equipment, and has managed to hit the smaller prey with any degree of consistency, probably will have no problem hitting the vital areas of the larger game. There is nothing that will substitute for practice, and small-game hunting offers some of the best.

Ranchers in Texas and other southern states like to have the armadillos eliminated for much the same reasons. They, too, dig holes large enough to break an animal's leg. The hardness of the shell on these throwbacks to a bygone era makes the armadillo a particularly challenging prey.

Another rather exotic critter hunted in the South is the nutria or coypu. A South American aquatic, otter-like rodent, it was introduced to the southern states as a fur-bearing animal whose pelts produced beautiful pieces. Severe storms broke up many of the original nutria farms, scattering the animals hither and yon. They have since reproduced to the point of being overabundant and somewhat of a pest. The nutria is a particularly sneaky animal and extremely difficult to hit.

While raccoons usually are hunted at night with dogs and rifles, they, too, may be sought out with a bow. Successful raccoon hunting means hunting at night with a light to find the animal in the limbs of the trees, and requires night shooting practice. Sharp broadheads are in order here, shot at an angle to prevent possible danger to the hunter during the arrow's downward flight.

The techniques used by a hunter in seeking out small game may be as haphazard or as specific as he wishes. Some hunters prefer to ramble around the hills and fields. When they spot game, they take the shots as they are offered.

Other bowmen prefer to use small-game hunting as a brush-up period in their stalking techniques. Trying to sneak up on a prairie dog, for instance, will take all of the stalking expertise a bowman has. Prairie dogs seldom are found alone, and a hunter will find sneaking up on them, without at least one of the dogs spotting him and sounding the alarm, quite a challenge.

While some hunters switch bows when they go for small game, laying aside the heavy bows used on large game and

choosing a lighter-weight bow instead, most prefer to shoot one bow for all game. As a rule, the more a single bow is shot, the more confidence the bowman has in that bow and the greater his percentage of hits.

For those who really enjoy a challenge, there is snow-hunting. The rabbit is king here, since other animals usually are in hibernation. It might even be the snowshoe rabbit being hunted, an animal whose coloring blends in with the white terrain, making sighting all but impossible. The order of the day for snow-hunting is to use the brightest arrow available. If the arrow is extremely bright in both shaft color and fletch, the chances of locating it in the snow are fairly good. Some of those old shafts can be redipped for just this purpose.

Perhaps one of the greatest drawbacks to small-game hunting is that many bowhunters find they prefer to stay with the small game and never go on for the bigger animals.

Opposite page: Game spotted, author begins slow stalk into bow range, deftly dodging brush. Below left: Arrow loosed, author shows advantage of shooting from strange positions. Note lugged-sole boots. Below: Again, terrain variance can be helpful in scoring hits on trophy game.

Chapter 19

Iᖴ THERE IS one sure way to get a novice started in the field of bowhunting, it is by taking him on a carp shoot. This is one of the fastest and most prolific of game hunted by bow. True, you must have some fish to make the sport worthwhile, but if you're near a body of water that has a school of carp, you can have year-round fishing fun.

Many target archers shoot fish as a form of practice, but once they have tasted the fun of the fishing system usually continue on to bigger and better things. Most lakes and sloughs are teaming with carp, unwanted scavengers which damage the game fish population, so your efforts in helping rid the streams of these rough fish will be appreciated.

There are only a few items you need add to your regular bowhunting gear. You can make all the needed equipment with the exception of the line. You will need a fishing arrow with a barbed point — illegal for most big-game hunting, but required to get a large carp to the bank. You also will need some type of reel to keep the line attached to the arrow and the bow.

The bow used may be your regular hunting bow. The bow weight isn't critical and there are no restrictions, but the heavier the bow — a hunter model is ideal — the more fun you will have. You can use a light bow, but you will be limiting your range with the light tackle due to the weight of the fishing arrow, often up to one thousand grains.

There are mixed theories about the weight of the fish arrow. One says the heavy arrow will penetrate better with less deflection as it enters and passes through the water. This is basically true. Another contends that the regular hunting arrow with the barbed, fish point will do the same job. This also is true, but common sense tells us that the heavier arrow will penetrate with less deflection. The light arrow will work better from light bows; the heavy arrow works from any bow, but better from a heavy or regular hunting bow.

Bowfishing tackle is available in many sporting goods and archery stores. The arrows usually are solid fiberglass, hence the weight, and thirty inches long. They are long to prevent the line from becoming tangled in the reel and to give you some protection from the barbed head.

There are several methods of making your own bowfishing arrows from fiberglass or aluminum shafts. The fiberglass usually is used since it is heavier and easier to work with.

Now that you have the arrows, all you need add is the fishing point. This is different from the regular broadhead used for game and there are several reasons for this.

First, the barb must be big enough to hold the weight of a thirty-pound fish. If you try to use the broadhead, you may lose more fish than you land since they will slip off the arrow as you reel them in.

A good fish point is one that will be tough enough to take direct hits on unseen underwater rocks or other hard materials. You may not see that sunken car body under the mud, but your arrow can find it.

There should be some method of taking the fish off the arrow without having to carve the carp into shreds to get your arrow out. One simple method has a reversing barb with one end alongside the point. When you spear the carp, the barb will hold it with the other stainless barb that sticks out the side. After you have your flopping hit on the bank, all you need do is pull the closely set tongue from the retaining hole, pivot the barb and pull the carp off the end of the shaft. This is a simple, fast and about as clean a system as you will find.

Minimal Accessories Provide Another Facet To Bowhunting; But It's Not Quite Like Shooting Fish In A Barrel!

BOWFISHING

You can make your own fish points, also, and should start with a good field tip. Drill a hole the diameter of the stainless wire you will use for the barb and, after passing the wire through the hole, cut it long enough to give a double-barbed head. Cut the wire, solder the hole to keep the barb from turning, and bend the wire back on each side to form the fish point. This is relatively simple, but to get the carp off the arrow, you either pull the arrow through the carp, after removing the line, or carve the carp to get a hole big enough to pass the barbs back through.

When you first start in the bowfishing game, it might be easier and certainly faster to purchase one, or better yet, two fish points for that first trip. Always take at least one spare arrow, complete with barbed point, in case you hit a submerged log or break the line and lose the arrow.

The simplest part of bowfishing gear is the fishing line. You could use monofilament, but it stretches too much and

kinks. Best choice is the braided nylon line often used for throw lines that can be purchased in any fishing tackle department or store. Be certain to insist on the braided style. Never try to use twisted line — you will wish you hadn't.

When you reel in the line after a shot, hit or miss, the line wraps around the reel attached to the bow. The twisted line will kink and snarl, since it either will go with the twist, creating many snags, or against the twist, making a worse problem. Braided line also tends to twist, but is less of a problem overall. Strength of the line usually is in the seventy to ninety-pound class. You don't catch fish that big, but you do put undue stress on the line.

You should have enough line to be able to shoot the

Carp is a quarry that can really sharpen a bowhunter's aim, or lead to immense frustration. Getting one on the receiving end of an arrow (below) takes adjustment.

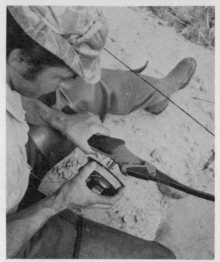

Bear Archery makes an assortment of fishing systems, as seen (above left). The most common way of attaching a bowfishing reel to the bow is by employing black electrician's tape, and wrapping it over the metal legs of the reel (center). For those who have purchased a Bear take-down, the reel slips into the stabilizer insert's threaded bolt. This saves time and energy.

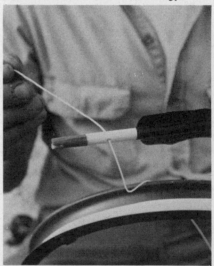

Black electrician's tape again is used to hold reel to bow, in this case a center-shot reel (above left). When the braided nylon line is wrapped on the hoop-like reel, the loose end is fed back through a hole drilled in the shaft near the nock (above right), then forward through another hole in the head. When completely ready, the archer shoots through center of the round reel.

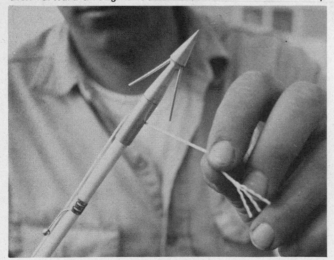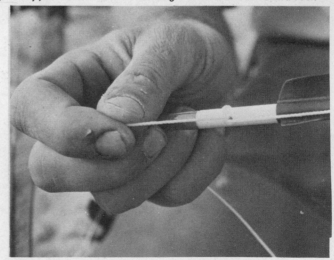

After the string has been passed through the hole near arrow nock, it is brough down and run through hole near point. Note the pencil clip used to hold the line.

To assure firm coupling of arrow and line, a half hitch or two should be taken below the nock. The line now passes back to reel, comes off smoothly.

Just a sampling of the fish points available to archer's is shown above. Point on extreme left is too large for carp, but right for frogs. Others have screw-on tips or collapsible barbs, and some have no release system.

fishing arrow twenty to thirty yards. You may not shoot that far — seldom, in fact — but if you are shooting down from a bridge, for example, you will need sufficient line not only to reach the water, but enough to reach the fish.

Wrap enough line on the reel to have extra in case the line breaks, but not so much it peels off when you don't need it. Fifty to seventy-five feet is enough for most bow-fishing.

The bowfishing reel can be a regular spinning reel, but often it is better to use one of the inexpensive bowfishing reels on the market. They attach to the back of the bow — the side toward the fish — and by several methods. One way to fish is to hold the reel in your bow hand. This allows you to lay the bow down as you wrap the line or play the fish. It has the disadvantage, though, of allowing you to become excited and drop the bow and the reel, perhaps losing both in the water.

Another method is to tape the reel to the riser of the bow with plastic tape. This won't harm the bow. Bear Archery came out with a new wrinkle when they made a fishing reel with a threaded bolt that attaches the reel to the stabilizer insert on the Bear take-down bows.

To make your own fishing reels, take a one pound coffee can and rivet a leather strap on the open end for holding. Take an eye bolt and put it in the center of the solid bottom with a double nut, one on each side. Attach the line to the eye bolt, wrap it around the circumference of the can and hold onto the strap with your bow hand. This is simple, cheap, and it works. You could arrange a metal strap that would tape to the bow if you wanted, but the holding system works unless you get too excited.

There is another style of bowfishing reel that mounts on the bow, usually with tape, and you shoot through the center of the reel. This gives you less wraps to get your line in and the pull of the line is more even, instead of all coming from the bottom of the riser with the other styles. The pull of the line is minimal but, if you look at the two

styles, you can see advantages in both. If you're not sure, try both, then buy what you want or try to make it.

When you have all your tackle prepared, with spare line and arrows, points and maybe an extra reel, all you need is some action.

Carp spawn in the Spring of the year and most lakes have more than their share of these rough fish. Access usually isn't a problem. Rivers, sloughs and other areas of quiet water will also have their share of carp. It is permissible to shoot most of the rough or non-game fish in any state, but be certain to check the rules. In the South, you usually can shoot the alligator gar, a challenge and great fun, since they can literally become monsters.

When carp spawn, they swim into shallow water to lay their eggs. That is when you will get the most shooting, but they can be found any time of the year in many waters. The spawning time is when they are hyperactive, however.

When carp are in shallow water, they make a reasonably easy target. All you need do is calculate the weight of the heavy arrow, the angle of the shot, and the distance to the carp. A method used by many instinctive archers is to aim for the back sticking from the water and they usually hit in the body of the fish. If the fish is farther away, you raise the bow; closer, you lower it. If the carp are swimming in deep water or laying in a hole, it becomes a different game.

When sighting carp in a hole or deep water, most shooters pull up, hold where he is, and miss every time. This is due to a principle called refraction. To put it simply, light bends as it enters water, so what you are looking at is there, but not where you see it. It is lower than your eye tells you

During spawning season, carp cavort near surface of sloughs like this one, or where there is a muddy bottom. Here, there's no wind to cloud the surface.

it is. Hold your arrow below the carp and you will soon learn to connect. You can read all about it, but until you try fishing for carp with a stick and two sets of string, you won't think there is much fun in it. One outing, if the carp are moving, will make you an addict for life. There will be more shooting than your arms can take.

If the water is muddy, the carp often will stir up mud as they scrounge for food and you can shoot for the swirls. This is more a luck-type shot, since you have no idea which end is which, but after a few tries, you will start connecting. When you think you are getting pretty good, try taking one of the finny critters on a pass shot, in deep water. You not only have to calculate the speed of the fish, but the depth of the water and refraction. This may sound simple, but until you've tried it, you have no idea of the challenge a shot like this presents.

There may be a method of rigging sights on a bowfishing system but, if there is, the author has never seen it done. For the pin-sight shooter to take a bare bow and try the fishing game adds more sport to it. If you feel you can't shoot without pins, try rigging a system; it could work.

One thing about the fishing gear that may be confusing at first is that most fishing arrows have no fletch on the shaft. You may see fishermen with regular feathers, heavily dipped in waterproofing material, or rubber or plastic fletch on the shaft. You really don't need any type of fletch, unless you are using a light arrow. The weight of the solid arrow, plus the line being pulled from the reel, keeps it straight on target. Fletch means one more problem, and after a few trips you will agree it isn't needed.

Bowfishing can be enjoyed in even the most casual attire — providing the time of year and location deem it practical.

The banks of slow-moving rivers also can be good points from which to spot mud-loving carp.

There are several ways to attach the line to the shaft. Some attach the line at the end or back by the nock. Others run the line from the point and to the reel. If you attach to the back of the shaft, the point can, and sometimes will, pull off. If you attach only to the point, the line will be dragging the arrow sideways as it plays out. A better system is to attach to the point, run the line up the side of the shaft and through a hole in the back or nock end of the shaft, then to the reel.

When you use the latter system, you must be careful of the line by your hand. When you shoot a heavy line from a fifty-pound or heavier bow, it can result in a nasty cut if the line becomes twisted around a finger. Not only that, the line can break, resulting in loss of the arrow, too.

It is possible to lay the line along the shaft, from the back to the point, using a quick-release system that keeps the line away from the fingers and also prevents snagging. Take a clip from a pencil or ball-point pen — the type that slips over the pen itself — and slip it over the shaft with the clip pointing toward the nock end. Place the clip close to the point, but above the knot that attaches the line to the point. When you have your line reeled in and are getting your arrow into position, take the extra line and run it down the shaft, under the clip, and it will stay out in front of the reel and your hand. When you shoot the bow the arrow will pull the line from under the clip — there is not enough drag to worry about — the line will come to the anchored position on the nock end of the shaft and fly true to the target.

If you can't find a pencil clip, wrap a rubber band at the same position and run a loop under one section to achieve the same result. The line then is attached to the point and through the hole by the nock, then back to the clip or rubber band retainer and you are ready for the next shot.

Bowfishing can be enjoyed by all members of the family.

These two bowfishermen are utilizing a flat-bottomed boat to get within range of spawning carp. Keeping a close watch is essential (above), for carp often will drift into bow range with little fanfare. When one of the rough specimens is sighted, quick action usually results. Remember to aim somewhat low, and your chances of scoring hits on rough fish will increase.

The two archers (above) are utilizing the buddy system in their bowfishing endeavors: one paddles the silent canoe while the other shoots. They then change places. It isn't often that carp the size of this monster make it to the bank (left), since their sheer size makes reeling a task!

Youngsters too young for the big-game fields can enjoy the thrill of the hunt by bowfishing. It makes a fine family outing if all members are archers.

There is one other piece of equipment recommended: not a necessity, but you will be much happier if you buy a pair of polarized or Polaroid sunglasses. Reflections of the sun off the water, which hide fish, will be eliminated when wearing these types of glasses. You can use any type, but be prepared to lose them if you fish from a boat — unless they float. They make underwater visibility much easier, and reduce the glare from the water and sun which causes eye strain.

Rig your bow for rough-fish fishing. It will give you off-season practice and keep the bow arm and those muscles in shape. You might have trouble finding the carp, maybe more trouble hitting them after you do, but one session after carp in the shallows of a lake or river and you will become an avid bowfisherman. You might check with your local authorities, as they often are very responsive to any method that will help rid the waters of these fish which kill game fish and also eggs of water birds.

Try to find an angle that puts you above the water. Banks make good shooting areas, as do boats or even a ladder or boat dock. Try anything which will give you a slight advantage when you attempt this most amusing and fun-filled version of fishing.

Bowfishing from a canoe can be risky business, especially if the archer gets excited. The canoe could tip, resulting in loss of expensive archery gear and unwelcome bath.

Chapter 20

BIG GAME & TROPHY HUNTING

Renowned Bowhunter Jim Dougherty Vividly Describes A Whitetail Hunt And Defines The Qualifications Of A Trophy Hunter

During one of his safaris to Africa, Dougherty downed this greater kudu with his archery tackle. Hunting skills called for in the taking of whitetail deer in North America also apply when on foreign soil.

IT WAS A FINE, big Bois d' arc tree set in the junction where two smallish creeks came together to form a slow-moving little run of water a boy could jump standing flat-footed.

On this particular morning, the cream and coffee water was dotted with the widening circle ringlets created by a steady profusion of falling pin-oak acorns. Up and down the length of the creek that ran out of sight not too distant from the big, old tree, squealing groups of wood ducks skimmed the surface, scurrying occasionally to snatch one of the sinking nuts.

It was a perfect fall morning, just enough breeze to be right, with enough frost shimmering on the bordering meadow grass to provoke even the latest bucks to run the creek bottoms in search of lady deer; several had passed the blind in the big tree already.

They had been smallish bucks, but any whitetail buck is enough to start a little hammering in my chest and a strange trembling sensation in my knees. I passed a fair eight-point which came by the blind, nestled among the tree branches, in a stiff-legged trot, nose out above the ground, following the track of a sleek little doe that had passed just at first light. The second was a forkie, the third had been a spike and in-between another doe with twin fawns that seemed especially uneasy, their unrest caused perhaps by the steady plopping of acorns on the creek bottom floor.

One waits on mornings such as this in an atmosphere charged with anxiety and anticipation: Anxiety for having passed a good buck that may well be the best you'll see; anticipation of the bigger buck of which dreams are made. Such are the prime ingredients in the serious game of bow-hunting.

Deer are my thing and whitetail bucks top my personal list of the most challenging bowhunter's game. There in the branches of the ancient Bois d' arc, I was as happily excited in my quest for a nice whitetail as I've been in pursuit of any other game; from one end of North America to the other, or around the world to the animal-rich thickets and plains of Africa. I am a dyed-in-the-wool deer hunter, for whom the sight and pursuit of a skylined buck with a noble rack holds a special fascination. Despite over twenty years of hunting them with a bow, my throat still gets dry and my legs react violently when a big buck and I have one of those close range, personal bowhunting encounters. Nothing else seems to affect me the same way and, by now, I suspect that it never will.

It was well into mid-morning when the buck first appeared, his entrance to the creek bottom marked by the slightest flicker of movement caught by the corner of my eye. A slight, careful shifting of position gave me a better view: it was indeed a buck, a pretty good one at that.

My experience with mule deer and blacktails is many times that of my involvement with the thicket-dwelling flagtails. While there are similarities, they are few; common hunting tactics do not work with the regularity one might expect. There are those who say mule deer are dumb, compared with whitetails. I do not necessarily hold with this, for I do not feel the big-eared Western deer is dumb. His environment leads him to a different way of life: He frequents more open country and has a fatal habit of stopping often to look back; nor does he explode into action as completely as the whitetail, which oftentimes explodes for no apparent reason. The arguments for and against will go on, as they have, forever.

Bowhunter Bob Markworth dropped this exotic four-horned ram while hunting Safari Island, off California coast.

In my opinion, the whitetail is cleverer, his instincts for survival surer, his trophy status greater than the mulie; but both are fine animals to be treated with equal respect.

Screened by sixty yards of intervening creek bottom cover, the buck fed leisurely along the little run of water; the wood ducks let him enter their world with hardly a glance. It was one of those will-he-or-won't-he emotional moments. His feeding pattern moved him in the direction of the big tree, then he would turn, working off in another direction. With regular moves, he would suddenly throw up his head to look about, carefully, for long seconds before once again lowering his head to seek out another marble-sized acorn. Once on a steady course, he cut the distance between us by half and I felt that he would soon offer a shot. Then, for whatever reason, he fed back downstream, melting in the cover to a barely visible shape, a touch of brownish gray, a fleck of white amongst the briars and high grass. These are the supreme moments in the bowhunter's sport: the wishing, waiting game; the silently worded pleas to "come this way just a few more steps."

Over the years, I have become adept in the quick mental compilation of points, width and height necessary to field score a mule deer on the hoof. This has been supported by measuring many heads to a point whereby I, and many of my hunting associates, can quickly tell just how good a buck is, whether or not he would be a record list candidate. Whitetails, on the other hand, confuse me. I've not enough experience to judge them nearly so well. The adage that "the good ones always look big" is accurate enough, but

The late Ben Pearson worked hard and planned well to bag this polar bear in Alaska. Archery great Fred Bear says the great white is the most dangerous bowhunting quarry.

220

nice ones have a habit of looking bigger than they are and any branched formation atop a deer's head is cause enough for excitement.

This buck, to my uneducated eye, did indeed look good; whether or not he was good enough to meet the magic, minimum figure of 125 inches, I wasn't sure. I doubted it, but he was closer than any I had previously been fortunate enough to glass. By now, I was sure of ten points (Eastern count) and I am not in the habit of passing up ten-point bucks, at least not yet.

The weather had turned, the wind now blowing from the north, increasing the early morning hint of a cold front. With the wind now in cool gusts, acorns fell from the heavily laden trees with such intensity as to make the forest a confusion of thumping sounds. The buck didn't like it. His head came up and swiveled constantly, his rambling pattern taking him off downstream, away from my tree, away from my silent urging that he come this way.

It was the rut. The bucks I had seen were neck swollen and glassy eyed. There were six scrapes on the trail into the bottom, three more up and down the length of the creek I had walked yesterday. Several involved good bucks, seriously intent on making love in the area. The buck I watched did not seem as far gone, his actions more nearly normal than the others. He had once rubbed his antlers on a willow snag, but he did not sniff the trail or cast his head about seeking the scent of a doe as the others had done. The finger-thick willows along the three main trails were rubbed in many places; eleven rubs and nine scrapes in a quarter-mile area. I had sprinkled the trail by my blind with a dash of buck scent and hung a scent pad upwind of the tree: If there ever was a time to believe in scent, this was it.

There are ways to call deer that work with astonishing effectiveness. I have often called mule deer in the rut with a call that offers a low, guttural growl. I've heard sparring bucks make this sound as they circle one another, heads low, hackles raised. I've called bucks and does with a plaintive bleat, almost reedy in pitch, from a finely tuned varmint call. Does, in the summer months of the early Western seasons in California, Utah, Idaho and Colorado, respond in a feisty manner to a varmint call blown cry-baby like; looking to protect a fawn, I suppose. Occasionally, a buck answers this same call.

Whitetails are most often "rattled," a form of calling that's effective during the rut on just the right kind of day with the wind just so. To rattle, one uses a pair of antlers, not too old so as to possess the right tone. These are scrambled together, producing the sound of bucks in combat. When it works, it's beautiful.

Now, with the morning passing and my buck wandering away — obviously decided on a course that would take him to the bedding grounds down the creek — I decided to try something, for there was nothing to lose.

The results disproved my theory that this buck was not into full rut. In my pocket was the ever-present call, this one low-toned, raspy. Cupping the front of the barrel with both hands to lower the pitch, I bleated once, a drawn-out call of about a four count.

Jim Dougherty shows the result of prior planning, persistence and determination: a trophy mule deer. Being a trophy hunter calls for undying spirit and belief, even when it seems fruitless. Spending hours dressed as he is (inset photo) sometimes is required for success.

The buck spun about, head up and alert with ears cocked forward, about seventy yards away. One more time, with a bit more feeling. Nose pointed forward, head held low, the buck started towards the tree like a stylish pointer dog with a nose full of covey birds.

He was a puppet on a string, a bull brought on by the cape. Full of purpose, he came down the trail, stopping once briefly, perhaps only then catching a whiff of the buck scent that the gusty breeze had kept from his keen nose. The scent was the cape that drew him by the big old tree, quartering away as he passed. He stopped as I fought trembling knees and shaking fingers. Fifteen yards away, the picture-book shot presented, the kind that is so easily muffed. It's easy to see why so many shots are missed in final seconds such as this – Lord knows, I've done it countless times. With a deer in your pocket, you simply shoot the arrow – at the whole deer.

When you concentrate fully on that one special spot, your chances increase tenfold. In spite of trembling muscles and rattling knees, the arrow came back smoothly. Only one place existed in my entire mind, that thin line of white hair behind the shoulder, down low – making sure it was low; it's hard to shoot a deer too low.

The Switchblade went out smoothly ahead of sixty-five pounds of silent power, out of the off-side, fifteen yards down the creek bottom. A brief, violent explosion, a crackling of brush, and the buck vanished, swallowed up by the thicket. His flight would be short, the end but a few steps into the brush. Concentration, more than shooting skill, had put spot and broadhead together in a final, efficient act.

That he was not a buck for the record list did not lower his stature a single notch. He was a fine buck, a worthy representative of his tribe, our country's number one, big-game animal. There will be other days in the big, old tree, in other creek bottoms or hardwood ridges where I can seek that whitetail for the "book." I'll be there, happily pursuing the bowhunter's finest trophy.

I am often called upon to make statements about trophy hunting with a bow and arrow because, I guess, by a combination of luck and circumstances, there are those who consider me a trophy hunter.

Frankly, I am not a trophy hunter in the pure sense of the word. I know trophy hunters and mostly they are probably people you have never heard of. In the most accurate phrasing I can think of, I'm a bowhunter, a trophy hunter lots of the time — at least temporarily on any hunt — but mostly a guy who enjoys all there is of the outdoors, harboring the same dream we all share of taking the giant forest patriarch, but generally I willingly settle for less.

In my formative years, as I developed as a target archer — never good — and a bowhunter — somewhat better — my mentor made a statement that I have always felt to be accurate. "Small game," said Doug Kittredge, "is big game when hunted with bow and arrow." I've since added a personal addendum: all game is good game with bow and arrow.

I've been fortunate over the years as some very nice animals have come my way; some by virtue of careful planning, a good many by luck and the occasional critter good enough to grace the den wall to help me through the not-so-good seasons.

I've only taken one animal in my life that was a total record book commitment before and after the fact, a pure trophy hunt, if you will. I've taken a fair amount of the record book game since, most by careful selection and no small amount of planning, but none with a total record

Dougherty straddles a respectable Cape buffalo, taken while on safari on the Dark Continent. When attempting to bag such a dangerous adversary, all the skills the bowhunter has mastered on other types of game come into play. It's not mandatory to travel afar in pursuit of exotic game. The Corsican ram (below right) was nailed by Bob Learn on preserve in New Mexico.

commitment as was that bare minimum cougar brought to bay after many saddle-weary miles, deep in a New Mexico canyon many moons ago.

Yet, because I have trophy hunted hard — most often coming in second — and because I feel privileged to have shared many a fire with those who are committed to trophy hunting, I believe I can make a few observations on what it takes to occasionally — 'cause no one does it all the time — collect one-for-the-Book; the Holy Grail of all who follow the footsteps of Pope, Young and Bear, to name the ones with whom we are all most familiar.

Recently, I was called upon to sum up what it takes to be a trophy bowhunter. In my opinion, the answer is quite simple, an answer that precedes winning, whatever the endeavor: desire.

Trophy hunters are dedicated to the objective: the really good ones. They are unwavering in their commitment. Nothing but the animal that surpasses certain limitations in physical conformation will do, all others get a pass. And, if you're going to play the game by those rules, you've got to have your head screwed on pretty good.

The following, I feel, are the most necessary ingredients to be a trophy hunter:

Desire is the prime ingredient to being any kind of success. The first desire is to fill that first tag with a bow; the natural evolution is to desire a trophy buck. Whatever the objective, desire has to be there and compound itself to meet more difficult challenges. When it wavers, so does performance. Without desire, one takes the easy way, perhaps relying on luck. Luck produces lots of winning situations, but luck is not a consistent force. A consistent run of luck is self-made.

Once the desire has been identified as trophy hunting, new elements raise their heads. Each individual has to establish a pattern and outline the conditions that have to be met, if any form of success is to come along. Of the seven keys that I feel are essential to good bowhunting results, the second, patience, is perhaps the most important and difficult to achieve. Patience takes time to develop, it takes experience, it takes a track record of victories, and it takes some years to mellow the enthusiasm of young beginners. I've noticed that the consistently successful bowhunters are fellows who have taken a lot of game, who have shot at a lot of game, who have been through the rookie years and have settled down. When this point is reached, true patience can be achieved and true, day-in, day-out patience is one of the trophy hunter's most valuable tools.

Without desire and patience, it would be difficult to achieve the proper degree of tenacity or persistence required of the serious bowhunter. Patience is achieved after a plan by which you will hunt has been laid. The trait of persistence is believing in a plan after the patience wears thin. There are many, many times this will happen, and there are those exasperating moments when the animal does something different, takes another trail, or you miss the shot of a lifetime. Patience and desire can get a bit bedraggled when things really go wrong. Blind, determined persistence has to take over for awhile, until you settle down and achieve a second wind of patience.

Persistence is not giving up 'til the last waning moments of the last day of the hunt. Persistence is believing that there is more than one shot of a lifetime. When you're trophy hunting, every shot is the shot of a lifetime and at that moment, the most important shot you will ever take. If you don't miss more than a few, you're not really human and you sure don't need to be reading this.

Persistence is committing yourself and sticking to it, with the ability to blow a shot and get ready for the next one.

Believing in yourself is extremely important. It is nothing more than a commitment to your patience, your strategy and your persistence. You must believe you can do it, even when you miss. Simply believe without a doubt that you will hit the next one. Know that you'll make mistakes, but believe that you will find the causes and not make them twice. Believe that if you play the game right, work hard and stick to it, you will win, and sooner or later you will.

To be a consistently successful bowhunter takes more than a passing knowledge of the game you hunt. As the trophy hunter evolves, this knowledge becomes the sharp edge of his sword. While the best way to obtain this knowledge is in the field, there are other methods of learning that should be explored. Nothing beats talking to the guy who has been there. Seek out the bowhunters who have done it and learn from what they say. Read. There are an endless number of books on trophy hunting, covering game and methods. Absorb as much as you can, but select those methods which seem to fit your country and your hunting methods. No two people have exactly the same theories or methods.

Understand the subtleties of trophy hunting as opposed to just hunting. Good, sound techniques you employ to collect a deer will have to be refined to collect a big buck every year. Talk to game managers and game wardens. They are fine sources of information, particularly the ones in the area you intend to hunt.

There are trophies and there are trophies. While it's nice to make the record list, an animal does not have to meet those minimums to be a trophy. Making the list, however, is what it is all about; the goal that makes the whole thing so terribly difficult. You are seeking an animal that has to be

An incredulous moose stares at bowhunter from a distance of some thirty yards. Moose was resting until bowhunter finished his stalk. Trophy heads can result from care!

better than good just to make minimum and, if you're a real, hard-core trophy hunter, he'll have to be better than just minimum.

To be able to judge animals effectively takes a good deal of experience, but, fortunately, this can be done without spending countless hours in the field. Visit museums, look closely at the heads in zoos, study the books put out by the Boone & Crockett Club — Pope & Young soon will have one — mentally score every mounted head and rack you see. Physically score as many heads as possible. This will help you in field judging trophies. Zoos and mounted heads are especially good, as are dioramas in natural history museums. Many of the good books you read on hunting will have chapters on judging heads on the hoof. If you want to be a trophy hunter, you have to know what a trophy looks like. Remember, all heads look bigger in the field; they're running around while your adrenalin is pumping.

All of the ingredients I've mentioned are habits you'll require to get yourself into a shooting situation with your game. Sure, there are other elements involved in getting you there: Mechanical things like practice, scouting, selecting the right area. But these happen anytime we hunt, for whatever we hunt.

When you have exercised enough patience, persisted in following a workable plan, and have identified the critter you intend to collect, there comes a moment when the entire project can collapse in a hurry. An old-timer hunting buddy once told me, "It didn't do a feller a whole lot of good to suffer for a week or two to get that shot, only to forget why he was there when he got the chance."

If there is one sure way to mess up a lot of work, it's a gap in your concentration. It may be that ol' malady, buck fever, in one of its many demonic forms. Perhaps you'll get mesmerized by all those antlers. Whatever, concentration on the key spot on the animal you intend to place your arrow must be unwavering — not the whole animal, just that particular spot. Seems simple but, truth is, that's the hardest thing to pull off in this whole game.

It may seem strange, but being a red-hot dandy on the field range is no guarantee for a collected trophy. Sure, you've got to be able to shoot and shoot well under some pretty tough conditions lots of the time. But being a paper-punching wizard isn't the solution. It won't hurt, but there are better things to do. Shoot your hunting tackle a lot, with broadheads whenever possible. Stump shoot, hunt rabbits and pull your bow often, even when you can't find time to shoot. Take the time to practice a bit when you are on a hunt; pull your bow occasionally while stalking or sitting in a blind, especially if it's cold; keep your muscles loose, your body warm. Shooting skill is important, but not, in my opinion, as important as the other things we've discussed. If you concentrate and exercise some patience, you can make the shot. You don't have to shoot him five times for twenty points, just once!

Nothing has been said here that's going to guarantee you a trophy — there are no guarantees — but nothing I've mentioned will hurt. Fact is, I believe it'll help and hope it does.

*Bob Markworth cannot help but show a degree of satisfaction over
the spread of horns on this Spanish goat taken on Safari Island.*

Its Past Reputation As A Silent And Deadly Killer And Use As A Poaching Weapon Still Haunts This Ancient Forerunner Of Gunpowder.

THE CROSSBOW...

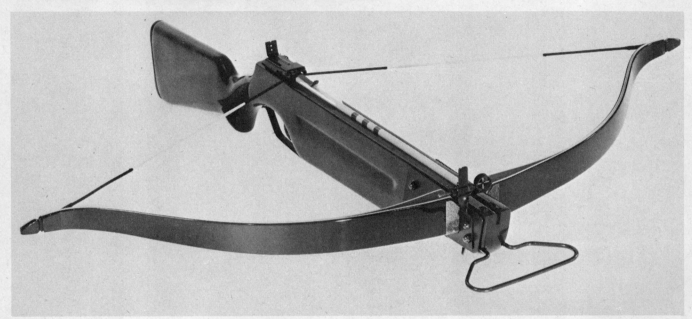

Instrument of Intrigue

Chapter 21

DATING FROM THE days of armor-clad knights in the Middle Ages, the crossbow was the forerunner of the rifle and remains, today, an accurate and deadly weapon.

Because, perhaps, of its historical aura of efficiency on the battlefields of medieval times, use of the crossbow for hunting is banned, or highly restricted, by the majority of the states. A few do allow hunting with the crossbow during established rifle-hunting seasons, but the majority of those states that do not ban it outright, limit its use to special seasons and areas.

In man's endless search for a better weapon, the crossbow evolved and reigned for many years, but eventually was replaced by gunpowder. It was renowned for its tremendous power, primarily limited only by the strength of the archer, or crossbowman, if you prefer. On some versions, windlasses were used to crank the limbs into the cocked position, from which a bolt could be fired through a suit of armor.

You could define the crossbow as a marriage of the longbow to a rifle stock; held and fired like a rifle, but propelling a bolt, or quarrel, as the projectile is called, instead of a bullet.

Most any good rifleman can pick up a crossbow and, after a few mental adjustments, start putting the bolt in the gold on the target. Hand the same rifleman a longbow, or one of today's composite models, and he probably couldn't hit the bales.

There is a certain amount of romance involved with the crossbow. Most of those seen today are still patterned after the archaic design, featuring a looping shoulder stock.

Although at one time manufactured of metal — which eventually became fatigued and occasionally fractured under the great strains placed upon them — the limbs of contemporary crossbows are made of laminated fiberglass, much on the same order of the composite hunting bows so prevalent today.

You can do anything with the crossbow that is possible with modern laminated bows. You can hunt, when and where it is legal; shoot targets; bowfish; and have just as much fun.

Like many archers, my curiosity became aroused and I decided to build a crossbow using modern methods. Several commercial models were studied and different people queried regarding this ancient archery system, and the end result is quite modern and accurate.

Made of a composite of laminated fiberglass and maple, it is thirty-six inches long with a draw weight of 125 pounds — a bit heavy for target work, but advisable since it was to be used mainly for hunting. The bow differs from some in that it is of center-shot — keyhole — design; an innovation flight archers have used for many years with great success.

The center-shot design allows the bolt to be placed on the barrel of the stock, with little or no downward string pressure on the stock itself. On many systems, the bow portion is mounted below the stock, resulting in a string angle which creates enough friction against the barrel to partially rob the limbs of power when the crossbow is fired.

There is one disadvantage to the center-shot design, and that lies in the fact the bolt, or arrow, must be inserted through the keyhole opening and then onto the barrel. A minor problem, but one not found on other designs where the bolt may be rested directly on top of the barrel.

Although the keyhole system reduced pressure and friction on the barrel of the crossbow, I decided to go one step further and added some Delrin, a DuPont material, to the top of the barrel to achieve the smoothest and most friction-free system that seemed feasible. Teflon could be used, but being softer than Delrin, the latter was used.

The stock of the crossbow was constructed from a semi-finished rifle stock obtained from Royal Arms. It was fitted with a rosewood tip and butt cap to enhance the white figure and color of the maple.

The forend was removed to allow for proper draw length of the string. Brace height of the bow is four inches, and the draw is eleven inches. This develops the 125-pound draw which was considered sufficient.

The thumbhole-style stock adds extra weight, but provides a platform for the mounting of a rear sight. The trigger was obtained from Dave Benedict — a maker of crossbows for many years — and beefed up to fit the stock and draw weight. A trigger guard was made from jeweler's brass, and the finished unit not only looks good, but is functional.

Cocking the bow — drawing the string from brace height to the trigger system — usually must be a hand operation in order to comply with hunting laws requiring that the crossbow be cocked by hand without the aid of any mechanical devices. Considering the bow's draw weight, some type of aid is essential and most crossbows on the market today feature a foot stirrup. This is a looped piece of aluminum that fits over the end of the barrel or stock. The foot is placed in the stirrup and held against the ground while the string is grasped with both hands and drawn back — up — to engage the trigger system. Easy enough at first, but if doing a lot of shooting, it can become something of an ordeal.

Crossbow sights may be as simple as a notched V at the

Dave Benedict, a well-known maker of crossbows, tests one of his creations prior to shipping to paying customer. His design differs somewhat from Ben Pearson Archery's Classic crossbow, pictured on the opposite page. Note the difference in appearance of the foot stirrups.

A close-up of the crossbow Dave Benedict markets as the model SK-I reveals just how complicated the system with scope is. The scope mount is adjustable, shown by knurled knobs, and the half-clothespin device is really a safety for trigger.

rear and a post or pin at the front, although in some cases the rear sight is adjustable for elevation and windage. Others come equipped with small, telescopic sights, which offer integral adjustments.

If a crossbow is bought for the primary purpose of hunting, be sure and select one that is equipped with some kind of safety device. Nearly all states allowing the use of the crossbow for hunting stipulate it must have a safety. Even though safety equipped, it isn't wise to roam through a hunting area with the crossbow at full cock and a bolt on the barrel for very long. The bow is under extreme tension

when at full cock and, if left in this situation for extended periods of time, the system becomes fatigued.

Strings for the crossbow tend to be rather large. Most are at least twenty to thirty strands and are made to withstand many shots. Keep a careful check on the string's condition. If it should break while you are bracing the bow, it could be quite painful. Check the ends that fit over the bow nocks for fraying. Keep a close eye on the center serving that slides down the barrel of the crossbow for any signs of wear. A center serving made of the monofilament material sold by the Easton Company works well. This nylon is slick

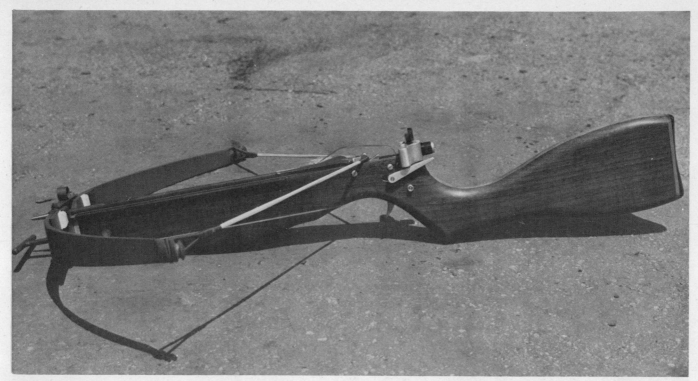

This is another view of Benedict's model SK-I crossbow, this one fitted with an open sight. For photo purposes, a bolt or quarrel was nocked; this is an unsafe practice when setting down a bow, and Benedict strongly advises bowhunters against it.

and, along with the Delrin track on the barrel, reduces friction to a minimum. It has held up well over some time and many shots, but is checked regularly.

Bracing the bow when first received often can be the worst problem you will have with the bow system. Instructions accompanying a bow that was tested a number of years ago suggested placing the metal limbs in a sturdy vise for bending by one person while another attached the string. This, of course, won't work in the field if you should break a string. The bracing system on the author's bow is a double-nock style — one for the shooting string and one for the bracing string.

Ben Pearson Archery Company is introducing a new crossbow which will have laminated fiberglass limbs and a pocket pouch bracing system.

The projectile fired from a crossbow isn't called an arrow. It usually is called a bolt, or sometimes a quarrel. The term "to pick a quarrel" comes from the old crossbow system. The bolt can be made of any of the arrow materials used for conventional bows, but is shorter. They range from about fourteen to perhaps (on the long side) eighteen inches. For target shooting, you could do some testing to determine the length and material that flies best for you. The bolt is not necessarily limited as to length, and can lay right on the channel groove of the barrel. Be certain, however, the width of the bolt is wide enough to prevent it from dropping into the channel groove. The channel groove is designed to allow the cock feather to ride in the down position: it fits into the channel, which must be deep enough so as not to interfere with the fletching.

The fletching on bolts can be as varied as on any arrows. Target archers use feathers and plastic vanes for a guiding system, but when a hunting broadhead is placed on the tip

of the bolt, more guidance is required than that provided by the minivanes or fletching on the target bolt. Some use a three-inch fletch, others a larger length, and as deep as the channel will allow. Most bolts are fletched with the standard straight fletch, since there is no way for a helical or spiral cock feather to fit the channel.

Type of hunting bolt is determined by two factors and legal length is the first of the two. Some states make no requirements, but Wyoming, for example, states the bolt must be sixteen inches long. The second consideration is that the bolt must be long enough to keep the broadhead in front of the end of the channel. If the broadhead lies on the channel or the barrel, it doesn't start turning as fast as the fletch, resulting in an erratic flight pattern.

Marketed under the trade name of Gun Bow, this close-up of action shows unusual scope-mount system employed. Fitted to the crossbow is a Bushnell 4X riflescope.

Some grit is needed when cocking the author's homemade bow, or any crossbow, for that matter. Foot stirrup is used and string is pulled upwards until it catches.

Broadheads for crossbow shooting can be of the same make and number of blades as shot with composite bows. There are differing opinions about wind-planing effects when using two-bladed heads, but two-bladed heads are lighter than the three or four-blade styles. The Bear Razorhead weighs in at about 115 grains, without the insert. The Zwickey Black Diamond weighs 110 grains. These lighter heads are a definite advantage, since they help offset the nose-down attitudes common to the short, light bolt, in comparison to a regular-length hunting arrow shot from a hand-drawn bow.

If you're a bit bored with conventional archery, you might like to take a look at the crossbow system, although there are problems never encountered with the hand-drawn bow in design and shooting.

Most triggers are of the rolling block design, some a clamshell opening. Whatever type, they must be kept clean or they drag the string and lose cast.

Sights alone can drive you up the wall, not to elaborate on the varying brace heights, draw lengths, and poundage for maximum efficiency; all of which can keep you working on new problems and systems without ever becoming bored. You may never get to hunt with it, but the knowledge gained most certainly will not hurt your efficiency with a regular bow system.

It is seldom one reads or even hears of any hunting with the crossbow. This is partly due to the regulations of most states. When I began building my crossbow, you could hunt predators in California. Now, about all that is legal to shoot is a rattlesnake.

An avid bowhunter, Peter Eichmann of Oshkosh, Wisconsin, recently conducted a personal letter survey of forty-nine of the United States and thirteen Canadian Provinces in an effort to determine if hunting with the crossbow was illegal and, if so, why. Of the thirty-eight replies in the affirmative, only fifteen included any reasons why.

Almost half of the reasons stated related to the crossbow's potential, or past, use by poachers. Several of the replies emphasized that, because the crossbow is silent, accurate and deadly, controlling its illegal use would be an almost impossible task.

The State of Nevada rationalized its crossbow ban by saying, "It must be historical, because such laws have been on the books of most states for many years. There probably isn't anyone still alive who could give you the original thinking behind such laws."

Vermont hunting laws state that game can be taken only by two methods: a gun fired from the shoulder or by a bow and arrow, and the crossbow doesn't fit either of these stipulations. Vermont's reply to Eichmann also noted that all over the country there is a philosophy that all hunting should be abolished, and to try and add more and varied methods would give anti-hunting forces more to complain about. "Vermonters don't seem to be asking for relaxation of the laws to allow crossbows, compounds and the like. One-hundred percent of these requests come from elsewhere."

Pennsylvania's primary objection to the crossbow is that it can be built to an almost unlimited pull and has no safety device to prevent its accidental discharge.

Hunting with the crossbow is banned in Eichmann's home state of Wisconsin, to "maintain bowhunting as a primitive sport demanding a high degree of stalking and shooting skill. The crossbow is capable of more power, range and accuracy by the unskilled user and is, therefore, not in keeping with the original objectives of bowhunting."

"The gun and regular bow are sufficient for hunting and harvesting Alabama's surplus game, in addition to being much safer than the crossbow," the Southern state reported, adding there were no plans to allow the use of the crossbow for hunting.

In Michigan, the crossbow is prohibited because, "It is both deadly and silent."

New Mexico, Minnesota, Maine, Washington, and the Province of Alberta say the crossbow originally was banned because of its use as a poaching weapon.

Some other reasons given were: it rivals the rifle in accuracy for distances up to one hundred yards, but doesn't have the rifle's knock-down power, resulting in more

As depicted by photographs below, a functional and even handsome crossbow can be manufactured by the home handyman, this one from a rifle stock. It's at full-cock (left) and author inserts quarrel (right). The crossbows are deserving of respect!

This is how crossbow, in this case a Benedict Gun Bow, looks when viewed at full-cock from above (top). Bob Learn carefully scoots bolt back into string (right). If bow misfired now, he could lose end of his finger, if he didn't remove it quickly enough!

Author draws a bead on imaginary target with his homemade crossbow, which even is outfitted with a rubber recoil pad! The main advantage of crossbow rests with accuracy: because of rifle-like hold, accuracy in the field is much improved.

cripples; it is more dangerous than the gun or longbow, because these require a special cocking device, but once the crossbow is loaded, few hunters will unload, even when in a moving vehicle or when in a group; when loaded, the shape makes it more difficult to carry through heavy brush and the chance of accidental discharge is greater than with a gun; makes little noise when fired, facilitating use by poachers and night hunters; if legalized, problems of poaching and night hunting would increase in proportion to the number that would be purchased.

The Canadian Provinces of British Columbia, New Brunswick, Nova Scotia, Ontario, Quebec and the Yukon Territory either have no restrictions on hunting with the crossbow, or classify it under their firearms' laws.

Newfoundland and Labrador allow its use on big game "under certain requirements" not furnished. In Saskatchewan, the crossbow can be used only for hunting non-game animals.

Alaska, Arkansas, Missouri, Oregon and Wyoming allow its use on all game animals, or when and wherever a rifle is permissible. Arkansas reported only two counties — Madison and Franklin — where there is a crossbow season.

Crossbow enthusiasts are advised, however, to check with the respective department of fish and game, et al., before venturing afield for hunting purposes; some of the states surveyed had legislation pending which could affect the information furnished.

Just a few of the many calls favored by the varmint hunting fraternity are shown at left, and each has its advocates. All can be effective when used properly and conditions are right. Dougherty classifies the coyote (above) as King of all varmints, for his stealth, speed and cunning. He's not fooled by careless calling and has been known to drive varminters up the wall!

Calling Up Varmints

Master Caller Jim Dougherty
Relates Not Only When And How To Use A Call
But Most Important, When To Shoot!

Chapter 22

Bowhunter George Wright was waiting at full draw when the coyote he called up came into range (left), and he shows the result of a well-placed broadhead (above).

"**W**ELL, I AIN'T believing that!"

The speaker, a camo-clad, face-paint-covered fellow, was sitting on his knees in the shadows of a large Palo Christo on the Arizona desert, staring in plain amazement at an empty patch of sand that seconds before was full of prime winter pelt attached to a large dog coyote; the distance was about thirty feet.

Somewhere, probably still skipping its errant way across the saguaro-studded desert, was his arrow. It recently had passed through the area in which the coyote had been standing, some milliseconds after the coyote had departed.

My friend had just loosed his first shaft at a called-up coyote, a set-up shot he calculated as duck soup, but coyotes, even at thirty feet, are never duck soup.

If there ever was a sport made-to-order for bowhunters, it has to be varmint calling. If ever a critter was designed to teach a bowhunter humility, it's the coyote — number one in the varmint category.

It had been our second stand of the morning. The coyote had come in hot in his familiar, mile-eating lope, straight up a slight, low spot that was almost a draw to where it terminated before the green Palo Christo. It was a natural: my hunting friend in just the right spot to ventilate the critter who skidded to a stop precisely where he should, and exploded when the bow did.

In twenty-two years of serious varmint calling/hunting, I've learned one thing is constant: coyotes are not easy critters to collect. There are lots of hunters who have collected a wall full of trophy game, but most of them are still looking for that first coyote rug.

When I was guiding folks who desired a coyote or bobcat rug, I learned that the most important part of the operation was to offer no guarantees — no matter how much you believed in yourself and your country. Varmint calling's like that.

The caller's prime game animals are coyote, bobcat and fox. In order of difficulty, that's how I put them. To me, the coyote is King. He's smarter, quicker, bolder and cannier than the rest of the fraternity. His ability to adapt and survive is legend, and he lives up to the legend.

The Prince of the varmint world is the bobcat. Highly prized as a trophy, he's the epitome of stealth — the secretive one that comes out of nowhere and vanishes before your eyes. He relies on camouflage, slipping right in on top of you and going about his business, most often without you ever knowing he paid a call. He's smart but not cunning, simple but not stupid. He will provide the bowhunter with the best chance to score, providing the bowhunter can see him.

Then come the foxes, red and gray, same species, but different characters. The red is sharp, coyote-like. Tough to call, he's tougher to hit. The wily fox of fable fame was a red. Comparatively, the gray is a dunce who makes kamikaze charges to the stand and oftentimes refuses to leave. I've seen as many as eleven arrows shot at a single gray fox. He never got the message, probably because he didn't get hit.

Lots of other critters come to a call. Mountain lions and bears are called fairly often, regularly by some hard-hunting fellows in Arizona who have perfected special calling patterns and techniques. I've called wolves who reacted like coyotes, and have had coons and badgers cover me up. But the coyote's my favorite because he offers the biggest challenge. "If you can call a coyote," said Wayne Weems many years ago, "you can call anything."

Varmint calling in Australia is somewhat different than in the U.S., simply because most varmints never have heard the sound of a jackrabbit! However, Rodney Scott (left), Graham Bellamy (center) and Paul Scott did manage to call up some goats! They use calls for communication with each other when moving through the dense brush when pursuing Russian boar.

The best months to call start in August, peak out in October through December, and begin to slow down in January. Critters can be called year-round, but these are the best months. Most conscientious callers lay off after the first of February. The females then will be carrying young, the denning season approaching, so ethics and morals dictate abstinence. Varmints, in my opinion, should be treated with the same respect accorded any game animal.

Spring can be a fairish time to call, but there's a lot of youngsters running that are wet behind the ears and as trophies, they're valueless. We've never bothered 'em much unless it was a depredation situation where predatory acts were getting out of hand. This happens a good deal in late Spring, when attacks on lamb and calf crops are historic problems requiring corrective action. Over the years we've corrected quite a few wayward critters with a taste for lamb chops.

The cooler days of Fall with light breezes and high overcasts are the very best. All animal activity is at its peak this time of year, when the cooler days with low light prompt predators to hunt late or all day.

There's been so much said and written on calls it tends to get confusing. When to call, how to call, what call, why that call, which pitch for which, on and on. There's a world of good, workable theories for the which-call-when theme, like fishing and baits which I often use as a parallel for the two sports.

We're talking about the constants, however, the overall best-producing theories for calls which I think boils down

to this: Big, open country, sagebrush flats, plains and washes — typical Western coyote range — takes bigger calling, louder, with more frequency.

Close cover, brushy woods, thick creek bottoms, and steep mountain canyons dictate a higher pitch, quieter calling with a little less frequency. For both types of calling, however, never fail to have a close-range squeaker on hand for back-up; you'll need it.

If you prefer the electronic calls, keep the same patterns in mind.

Stand selection for the bowhunter is infinitely more important than for the rifleman. The tendency to want to be able to see a long way must be suppressed. It's better to be a bit surprised up close than be spotted by an incoming customer that's fifty yards out. I prefer to be in a draw or wash, down where the contour of the land makes a natural game path. Get below the crest of a ridge, rather than on it. Remember, you have to move a lot to get an arrow off, so don't get skylined. Seek the shadows and get some bulk behind you to help cover those movements — a big boulder, tree trunk, hillside or brushpile.

During morning and evening stands, keep the sun at your back, let it work to your advantage. The sun's low glare will disguise a lot of your motion and will help illuminate incoming game that might be hard to see, like a bobcat whose hide will throw off just enough reflection to alert you.

If you're calling in groups larger than three, have a nice day, enjoy the country and don't expect to sack 'em up. Three is a crowd; workable, but poor odds. Two make a

Well-known bowhunter and varmint caller John Alley hides in what he calls a perfect blind: well concealed with a clear view (left). Another good stand is shown (right), with trees breaking up the human outline which tends to spook varmints.

good team, with the caller keeping well behind the shooter while trying to bring the game up a natural depression. One on a stand is perfect. You may miss seeing a critter or two, but you'll get run over often enough to make it worthwhile. If you're scared of coyotes on collision courses at ten feet in these down, out-of-the-way spots, trade your bow for a shotgun or give it up: Sometimes this is no sport for the faint-hearted.

Varmint callers and bowhunters keep the camouflage-clothing manufacturers in business. Camouflage is a must, from head to toe, with all the bumps and digits in-between. Face paint is fine; a head net with holes for your eyeballs is better. I prefer the type with glasses sewn in and the lenses knocked out. Unless it's a dark day and you're in good shadow, faces and hands are the first giveaways. Camo patterns should blend: I like to match the colors even though I know the game is color-blind. A bow with a high-gloss finish is a real flashy-looking piece of equipment, so cover it up with a bowsock, or paint it, or throw it in the mud to get rid of that flashy look. Not many critters are going to stand around and admire your bow. The object is for you to stand around and admire them.

Rifle-wise, we just hunker down in some good cover, camouflaged in moderation, keep our faces from shining, and drill 'em anytime we feel like it inside of a couple-hundred yards. Very effective when you're doing a bit of control work, but with string guns, that coyote has to come another 180 to 190 yards, and if he sees you he isn't coming.

I've always felt that a bit of scent helps when bowhunting for varmints. Wind is an important factor in this game and it stands to reason that the downwind leg of your call is going to carry farther. Lots of animals will try to come up downwind, and if they smell you, the jig's up. It probably doesn't matter what you use. I remember when all the Arizona guys started out using garlic oil; pretty rank bunch around camp but the coyotes kinda liked it. I've used rabbit scent with good results; just a dab or two on top of my hat where the wind kind of swirls it about. It's a good gimmick to carry some in an atomizer if wind's a problem. A dash carried downwind from a squirt in the air while calling can certainly reduce the chances of spooking game.

One of the hardest lessons I've learned over the years is when to shoot. I believe that knowing when to shoot in any bowhunting pursuit is probably as important a factor as any other element. The difference with varmints — coyotes, at least — is it's better to shoot at them moving than standing — providing it's a good, close-range set-up.

Granted, if you're looking at a forty to fifty-yard shot, it's much better to shoot at a stationary target. But most good shots in calling situations, if everything is clicking, are going to be inside of fifteen yards. These are the shots I most often get, and I like to take them when the coyote is making his purposeful lope or trot through the shooting area. His direction and speed are easy to calculate, he won't bolt quite as much at the shooting movement, and chances are good he won't be looking right at you.

A standing coyote at these ranges will see you move. He

Opposite page: In a nearly ten-year-old photo, a much younger Jim Dougherty pits his calling skills against California varmints. Left: The least intelligent of varmints hunted, this gray fox is about to be dispatched. Above: A successful outing resulted in this fine coyote rug for Dougherty's trophy room. He was taken at less than fifteen yards, about average in this varmint game.

is extremely alert and can recoil faster than a woods-wise whitetail buck. Sometimes you will catch a glimpse of an incomer, allowing enough time to get partially set. If you're up to full draw when the critter gets in close, the edge is in your favor.

This does not apply with cats or the gray fox. They will give you a pretty fair shot under most circumstances. Cats often will simply sit and watch you. Sometimes they'll hunker down and flatten out, just as often they'll sit up straight, posing for a picture-book shot. With slow, deliberate movements, you'll get a good shot. Red foxes are quick to skedaddle and may be the most difficult to collect with a bow. Incidentally, making your stands from a tree is an excellent way to avoid detection and it's popular with red fox callers.

Any member of the varmint fraternity is long on raw, lean tenacity. Sharp broadheads are a must, every bit as important as when hunting any of the so-called big-game animals. I prefer multiple blades and look to their condition with care. Varmints are not big: The forty and fifty-pound bobcats you hear about seldom see a scale. The average weight for a mature cat is eighteen pounds of thin-skinned dynamite. Coyotes are a bit bulkier — there's heavier fur to contend with and larger bones — but they're a lot smaller than they look, averaging less than twenty-five pounds. Sure, there are big ones. I've seen a lot of big dogs go over thirty-five and a bunch of cats push thirty, but I've seen hundreds of them weighed. The biggest coyote I ever saw on a scale was fifty-six pounds, the biggest I ever took, fifty-four. Bobcat-wise, a forty-two-pounder tops the list of cats I've seen hit a scale.

Varmint calling has helped make a whole lot of people better bowhunters. It's a fascinating sport where the game wins almost all the time, offering the bowhunter a unique challenge and unparalleled excitement.

Chapter 23

For Tuning Tackle And Muscles —
And Solving Shooting Problems —
Range Practice Is Needed.

BOWHUNTING SUCCESS SECRET:
TARGET PRACTICE

BOWHUNTING FOR SMALL GAME or rough fish is a fine way to tune both equipment and archer for upcoming big-game seasons, but there are times when the fur and fin segment fails to cooperate. Also, there are times during the year when seasons are closed on small-game animals, so how does the bowhunter derive the needed practice that so often spells success in the hunting field?

The answer lies on a range, where animal targets are affixed to hay bales or cardboard and placed in lifelike situations. Just about every local club has some type of range established and, if you check the attendance roles, you'll find most of the successful bowhunters have been shooting with some degree of regularity; perhaps even as frequently as once per month.

While there are some disadvantages with standard field ranges — most notably that broadheads are prohibited, because they damage hay bales in short order — there is much the individual bowhunter can derive from shooting these courses, aside from practice.

For one thing, it's an opportunity to study and occasionally shoot new bows that have been introduced and purchased by a shooter. Also, you may discover your next hunting partner while shooting. If you don't have objections to shooting with standard target tackle, this can provide a source of pleasure and familiarization.

When you shoot with a group, follow their rules and type of shooting. You might prefer animal targets but, if they use the standard round face, shoot anyway; the practice won't hurt.

Another solution is to form a hunting club or get a group of hunters together for fun shoots — if you can. There are many bowhunters who shy from joining any organization. These hunters basically are loners and prefer it that way but, if you can find a dozen or so bowhunters who like the idea and are compatible, you can set up your own ranges on the terrain of your choice and shoot broadheads.

One big problem is finding a place where you can conduct a shoot with broadheads. Bales are becoming more expensive and, unless you can leave them set up, it's too much to carry them from shoot to shoot. A simpler solution is to use free-standing, cut-out targets. These are made easily by taking the animal face from a regular target round, pasting it to a piece of cardboard, then laminating several other sections of cardboard to the first. You usually can get by with four layers to stop a broadhead from a heavy bow.

After the laminates are dry, cut the outline with a saber saw. Several targets can be carried with ease in the trunk of a car. All that's left is to locate a willing landowner or some safe public ground and set up a roving range for broadheads.

A practice bowhunting range should include several up or downhill shots, to more closely resemble hunting situations. A pocket is not the place for broadheads!

This is the best method of practice and many bowhunters really enjoy this type of shoot. You can place the cutouts under limbs, in brush or other natural surroundings, held in place by wooden stakes driven into the ground. If the stakes are behind the targets, they will be shattered by a marginal shot. It's easier to pound the stakes in a few inches from the target, then wire the target to the stakes with light baling wire. This holds the target upright and will not interfere with the target when hit.

You can take fourteen animal targets, ranging from moose to crow, and arrange them around a cutbank area that will allow safety while shooting. The course should be laid out so there is no danger of errant shots from one target hitting archers on another; by zig-zagging the course, you can have safety and variety at the same time. Try to pick areas that will allow misses to be found without having to tear up a hillside, and don't place targets in front of a rockpile: Jokes like this might be fun, but they also are expensive.

You can set stakes for the shooting marks, assuring all shots are taken from the same place. These can be marked, with the number of the target being shot at, if desired. For added challenge, change the shooting stakes for the afternoon session. This makes the shoot more fun and gets the target practice back to being more like an actual hunt.

There are some archers who dislike shooting at any type of formal target, so the following system is for them. Take a group of four or more archers and have one pick a target, anything from a clump of green grass on a stream to a bank, a rotten stump or some other natural target. All archers will shoot one arrow at that target, the person who is closest to

Bowhunter in foreground waits while previous shooters pull arrows and score hits. Safety is the byword on the practice range, and the shoot should be designed so that no archer's arrow can miss one particular target and hit other shooters.

Trees can change a simple shot to anything but! Assure that there is ample support, so that archer can't fall from the tree and hurt himself.

Seen from behind this pig target, a sand pit and sandbags are visible. These protect arrows from rocks.

the mark picking the next target. You may damage a few arrows on unseen rocks, so don't use top-notch shafts.

When you carry broadheads into the field for target work, it's safety first. Don't shoot when it isn't safe; and watch the steel edge as you pull the arrow from the target, for it can cut from the sides, too.

If you do much shooting of this type, you'll soon learn a few target tricks, like always carrying a pair of pliers. When you bury a broadhead into a one-inch pine stake, pliers aid in getting it out. A stump that looks rotten may have a solid core — try pulling the arrow from it and you'll have an arrow sans head!

When shooting at laminated cardboard targets, round off the back edges of the broadhead with a file or grinder and they will pull out much easier. If using Converta-Point arrows, unscrew the head and withdraw the shaft.

Common sense and courtesy make an outing more fun, so keep the little things in mind and the big ones will take care of themselves. If you decide to organize a club, make certain you have a method of eliminating troublemakers or those who just won't work with the group. If not, you'll soon find you have no group, which is probably why some clubs fail after a short burst of popularity.

Above all, don't forget the women. They like to shoot, too, so don't make it a stag club. Some men don't want the girls to show up, since some can outshoot the males!

Try to vary the shooting system so there is a new style or a new idea from time to time. You can make flingers that will throw aerial targets for wingshooting practice, make new types of targets from cardboard, or just draw an outline on a large sheet of cardboard and tell shooters to find a vital.

Make shoots realistic, but not so difficult that beginners will become discouraged. You can design a course you think is terrific, and still get negative reations, since others think it's too difficult shooting between limbs and over branches. Have a few shots that require a kneeling position and, if there are trees, have one or two shots from a tree, similar to a shot from a stand. The variety is endless.

Another needed decision concerns the award system, since there always are winners and they want recognition. Do you give them a ribbon, a trophy or a gift certificate from a local shop?

Awarding trophies or prizes does, however, present problems. There always are better-than-average shooters in any group, and they usually take the prizes, month after month. This is discouraging to the beginner or advanced archer, since he knows it will be a long time before he can beat that winner.

There are ways of getting around this, however. One club has drawings during a meeting to award a prize to a member who attended the last shoot and is present at the meeting. If they don't attend the meeting, they forfeit the award. This builds meeting attendance and gives all archers a chance at the award. A simple drawing of names from a hat often will keep peace in the group.

Group shooting and meetings can be fun and beneficial. If you don't have a group in your area, set one up and give it a try. You might find your next hunting partner that way!

This is a perfect broadhead target that really can tune a bowhunter. The pig is heading across the sand wash — a lifelike location — at an angle, which is compounded by the slightly downward shot. The target is constructed of numerous layers of cardboard laminated together with the face painted over the top. The cardboard is cut around the pig outline, and held in position with baling wire strung between stakes. This keeps the target from falling, should an arrow hit a sole supporting stake.

Skulking bobcat is concealed behind brushpile and a large boulder (below). At a slightly downward angle, this shot takes on new dimensions for the bowhunter.

Many archers have trouble — both in the field and on target ranges — with downhill shots. It is easy to misjudge the distance, which makes practice vital.

Chapter 24

BOWHUNTERS ASSOCIATIONS

There's More Involved Than Just Belonging; Your Support Is Essential To Your Own Future!

EVEN THOUGH BOWHUNTERS basically are loners, they are well aware that, in order to be considered when hunting regulations are being decided, they must have representation; and representation by an organized group usually produces the best results.

There are such organizations — in just about every state that permits bowhunting — which work with the respective fish and game departments of the various states in furthering good game management.

Another good, and urgent, reason for affiliating with a bowhunting organization is to assist in the education of the non-sporting public — particularly the anti-hunting segment — of the one fact most are not familiar with! It is the money derived from the sale of hunting and fishing licenses and permits which funds this country's wildlife management programs.

One such organization, the National Field Archery Association (NFAA), allocates a part of each bowhunter members' annual membership fee to a bowhunting defense fund which is used to pay for legal counsel in defense of bowhunting rights in the United States.

Conceived by bowhunters more than thirty years ago, today the NFAA is the largest organization of archers in the world. Members receive twelve monthly issues of Archery Magazine free, and are eligible for all NFAA bowhunting awards. Initial bowhunter membership fees are $3 a year — $1 of which is deposited in the defense fund — and renewal fees are $5 per year, $2 of which goes into the defense fund. Additional family memberships are $1 each, half of which is deposited in the defense fund.

Another prestigious association is the Pope & Young Club, in which regular membership is limited to that exclusive few who have recorded three North American big game trophies and are accepted by the membership committee. Established in 1957 as a bowhunting activity under the guidance of the NFAA's Hunting Activities Committee, the club also offers associate memberships to bowhunters accepted by the membership committee.

Now a separate scientific corporation, Pope & Young is the sponsoring organization for bowhunter competitions — patterned after the world-famous Boone & Crockett Club of New York — and is recognized throughout the sporting world as the authority on North American big game trophies taken with the bow and arrow.

The club maintains representatives throughout the country who score bow and arrow trophies for registration in the continuing competitions, which cover the skull, tusks, horns and antlers of animals. Data secured from the heads and horns submitted are placed in the archives as part of the file on records of North American big game.

Pope & Young competitions are open to anyone, but the animals must be taken with bow and arrow under the rules of Fair Chase during legal hunting seasons. Preliminary entry is made by filling out a scoring form for the particular type trophy entered.

If the trophy meets the preliminary minimum requirements, it can be entered in the competitions by having a measurement made by an official Pope & Young measurer. Scoring forms and a list of official measures are available upon request from the Pope & Young Records Committee, Box J, Bassett, Nebraska 68714.

New world records are awarded special plaques. First, second and third places receive medals. Honorable mention certificates may be presented for other trophies judged outstanding.

To be eligible, the trophy must equal or exceed the minimum scores listed for the Big Game Competition, and have been taken by the individual entering it — entirely by means of bow and arrow — under the club's Fair Chase rules. No aid in the form of tranquilizers, poison or firearms may be used, and the term Fair Chase does not include the taking of animals under any of the following circumstances:

1. Helpless in or because of deep snow.
2. Helpless in water, on ice, or in a trap.
3. While confined behind fences, as on game farms, preserves, etc.
4. In defiance of game laws, after legal hours, or out of season.
5. By "jack lighting" or shining (lights) at night.
6. From any power vehicle or power boat.
7. By the use of any aircraft for herding, driving, landing alongside any animal or herd, or using an aircraft to communicate with or direct a hunter on the ground.
8. By any other method considered by the Board of Directors of the Pope & Young Club as unsportsmanlike.

An even more exclusive group until 1973, the Fred Bear Sports Club is named after the world's foremost living authority on the bow and arrow, world-renowned bowhunter Fred Bear. For several years the entire membership was comprised of only ten prominent Americans: Astronauts Joe Engle and Walt Cunningham; former astronaut trainer Joe Garino, Jr.; actor William Shatner, Captain Kirk of Star Trek; actor James Drury, The Virginian; and five of the country's best known professional archers: Vic Berger, the White Knight of archery; Frank Gandy; Vince Delorenzo; John Klemen; and Clarence Kozlowski.

In honor of Fred Bear's sixty years of bowhunting, Charter Memberships were opened "to qualified outdoorsmen and women through the end of the 1973 hunting season." Those accepted as charter members compete for awards for game taken only under the Rules of Fair Chase, identical to those of the Pope & Young Club.

Objectives of the club are the protection of outdoor ecology and the proper wildlife management of the woods, fields and waters of the country. Members pledge to uphold the rules of Fair Chase, the State Game and Fish laws to which they are bound, the preservation of natural resources, and the honest fulfillment of the restrictions under which they compete in all outdoor sports.

You may, perhaps, feel that membership in such organizations is not for you: you bowhunt infrequently and never expect to even catch a glimpse of a record-size trophy. But, it is becoming more and more evident that, if hunting is to remain legal in any form, the individual support of every bowhunter is required to ensure continued representation of the sport.

That I will assist all bowhunters in locating places to hunt, but I will not impose myself knowingly on another bowhunter.

That I will enjoy the challenge of the hunt and will study the habits of the game I hunt.

That I will use legal archery equipment and will search long and diligently to track down and recover any wounded game.

That I will not undertake or commit any act which would be construed detrimental to the ancient and honorable art of bowhunting and to the National Field Archery Association.

Route 1, Grayling, Michigan 49738

We believe that man has a right to use his natural resources, but that he has a duty to use them wisely, carefully and with reverence.

We believe that wildlife of all sorts must be intelligently managed in a natural environment, and we will work to make it happen.

We believe that clean, pure water is essential to the well-being of all creatures, and we will not pollute it.

We believe that clean air is vital to the survival of all and we will constantly be alert to those who would have it otherwise.

We believe that litter and waste are spoiling our heritage and we will not tolerate it.

We dedicate ourselves to these goals for our own generation and for the generations to come. For we believe this to be the fulfillment of the American Dream.

NATIONAL FIELD ARCHERY ASSOCIATION

Route 2, Box 514, Redlands, California 92373

Bowhunters Creed

I firmly resolve, without reservation or equivocation, to uphold the following Bowhunting Principles.

That I will support National, State and Provincial regulatory agencies and conservation organizations in the propagation and management of all game.

That I will at all times actively support and promote hunting with the bow.

That I will abide by current Game Regulations and at all times conduct myself as a sportsman so as not to bring discredit to the Bowhunting Fraternity.

That I will respect landowners' rights.

Box J, Basset, Nebraska 68714

Under the heading of North American big game are included the following with the minimum point score requirements (Boone & Crockett scoring system). The entry fee to enter a trophy which meets or exceeds these minimums is $10. All trophies entered are awarded a Record Class Trophy Citation.

Whitetail Deer, typical	125
Whitetail Deer, non-typ.	135
Mule Deer, typical	140
Mule Deer, non-typ.	150
Columbian Blacktail Deer	90
Coues Deer, typical	68
Coues Deer, non-typ.	78
Yellowstone Elk (Wapiti)	225
Roosevelt (Olympic) Elk	210
Woodland Caribou	220
Mountain Caribou	265
Barren Ground Caribou	265
Pronghorn (Antelope)	57
Wyoming Moose	115
Canada Moose	135
Alaska-Yukon Moose	150
Bighorn Sheep	130
Dall (White) Sheep	120
Stone Sheep	120
Desert Bighorn Sheep	115
Rocky Mountain Goat	35
Alaska Brown Bear	20
Grizzly Bear	18
Black Bear	17
Polar Bear	17
Jaguar	12
*Cougar	13

Cougar taken in any area where a bounty provision of any type is allowed are not eligible for entry in Pope & Young Competitions, or for Record Class Citations.

EXCLUSIVELY FRED BEAR

Bowhunting's Living Legend And Foremost Innovator Passes On His Proven Techniques

RARELY DO BOWHUNTERS get together that the name Fred Bear doesn't come up. When it does, it usually is uttered with no small amount of reverence.

For Fred Bear, bowhunter and archery pioneer, is at the zenith of the bowhunting world. His feats with bow and arrow are unmatched, and have been witnessed by millions on ABC's American Sportsman television series.

The legend of the man with the thin, dimpled face goes back to his early childhood. Raised on a farm in Pennsylvania, Fred Bear's first exposure to the outdoor life came when he ran a trap line along the creeks surrounding his home and hunted with his father.

Settling upon a career as a patternmaker, Bear was lured to Detroit in the early Twenties; not so much by the economic picture, but by the near-virgin hunting areas of Michigan. But it wasn't until 1927 that archery's Fred Bear surfaced: After viewing a movie made by Art Young — the latter half of the Pope & Young team — on bowhunting in Alaska, Fred Bear turned from patternmaker to bowyer.

His first bow, primitive by today's standards, was of lemonwood. Bear taught himself to shoot it and, during the Thirties, gained quite a following through his excellent performances in both outdoor and indoor archery tournaments.

Soon, he began making bows for friends and his one-man operation began to grow. He continued to hunt throughout Michigan and, following the second world war, decided to move his manufacturing facility to the then-tiny town of Grayling, where the hunting and fishing were better. His corporation has continued to expand both in size and importance, but has remained in Grayling ever since.

While his expertise in the hunting field is well known, few archers today realize the impact Fred Bear has had on the sport in general. For example, no matter the name on the bow you use, it's built on principles Bear discovered and initiated. And part of the beauty of the man is that he has never sought royalties from competing firms for use of his patented designs, which gives just an inkling of his personality.

Just one of his achievements relates to the composite bow. Archers have for centuries sought to duplicate the performance of bows carried by the Turks, who wouldn't divulge their secrets. After years of study and experimentation, Fred Bear found the combination so long sought: high compression, fiberglass and exotic hardwoods.

Another couple of his innovations which have become standard today are the built-in, adjustable arrow plate, and bowsights which are integral parts of a bow's design.

One of his best achievements, so far as bowhunters are concerned, is the bowquiver. When stalking through the brush in pursuit of game, Bear was something less than satisfied with either the back or belt quivers, finding them troublesome under normal conditions and unruly under conditions other than normal, in which bowhunters often find themselves.

His first reaction was to discard the quiver and carry the arrows in his hand. It then was a natural outgrowth to fashion into the back of his bow a slot into which his spare arrow would fit. Constantly upgrading his equipment, he came up with a hand-held quiver, which later was attached directly to the bow. Such was the birth of the bowquiver as we know it today.

His next improvements were made on the arrows and hunting heads. His Razorhead, a two-blade design with available inserts, was the first of its kind on the market and now is the most widely used of any head.

He was long perplexed by the permanent attachment methods of affixing broadheads or other tips to the shaft, necessitating three sets of arrows for use in big-game hunting, target shooting and small-game hunting. After studying the problem, he came up with the Converta-Point tip which allows interchangeability of heads by a screw-on method. This resulted in substantial savings for hunters who could tip the same shafts with blunts, field points or razorheads.

While other companies have the distinction of being the first to offer a take-down bow, Bear surely holds the record for time-testing a product before availing it to the public: Would you believe twenty years?

He first began studying the problem of portability back in 1947. He realized his bow was too long and could easily be damaged by careless baggage handlers, so he invented his first take-down bow in that year. But he wasn't satisfied with the product and, until he is, you'll never see it on the dealers' shelves.

He continued to study the problem, fiddling with one piece, then another. In the meantime, other makers brought the product before the public. Fred Bear didn't rush to get his model into production, though, and it wasn't until 1967

Chapter 25

The arrow rest on this Bear bow was left intact, as the photo was taken for advertising purposes. Still, it's easy to see how the arrow rides over his finger — the manner of shooting he favors. He's been successful, so why bother to change?

that he felt satisfied his bow had all the bugs removed.

Much to the chagrin and knuckle-gnawing of his sales and marketing staff, Fred Bear still wouldn't turn it loose. It had to be field-tested to discover whether it'd do the job for which it was intended.

Spending thousands of dollars and traveling still more miles, Fred Bear put his bow to the test in Alaska, South America and Africa against the toughest game those areas had to offer. After three years of hunting and field-testing, Bear gave the okay: his bow was ready. And it has become

one of the all-time favorites of bowhunters since its introduction in 1970.

These are some of the facts that have contributed to the legend of Fred Bear. But more than anything, it is his hunting ability that has brought him notoriety. This is a subject that hasn't before been expounded in the millions of words printed about him, or the infinite feet of film showing him in the field. What follows are the master's comments on the tackle and hunting techniques that he uses.

The bow Fred Bear has used for more than thirty years

Where conditions permit, Fred Bear favors a pair of tennis shoes over any type of footwear. Perhaps their quietness aided the successful stalk of this braggin'-size mule deer, taken by the famous bowhunter/innovator several seasons past.

measures sixty inches. "I prefer this length over a sixty-six-inch or fifty-four-inch bow because I use a bowquiver," says Bear, who has dropped a bull elephant in its tracks with a single arrow. "I want the lower limb of the bow to be long enough so that I can lean the bow against a tree and not have the nocks dig into the dirt. Longer bows will perform as well, but are more unwieldy in the brush. The shorter bows might be more delicate to shoot accurately."

Bear prefers a bow scaling sixty-five pounds at his twenty-eight-inch draw, and shoots the bow left-handed.

"It's really puzzling that I should shoot a bow left-handed," he confides. "I shoot a rifle or shotgun right-handed, and my master eye is the right one. However, I play golf and throw a baseball left-handed. I have been successful with this left-handed shooting style, so I haven't tried to change it."

The string Fred Bear uses on his sixty-five-pound bow is identical to those available on racks in any archery store. "I prefer a heavy string," he notes, "for several reasons: The heavier string will make a quieter shooting bow since there

times when there isn't any game around. I remove the broadhead from the arrow, screw in a blunt and shoot stumps, clumps of dirt — anything to keep my eye 'in' as I move around. Many bowhunters never shoot the bow until they see game and the muscles are stiff. I prefer to shoot often and keep the muscles limber."

Bear's arrows are cut twenty-nine inches for his twenty-eight-inch draw which gives an extra inch behind the broadhead for safety. His arrows come off the shelf, just as you would buy them in a store.

"I prefer a helical fletch, and I have shot both right and left-wing styles with three feathers," he notes. "When I place the first arrow on the string for a shot at game, I usually will place the cock feather out. But for the next shots, if needed, I don't consider which feather is out, and shoot the arrow as I nock it.

"I use a factor of nine for my arrow weight," continues Bear. "Since I am shooting a sixty-five-pound bow, I like to have the total arrow weight at from 575 to 600 grains. This gives me an arrow that will fly well, with sufficient weight for good penetration."

The fletching color Bear uses is not necessarily what he prefers, but what is dictated by filming requirements. "I use a white color now, but I would prefer a darker one," relates the bowhunter. "Darker fletching won't show up on film, so I use white. It is easily followed by the audience and I can tell the point of impact readily."

The nocks he uses are the index style, which are deep and assure a solid seating on the string.

When sharpening his Razorheads, Bear uses only a file. "I've found that a stroke system gives a fine-toothed cutting edge, and I prefer it to a honed edge," he notes. "I alway carry a file in the field with me and touch up any broadheads that need it."

The master bowhunter's shooting style often is termed "snap-shooting" by viewers who have seen his hunting feats on television. "I might be considered a snap-shooter, but with several exceptions," he explains. "The true definition of a snap-shooter is one who freezes and often will release the arrow before coming to full draw. The release might come anywhere and never twice in the same spot during the draw, due to the freezing problem.

"I suffered from this problem and fought it for three years," he adds. "In the field, a clicker is out of the question, so I merely concentrated to the point I overcame it."

While it appears Fred Bear snap-shoots, in reality he comes to a full draw each time, using a three-finger pull. When he anchors, the second finger in the corner of his mouth, he releases the arrow rather than holding on target.

The bow is canted at fifteen or twenty degrees and he leans over from the waist to look right over the arrow toward his target. "I don't worry about distance in yards, but judge the distance by feel," Bear notes. "This is purely instinctive shooting and, if I miss with the first arrow and try to correct, I usually will miss with the second arrow, too. The only way that I can correct for a miss is to draw farther or not so far."

Bear doesn't shoot all year. In fact, dependent upon his personal workload and weather conditions, he has gone as long as six months without even picking up a bow.

When he does practice, he uses a small range — built on his property — with seven targets. These targets are life-size

is less sing from the string. Also, if I accidentally sever a strand or two, I know I can continue shooting safely because the heavier string is actually over the maximum required. I always carry a spare and put it on when needed."

The spare Fred Bear totes in the field isn't factory new. In fact, it has been shot numerous times and already is outfitted with a nocking point. It won't stretch in the field, assuring consistency in shooting.

Bear uses only one nocking point — above the arrow. "By using this type of nocking point, I don't have to look at the arrow or string when I nock an arrow in the field," he says. "I can place the arrow on the string, bring it up against the nock and come to full draw without ever taking my eyes from the game."

The sight window of Bear's bow is built out to the side, and he can be termed a knuckle-shooter. He will test a bow by taping a piece of wood, leather or some material with thickness, against the sight window. When he finds the point on his sight window where the arrows will hit accurately, he measures this thickness and makes a permanent one from leather.

Bear uses a bowquiver extensively, usually fitted with five arrows. "I will slip eight arrows in the quiver if I'm going a long distance from camp," adds the archer, one of a handful who has taken a Bengal tiger with a bow and arrow. "I use the two-bladed Razorhead with the inserts, and my shafts are outfitted with Converta-Point heads."

Bear changes tips frequently on his hunting expeditions, and for good reason. "I feel one mistake most bowhunters make is not shooting enough in the field," he says. "I always carry some blunts in my pocket and shoot a few

Note the enormous size and girth of the arrows Fred Bear used to collect this trophy tusker several years ago. The heavy weight was needed to penetrate the thick hide and reach vital organs. White fletching was used for better visibility.

whitetail deer, the outlines cut from laminated cardboard in triple thickness. They are fitted with stakes and driven into the ground at the same height as a whitetail would appear when standing. The ranges can be varied, and he shoots at them from different positions.

"When hunting season is rolling around, I'll take my hunting bow and shoot at these targets to get my muscles back into condition," says the president of Bear Archery Company. "At first, the bow feels heavy and that first evening I probably will shoot only a dozen arrows. I quit before I get tired to prevent bad habits from forming."

As an experiment, he conducted a test over a three-year period. He hadn't shot the bow for about six months and, when he went to his range, placed his first arrow right into the rib cage of the target. He feels this might not prove anything to some, but, as far as he is concerned, the instinctive feel some archer's have with this style of shooting needn't be practiced as much as other systems.

He compares it to swimming: "If you haven't been in the water for some time, you still will know how to swim when you jump in again," Bear says. "It's the same thing with the instinctive archer."

Bowhunters need practice and Bear says they should always concentrate on making that first arrow count. He feels bowhunters should warm up at the hunting camp before going out after game.

"You don't have time to warm up when a deer comes into the picture," he comments. "You only have one shot most of the time and that first shot should be the one you connect with. By concentrating on making that first shot count, you will have greater success in deer or any other type of hunting.

"And, just because you hit a vital area on the first shot, you shouldn't stop there and say you need no more practice," he adds. "You have to keep your skills refined, so you can duplicate that shot in future hunts."

When in the field, Bear likes to carry a couple of blunts in his pockets. "I'll shoot at stumps or trees when there are no deer around, or there isn't any possibility of spooking any," he says. "When you are coming in at the end of the hunt, you can shoot on the way back and keep the muscles toned. If there is a chance of finding game in the area, however, hunt your way back."

In describing his hunting technique, Bear confines his discussion to the whitetail deer: an animal most bowhunters go after, and one for which he has a great amount of respect. The technique varies only with the type of terrain being covered and its limitations.

"If there are trails and crossings that deer are using and a blind or a tree stand is available — or not much trouble to construct — I prefer to hunt from these in early morning and late evening," he elaborates. "Those are the times when deer are moving and when you will have a chance for getting a shot. Between the morning and evening stands, I like to still-hunt."

Bear feels there is some misunderstanding about still-hunting and stalking. "Still-hunting is when you move through the area with caution until you spot game," explains the hunter. "Then you can move quietly and stalk the game until you get within bow range."

Indian beaters and elephant used for transportation frame background as Fred Bear and his guide examine Bengal tiger arrowed while on shikar. Bear is one of the few archers ever to have collected this cagy, dangerous, striped feline.

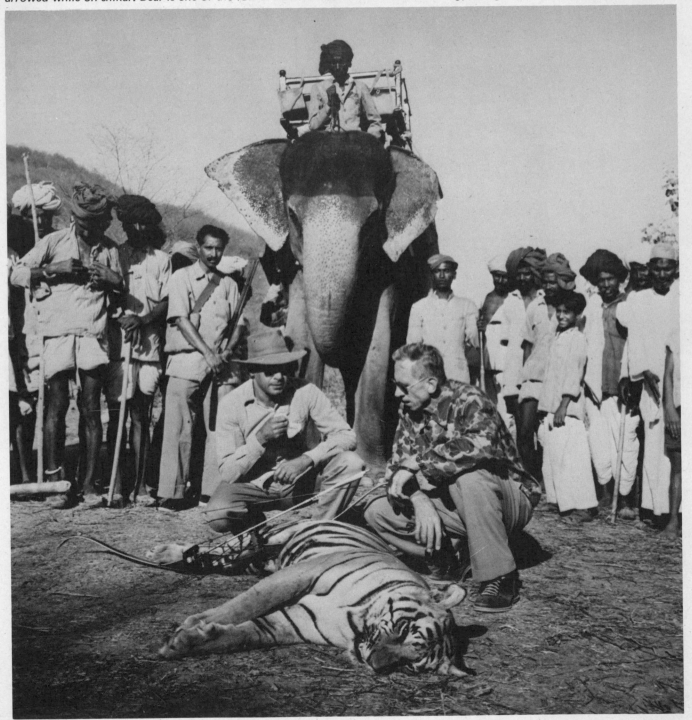

While Fred Bear is well known for his hunting feats, few archers are aware of his overall contributions to the sport.

This brace of monstrous moose fell to a sixty-five-pound take-down Fred Bear was testing near Mt. McKinley, Alaska, in 1967. The moose at top was arrowed at sixty yards, then ran another eighty before dropping. It now is a full mount in the Fred Bear Museum in Grayling. Bottom moose also was taken with test bow but Bear didn't market the bow until 1970.

Still-hunting is a favorite of many bowhunters, but Bear feels they spend too much time looking at the ground for signs or where to place their feet as they move. He advocates training the eye to pick up at least five or six steps at a time, so you can keep your eyes above the ground where you will have a better chance of spotting game. By walking quietly along logging trails, a deer trail or an abandoned road, there is less chance of breaking twigs or rolling rocks which will spook game.

"When you start looking for deer, don't look for the entire animal," Bear warns. "Rather, look for a part of the deer. Most objects in the woods are vertical, so if you see something that is horizontal, give it a closer check before you move.

"Look for pieces of deer, such as a tip of the antler, the small, white V formed by the tail on the rump, or maybe nothing more than light reflecting off a glossy coat," he adds.

Bear seems to have aged little since 1964, when he collected this greater kudu on the African plains with his sixty-inch bow. As tennis shoes wouldn't protect against burrs and thistles in African dongas, Bear donned kangaroo-hide boots.

"When you spot the deer you are after, don't get excited and start stalking for the kill right away. Watch the deer and, at the same time, check the area for other deer that could be traveling with the one you've spotted. Quite often, it is the deer you don't see that spooks the herd.

"After you have surveyed the situation and you know you can approach with caution, make moves only when you know which way the deer is looking," he continues. "The deer can look right at you and, if you're standing still, he probably won't see you. But if you move, he will pick up the action, which spells danger to him. When you know which way the deer is looking, or when the head is down feeding, you stand a far better chance of taking a few cautious steps to get closer and within bow range."

Still-hunting and stalking can be successful only under the right conditions. "If the wind shifts and blows from you toward the deer, your scent will spook the game," advises Bear. "Keep the wind in your face and try to move

only in that direction. You might get by with some quartering wind, but if it is gusting or eddying, you could ruin the stalk by being too eager."

Fred Bear generally uses the same type of clothing for all types of hunting. His standard garb consists of a camouflage jacket, a green-felt, brimmed hat, and khaki wool trousers.

For footwear, he favors the common tennis shoe over anything and will use it exclusively except in prohibitive terrain, such as snow country or in the watery areas of Canada and Alaska. He wears a lace boot with rubber soles for snow hunting, and hip boots in the swampy areas.

Bear prefers wool clothing for several reasons. "First, it is very quiet when moving through the woods," he says. "The limbs will brush on it, but no scratchy sound comes from the material. It also is one of the warmest materials you can wear and will hold in heat even when wet."

Bear usually refrains from using the face and hand camouflage that many hunters like, this being a result of

All the stories of Bear's hunting secrets are a smokescreen to camouflage his real secret: He has his neighborhood witch doctor put a lucky spell on his bow every morning before hitting the trail! In Africa, he works all the angles!

Fred Bear rarely dons full camouflage outfit, complete with face paint, due to filming requirements. He says he has to work harder to make up for this handicap, which just proves what a truly great hunter he is. Note Razorheads in quiver.

filming requirements. He feels he should appear as normal as possible, but realizes that the exposed skin is a detriment to his hunt. He simply must hunt more skillfully to overcome this handicap.

While Fred Bear enjoys hunting camps and participating in drives for game, he prefers solo hunting, pitting all of his skills against the instinct of the game he seeks.

"I have other preferences, too," he says. "For one thing, I never wear gloves to shoot unless I'm on horseback or hunting polar bears, because I don't feel I have the same accuracy."

To overcome the problem of cold hands, he carries the bow under his arm and tucks his bare hands into the wool-lined slash pockets of his jacket. When he sights game, all he has to do is remove his hands from his pockets and shoot.

While he prefers to hunt alone, there are times and situations that demand another person be along, usually a guide. "A good guide can be a definite asset on any hunt, and there are some areas, like Canada and Alaska, that require a guide," he says. "If you're after dangerous game, grizzly or brown bear, for example, it is wise to have a back-up man with a rifle, just in case.

Walking back to camp following a successful hunt for Dall sheep and caribou are Bear and companion (left). On a 1963 hunt for Life Magazine, Bear looks for grizzly sign along the Kispiox River, B.C. (below).

Fred Bear hunts from blinds during early morning and late evening hours, when game is moving (above). When in wet country, the bowhunter uses hip boots to keep his feet dry (below). Here, he crosses Little Delta in Alaska.

The master bowhunter whips up some breakfast at one of the many hunting camps he's frequented. While he enjoys the camp life and sharing a fire with other hunters, he prefers to hunt alone in the forest. It's proved a successful method.

"When after dangerous game, I sometimes carry a handgun, usually a .44 magnum. On one occasion I had a Kodiak bear come charging right at me, so I drew the pistol and prepared to shoot him. Luckily, the bear swerved and I didn't have to shoot. A bullet hole nullifies it as an archery kill, but it's better than getting mauled or killed yourself!"

During his years of hunting, Bear has taken dangerous game from all over the globe. He has spent many hours treed, with raging bears rumbling their displeasure below him. He has remained in a blind for six hours with a growling lion thirty yards away. He has collected tiger, Cape buffalo, lion and grizzly, among others. Which species does he consider the most dangerous to a bowhunter?

"The great white bear of the North, the polar bear!" he exclaims. "It took three trips before I finally bagged one

that could be classified as an archery kill. We found bear on the first two trips, but as I arrowed them they charged and the guide had to drop them both. They are so unpredictable you never know what they're going to do."

Trying to select one specific trophy as the greatest he has taken was difficult and took some time. He recalled the chases, camps and friends, and finally settled on the Stone sheep he took in British Columbia. The chase was exceptionally difficult, but resulted in a ram with more than a full curl, without the tips broomed off.

Fred Bear, now in his 70s, is still found in hunting camps. "I have taken my share of game animals with the bow, but there still are many out there to be hunted," he says. "If I had to choose which animal to hunt as a future trophy, it would be a difficult choice."

Chapter 26

STATE BOWHUNTING SURVEY

Where You Can't, Where You Can And How, And For What And How Much

We ASSUME THAT each hunter knows his state's regulations and seasons, therefore he usually is more concerned with regulations and cost of non-resident fees for other states.

This can be confusing, since most states have different systems. Some states charge a flat fee whereby one buys a big-game license for hunting game in season. Some states require a basic license and separate tags for each species of game hunted beyond the basic fee. Another system is to charge only for the game being hunted. The combination fee may be less expensive if you plan to hunt more than one species, provided they are in season at the same time.

No bowhunter should venture into strange territory before he knows the seasons and the rate that state will charge for hunting. Some states have one long bowhunting season that lasts over one hundred days. Another state may have a long season, but it varies within that state. Another problem is that exact dates on which the deer seasons open vary each year. Many states have the same starting day, such as the third Saturday in August, but the exact date, of course, changes each year. Some states allow no hunting on Sunday.

With so many variations in seasons and starting days, for simplification in the accompanying chart, the total number of days one can hunt in the field during the archery preseason or special seasons is included. This doesn't mean one can't also hunt during the rifle seasons.

Some states allow no bowhunting at all during rifle season, others allow bowhunting during rifle season, but one must buy the rifle season license, as bow or archery tags can't be used then. Check each state for these irregularities.

As of this survey, no state required a hunter safety course for anyone over 18 years of age. If you plan to take your son hunting out of state, be certain he has his hunter safety card with him. This regulation now applies to minors 18 or under and, in some states, those under 16.

Bowfishing for rough fish such as carp, rays and other non-game fish is allowed in most states, but there are exceptions. A quick look at the chart will indicate those states that do not allow bowfishing. One unusual situation relates to Iowa, which allows no non-resident big-game hunting, but one can bowfish with the crossbow.

The game animals listed by state are those popular in those specific boundaries. (There are footnotes for the states that offer different species of game.) Wyoming and Montana are two that offer a great variety of game, but some of this hunting is licensed on a drawing basis. One must file an application early to be considered for a game animal such as grizzly bear, as the state puts out only five tags a year.

When you decide what you want to hunt, the next problem is where. This determined, one should plan to hunt the following year, except for deer and perhaps black bear. Any animal on drawing — with the possible exception of antelope — has a waiting list.

Camouflage clothing is allowed in practically all states. Common sense tells any good hunter that, if he wants to hunt during the rifle season, he should wear bright orange colors.

Many states allow predator hunting with the bow, the type varying with the region. Western states offer coyotes, bobcat, fox and similar non-game animals, while some Eastern states limit bowmen to fox, opossum or raccoon.

Practically all states have regulations regarding the hunting tackle used. The lightest bows found acceptable are in the thirty-pound bracket, while the heaviest draw was fifty pounds. Heavy bows were required for elk, moose and grizzly bear. Some states limit the size of broadhead used to seven-eighths of an inch. This means the broadhead can't pass through a hole seven-eighths-inch in diameter. If it does, it is illegal. Other states require the broadhead to have cutting edges and that is all. One state outlaws the four-blade head. Before you buy a batch of broadheads for an out-of-state hunt, you should write for information.

Most states have few restrictions regarding arrow materials. Some specify a minimum length of twenty-four inches. Texas requires that the bowhunter have his name and address on the shaft in indelible writing.

A few states have made no decisions regarding the compound bow. Some states say it is not a longbow and make it illegal for hunting. Status is noted in the chart.

Crossbows are becoming more popular, but some states allow them only on target ranges. Other states allow hunting with the crossbow on any game animal, except during rifle hunting season. Some states have a special primitive weapons hunt and allow the crossbow, along with muzzle-loading rifles. Wyoming allows crossbow hunting with specific regulations regarding the type that is legal to use.

Montana is the only state that requires a guide for all bowhunting. Utah requires a guide for cougar or bear. There is some controversy regarding the legality of requiring guides, as the definition of a guide is sketchy. But common sense says you don't go after a grizzly bear in unknown country with no backup.

A guide who knows the area and is responsible for a group could save the state many dollars looking for a lost hunter.

The last column on our chart is an estimate by the fish and game departments of the number of bowhunters in the field for 1972 or 1973. Some states hadn't computed 1973, so their figures are based on a previous count. Other states have no way of checking on bowhunters, since they sell a basic license with no special archery tags. NA in the column means figures weren't available.

STATE	NON-RESIDENT FEES	DAYS ANNUALLY	ARCHERY TAG	DEER TAG	BEAR TAG	TURKEY TAG	SMALL-GAME TAG	BOWFISHING LICENSE	PREDATORS TAG	COMPOUND BOW LEGAL	CROSSBOW LEGAL	BOWHUNTERS LICENSED
Alabama	$25.15	100		X	X	X	$5	X		No	No	NA
Arizona	$30	50		$30	$25	X	$12	X	Yes	No	No	12,000
Arkansas(1)	$20	60		$10	$1	X	$6	X	Yes	Yes	Yes	NA
California	$35	30		$25	$25	X	$15	SG	Yes	No	No	26,700
Colorado		30		$25		$50	$10	X	Yes	No	No	NA
Connecticut	$13	60	$5	X			$8.35	X	Yes	No	No	1,500
Delaware	$25.25	90		X		X	$9.50	X	Yes	No	No	3,000
Florida	$26.50	21		X	$10	X	$10	X	Yes	No	No	10,000
Georgia	$25.25	30		X		X	$10.25	X	No	No	No	20,000
Idaho	$135	120		$75	$25	$35	$15	$5	Yes	No	No	NA
Illinois	$35.50			NO NON-RESIDENT BIG-GAME HUNTING		$16.25	$4.25	X	Yes	No	No	15,000
Indiana	$25.75	25		NO NON-RESIDENT BIG-GAME HUNTING				X	Yes	No	No	18,000
Iowa(2)	NO NON-RESIDENT BIG-GAME HUNTING					$25	$10	X	Yes	Yes	Yes	9,000
Kansas	NO NON-RESIDENT BIG-GAME HUNTING					$25	$5	X		No	No	5,490
Kentucky(3)	$27.50	60		$10		X	$10		No	Yes	Yes	13,080
Louisiana(4)	$25	100	$2	X		X	$6	X	Yes	No	No	13,000
Maine	$26.50	33		X	X					No	No	NA
Maryland	$25	100		$5.50		X			No	No	No	NA
Massachusetts	$35.25	21		$5.10			$14.25		Yes	No	No	1,000
Michigan				$20	$25	$25	$6.25	X	Yes	No	No	40,000
Minnesota		90		$10	$25	$27		X	Yes	No	No	5,000
Mississippi	$25	45	$3	X		X	$12	X	Yes	No	No	11,000
Missouri(5)	$15.30	90		X	$35	X	$7.80	X	Yes	Yes	Yes	24,000
Montana(6)		36		$35		X	$15	X	Yes	Yes	Yes	6,579
Nebraska		120		$30	$25	$25	$10	X	Yes	Yes	Yes	9,000
Nevada	$10	30		$35		X	$15	X	Yes	No	No	1,200
New Hampshire	$15.50	31		X	X		$15.50	X	Yes	No	No	2,500
New Jersey	$25.25	30		X			$10.25	X	Yes	No	No	31,000
New Mexico	$15	120		$2	$25	X	$10	$10		No	No	8,000
New York	$36	16		X	X		$11		Yes	No	No	NA
North Carolina	$23.75	40		X	X	X	X	X	Yes	No	No	30,000
North Dakota	$25	90		X	$35	$35	$6	SG	Yes	No	No	7,000
Ohio(7)	$34.50	100		X		X	$10	X	Yes	Yes	Yes	10,000
Oklahoma	$25	60		X	$15	$15	$3.25	SG	Yes	No	No	17,000

State											
Oregon(8)	$52.50	100		$15	X	X		X	Yes	Yes	6,000
Pennsylvania	$40.35	60	$2.20	X	X	X	$12.50	X	Yes	No	175,000
Rhode Island	$20	120		X			X		No	No	600
South Carolina	$25.25	120		X	X			X		No	NA
South Dakota	$31	90	$3	$35		$25	$8	X	Yes	No	5,000
Tennessee(9)	$25			$5		X	$15	X	Yes	No	4,000
Texas(10)	$37.50	75		X	X	X		X	Yes	No	12,500
Utah(11)	$75	16	$7	X	$100	$15	$15	X	Yes	No	25,000
Vermont	$30.50	16	$5	X	X	$15	$6.50		No	No	21,000
Virginia	$15.75	30	$20	X	X	$2	$10	X	Yes	No	25,000
Washington	$50	60		X	$2	$2			Yes	No	NA
West Virginia	$30	90		X			$15		Yes	No	NA
Wisconsin	$25.50	70		X	X	X	$12.50		Yes	No	100,000
Wyoming(12)	$50	10	$5	X	$30	X	X	X	Yes	Yes	4,000

X indicates included in basic fee. SG indicates included in small-game fee. Blank spaces under species indicate no bow season.

1. Arkansas — Big-game hunting with the crossbow is legal during the regular rifle hunting season and for small game and varmints. Minimum bow draw weight of seventy-five pounds and a basic hunting license is required.

2. Iowa — Although non-resident big-game hunting is not allowed, visitors may purchase a regular hunting license and use the crossbow for hunting small game, varmints and rough fish.

3. Kentucky — Big-game hunting with the crossbow is limited to designated Pioneer Weapons' areas, in season, and a minimum bow draw weight of eighty pounds is required.

4. Louisiana — May take five deer during regular bow season for the basic $25 license, or buy a five-day permit for $5 plus a $2 archery tag and shoot the same number of deer.

5. Missouri — No restrictions on use of the crossbow during regular rifle season for big game, small game and varmints, as well as rough fish. License rates, tags on chart.

6. Montana — Crossbow legal during rifle season for big game, small game and varmints, but regulations call for licensed professional guide, outfitter or qualified resident for hunting. Grizzly bear and big-horn sheep permits issued on a limited and draw basis.

7. Ohio — Crossbows may be used for rough fish only.

8. Oregon — Crossbow legal during rifle season for big game, small game, varmints and rough fish.

9. Tennessee — Arrow shafts must be at least twenty-four inches long and four-bladed broadheads are illegal.

10. Texas — Bowhunter's name and address must be indelibly printed on arrows.

11. Utah — Bowhunter must be accompanied by a guide when hunting for cougar or bear.

12. Wyoming — Crossbow legal in bow or rifle seasons, but must have minimum draw weight of ninety pounds, a bolt of at least sixteen inches, and draw length of fourteen inches. Crossbow must be equipped with a safety and be hand-cocked without use of cocking levers or similar aids. May be used for big game, small game and varmints, if properly licensed.

265

SELECTING A BOWHUNTING GUIDE

Chapter 27

When Entering Unfamiliar Territory, A Good Guide Can Spell The Difference Between A Good And A Bad Hunt.

THERE COMES A time when the lure of the unknown becomes irresistible, and the hunter begins making plans for his first hunting trip. It may mean traveling only a few hundred miles, or possibly thousands of miles. Regardless of the specific area, it's new territory to him, holding a promise of varied game and plenty of challenge.

The first factor to consider when planning a hunting trip is time. Can you spend the time required to locate, stalk and down your prey in a strange area? Can you take two to three weeks from work to do the leisurely hunting of which most of us dream? If not, it might be more prudent to consider the use of one of the many guide services offered in most states. If hunting in Canada or the upper regions of Alaska, you are required to have a guide; it's the law. Although not required by law in most of the United States, there are, however, many qualified guides willing to help make that first hunt a successful one.

How does a hunter find a guide in the first place? There are several ways. He can look in the outdoor magazines' advertisement sections and write letters asking for information. Or, he can book a guide that a friend has used in the past, since this will give him first-hand information as to the services provided. If booking a guide via the mail, keep in mind that it will take additional time, so start early in the year, long before any seasons open. Even then, you may find it difficult to book a hunt during that same year, since most of the better guide services are booked twelve months or more in advance.

There are many services offered by guides. These range from actual accompaniment on a hunt to simply pointing out the best directions. Which services to choose will be determined by the hunter's own capabilities as both a hunter and a woodsman. Finding the way in strange country can be terrifying to the first-timer. He runs the risk of becoming lost with no references to draw upon. While the guide is familiar with the country being hunted, the hunter has little or no idea of the terrain. The guide not only knows the best areas to hunt, he also knows those areas to stay away from; the areas with little game population and private property lines.

Although specific services will vary from one guide service to another, there are some general services to expect. First is the matter of accommodations. Furnished by the guides, these can range from a series of surplus army tents set up along a stream, to plush cabins. Most bowhunters are frugal people and do not expect the plush lodges and the massive meals offered to the rifle hunters.

How much gear to carry will be determined by the degree of accommodations offered. This will range from the basic tackle required for the actual hunt, plus perhaps a sleeping bag, to a full kit including chow and tent. Be sure to determine just what is needed before making the trip.

Many guided hunts utilize the tree-stand technique of hunting, where the actual hunting is done at some distance from the camp. In the morning, the guide will take you to a designated stand. All you need do is walk to the stand, climb up and wait for your target. The guide knows his area and places the stands near waterholes, crossings or migration areas the game frequents.

At a predetermined time, the guide will return to chauffeur you back to camp. The same procedure will follow in the afternoon, going out early and sitting in the same stand until dark. In this instance, a sleeping bag could prove valuable, easing the discomforts of sitting in one place for an extended period of time. A bag of candy or light snacks also is a welcome addition as you wait.

The tree-stand system of bowhunting is quite simple and requires a minimum of effort by the hunter; a distinct advantage if he is in rather dubious physical condition. From his elevation he can easily spot approaching game without being seen himself, and need only wait until it comes within shooting distance. For the hunter unsure of his physical abilities, it may be the best system available.

Some hunters prefer to walk through the timber and still-hunt. Although they stand a better chance of becoming lost, the guide usually has procedures for this type of hunter, too. One technique is to place the hunter in a huge area, perhaps several miles in diameter, that is fully fenced in. If the hunter does get turned around, all he need do is find a fence and follow it. This has a further advantage in that the guide knows the general area being hunted and can go out looking if his charge fails to show for dinner that night.

One of the best protective devices a bowman carries, and one he should include in his gear even when hunting with a guide, is a compass. With this simple device, he should be able to find his way back to camp on his own, if need be. A word of caution, however: Never try to walk in strange country after dark. You're much better off to find yourself a secure area and wait out the night hours than to stumble around in the dark, possibly hurting yourself in the process.

Keep in mind that, when considering a guide service, the guide usually will prefer for you to follow his system of hunting, since he is set up for this style. If you do not like stand-hunting and cannot sit still long enough to wait, be sure your guide offers alternate methods.

Another popular method employed by guides is to locate hunters on stands, not necessarily in trees, but perhaps in rock piles or other places of concealment, and make drives. Driving can be very productive since it moves the game and, as it moves, the hunter gets more chances of filling his tags. This also requires that the hunter remain in one spot throughout the hunt. Many guides place hunters in chosen places, take horses and wranglers and move off in a circle. They will then come around the backside and whoop and holler to drive the game through the area and past the hunters. The hunt isn't necessarily over once the drivers pass by, however. Often game may become hunt-wise, themselves, and instead of running ahead of the drivers will let the horses and riders pass by, then circle around and go behind them.

When a guide drives game, he often will work his hunters in different areas on different days, giving each hunter an equal chance at the game.

There is another type of guide service available, although at a somewhat higher cost. This is the pack-in hunt. It requires a string of horses to take the riders, the camp workers and the tents, grub, and all that will be needed for

Guides not only help with locating game, but also with gutting and caping of trophies, like Corsican ram (left). Guides often spell success.

For hunting in remote locations, a guide often has string of pack and riding horses. These may increase the cost of his services somewhat, but are worth the cost in effort!

Unless you have intimate knowledge of the terrain you intend to hunt, you may spend many fruitless days in the field without a guide. He not only knows areas that hold game, but also those that don't. A Texas javelina hunter follows quietly behind his locale guide, and gets his hog. To him, success is worth the investment!

a week or two in the wilds. A ride of perhaps eight or ten hours, and possibly a saddle sore or two, will place the hunter far from any roads or other hunters, and closer to the trophies. A guide, or one of his men, generally will accompany the hunter when he goes out each day. He is then free to set up his own stands and let the riders drive the game to him if he wishes, or he can simply ramble over the hills. The guide will prevent him from wandering too far or in the wrong direction. While the pack-in admittedly is more costly and physically taxing, it also is a lot more fun for hunters who have tried it.

The costs involved in a guided hunt will depend on the guide's own outlay of cash and materials for the hunt. As that outlay increases, so does his fee. Most guides are ranchers during the regular working months, guiding only during the hunting months to augment their annual income.

There also are some low-budget hunts available to the hunter who feels he cannot afford the more expansive services. However, a hunter who jumps at these should expect the services to be limited. Many of the economy hunts are access hunts. For a hunter competent in the woods, perhaps this is all he will need. It will get him into an area where there is supposed to be game. No guide can guarantee a kill, regardless of the fee he charges, unless he ropes and ties the game to a tree. He has no idea of the hunter's prowess with the bow, but he can and does guarantee shooting.

In talking to those who have gone on guided hunts, a hunter will hear all sorts of stories. While some hunters tell of the lousy service they received, most will rave about the good time they had and the services offered by their guide. Many hunters return year after year to the same guide since they know what to expect from him.

Most states, especially the Western states, have a licensed guide system. The guides must be approved by the state and are issued a license to conduct hunts. A license can be revoked for poor or improper service. In addition, many guides also are members of the state guide association. These associations set standards and act as a clearinghouse for gripes from hunters who might feel they didn't receive what they felt was due them. However, most guides rely on return trade. For that reason they often will give a hunter much more than they advertise.

Any hunter who is a member of a guide association will work to retain that membership. A hunter often can obtain a list of guides in any state by writing to the respective fish and game department, in the state capitals.

Hunt camps can be fountains of memories for many years, where a hunter will meet local people who have an interest in his sport and often are bowhunters themselves. The other hunters he meets in camp often become firm friends. Should he be unfortunate enough not to bag a trophy that season, he will still have more than enough

pleasant memories from the companionship of new friends to make the trip worthwhile.

As already mentioned, before trying a guided hunt there are several things to do. Write for information from the guide service that appeals to you. Ask for references, preferably in your area, from others who have hunted with the guide in the past. If no one from your area has ever used the service, write to several references the guide furnishes and ask them. They paid for the service you hope to get and usually will tell you in no uncertain terms about the service of any guide.

Be certain of the accommodations offered, what you must bring and what the guide will furnish. A rule of thumb is to bring your personal hunting gear, bow, arrows and clothing, plus a sleeping bag. The food and shelter often are provided by the guide service. If it is an access-only situation, be certain to find out if you will need a tent and camping gear.

A few letters far in advance of hunting season could set you up with a hunting partner, not merely a guide.

Chapter 28

Common Sense Safety Suggestions

Bowhunting is One Of The Safest Sports. A Little Planning Is All That's Required To Keep It That Way.

WHEN THE BOWHUNTER takes to the field in search of game, he might well consider that he is potentially his own worst enemy. While it is rare to hear of an archer injured by another bowman, the incidents of self-inflicted wounds are all too common. Generally, they are the result of carelessness or lack of preventive measures by the bowman. The hunter would be wise to keep in mind that each step in archery hunting, from the initial stringing of his bow to the skinning of game, offers some degree of danger unless he knows what he is doing and how to do it properly.

Take, for instance, the stringing of the bow. The initial step involves bracing of the bow; firmly anchoring the bottom end of the limb and then bending the upper end until the bow is sufficiently arched to allow placing of the string around the string nock. There are several ways of doing this. Among the older methods used is the step-through, whereby the archer actually steps between the bow and bowstring, locks the bottom limb against the outer side of his ankle, and then slides the string up onto the nock as he bends the limb. While this is one of the more common means of stringing, it does have its hazards. In

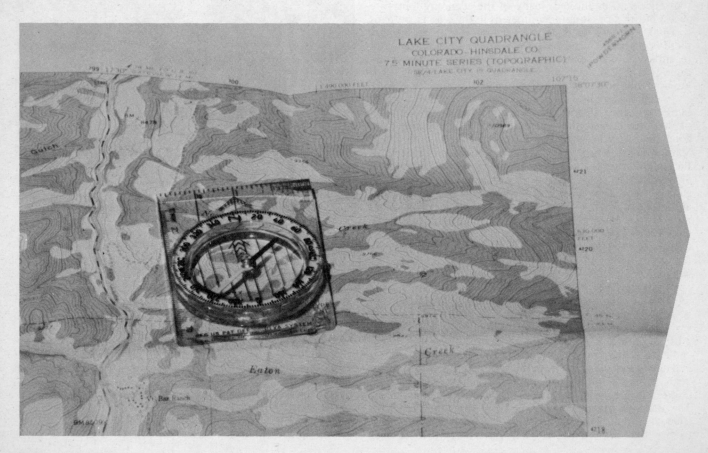

particular, it is prone to slippage, allowing the bow to twist as it's bent, thereby causing damage to the limb or even the hunter.

Another old system is the push-pull method. To string a bow using this system, the hunter places the tip of the lower limb against the instep of the right foot, with the upper limb held in the left hand. The hunter then pulls on the riser of the bow with his right hand as he pushes on the upper limb with his left. When these movements are coordinated properly, the bow will bend to allow placement of the upper string loop around the nock. This particular method, however, does place the tip of the bow in close proximity to the bowman's face, and slippage might easily result in serious facial or ocular damage. The extent of damage can be reduced significantly by simply turning the head away from the bow as the limb is bent. It isn't necessary to actually see the string being placed around the nock. The string can be felt slipping into place, and a visual check then made. With this method, if the limb does get away from him, the hunter will probably only sustain a slap to the side or back of the head, and suffer no real damage.

A word of caution: When using the bowsleeve camouflaged cover, the chance of slippage is greatly increased, as the cover slips easily.

There is no need to use either of the above methods, however. A simple investment of a few dollars toward the purchase of a bowstringer will solve the problem. The bowstringer basically is a length of high-test nylon cord with leather pouches on either end. The pouches slip over each end of the bow and are seated there. The bowman then simply places his foot across the nylon cord approximately midway, and pulls up on the bow. With the center firmly anchored by his foot, the upward pull causes tension on either end of the bow, bending it until the archer is able to slip the bowstring into place. At its fullest extension, the bowstring and stringer will resemble a triangle — the bow forming the rounded top and the stringer the two sides.

For the bowman who favors the narrow-tipped bows, the original version of the bowstringer may not prove satisfactory. If so, Saunders Archery has produced a variation of the original. They use the standard pocket on the lower limb, but instead of an upper pocket they use a moulded section that grips the upper limb along its length, down from the tip but high enough for use as an aid in stringing.

Still another system available is the DEI, a telescoping, channeled aluminum device that will extend to approximately six feet. It can be locked into place, forming a rigid brace. There is a long loop of high-test nylon cord attached to the base of the DEI, and a small saddle of the same material held to the main channel at the top and to an arm pivoting out to the side. To use the DEI, the archer places the lower limb into the lower loop, then cradles the riser at the grip in the upper nylon saddle. As he pulls down on the upper limb, the bow is safely braced. Bows up to and including eighty-five pounds have been braced using the DEI with a high degree of success. Should the bow slip from the archer's grip, it will fly away from him.

Both the pocket-cord style and the Saunders stringer offer the added advantage of compactness. With their small weight and space factors considered, they can become valuable assets for the tackle box or hunting jacket. With either system, the hunter is prepared for a safe method of bracing in camp and in the field, should the need arise. While the DEI is much too large to carry in the field, it can prove to be a valuable asset in camp.

The step-through method of bow stringing is not only potentially dangerous, but one of the best ways known for twisting the bow's limbs. If this system must be used, step over bow with the left leg, bracing curve of lower limb against right ankle. Attach the string to lower limb, then bend bow at riser and pull upper limb toward string. Two-man string-bracing method (above) is safer. Place riser on knee and pull limbs back while partner — standing behind bow in event you let go — places the string in the nocks.

There are few animals from which a hunter need fear attack in most hunting fields, but there are a few rules to keep in mind. Any wounded or cornered animal will fight to escape, even a rabbit. And any female accompanied by her young also is prone to attack in their defense. It's best not to test them.

Perhaps the deadliest animal in the hunting field is the one most archers hope never to spot — the snake. Unfortunately, much of the hunting terrain favorable to game also is favorable to rattlesnakes, copperheads and cottonmouth snakes. The wise hunter will carry a snakebite kit with him, preferably inside his jacket or trouser pocket. Hopefully, he will never need to use it, but he should take the time to learn how. It's also a good idea to check with your family physician to make sure that the serum inside the kit is safe to use. Some people are allergic to various anti-snake serums.

In the event of snakebite, survival becomes an immediate but restricted problem. A snakebite victim must, of necessity, severely restrict his movement to prevent the blood flow from circulating the venom. While calmness may seem impossible, it is imperative. Snakebites can be deadly, but more people die from heart attack and panic than from the bite itself.

When bitten, the hunter must do three things. First, determine the whereabouts of the snake, and either kill it or chase it away. Next, tend to the wound itself. And, finally, get help. While there is no universal distress signal available to bowhunters, there are various methods of attracting attention. Even a police whistle can be used. Three blasts on the whistle in rapid succession will alert hunters that someone is in trouble. Three of anything is an emergency distress signal, and should be considered as such.

There also are various types of flare devices on the market and, if there is little danger of fire, they make an excellent signaling system. They take up little space, can easily be carried inside a hunting jacket, and are well worth their cost.

Another welcome addition to your hunting garb is a small piece of brightly colored material, easily visible by hunters or searchers. Orange colors have proven excellent for this purpose, and can be used as a flag to attract attention. For the hunter who favors camouflaged gear, the orange material is particularly valuable, and some hunters wear reversible style jackets that have an orange lining on one side and camouflage on the other.

If hunting in a familiar area, this safety equipment may be all that is needed. However, for many hunters there is nothing more challenging and enticing than a new hunting area. Unfortunately, it also is an area where the terrain, shelter and dangers probably are unknown. It is possible, however, to obtain advance information on new hunting areas by simply writing local government offices and requesting topographic maps of the area in question. Ranging in price from seventy-five cents to $2, the maps indicate important terrain features in the area, from improved roads to footpaths, water, forest and marshes.

Again, a word of caution: Many of the topographic maps were made as much as twenty years ago and, consequently, some of the landmarks — particularly manmade ones — may have changed during that time. But the basic layout of the area will be there and, with sufficient study, any hunter should be able to find his way into and out of any new area using the maps as a guide. It's always best to carry a map into the field for quick reference when needed.

No hunter should ever venture into new country without one of the simplest lifesaving devices in his pocket: a compass. There is nothing more frightening than realizing that

DEI stringer (upper) is simple, efficient and telescopes for carrying. Nylon cord loops over lower limb and nylon cradle on arm — braced against foot — holds bow at handle giving even displacement of strain as upper tip is pulled back. Saunders stringer (lower) has cradle on one end, pocket on other which fit on limb tips. Attached nylon cord is placed beneath foot and bow is braced by pulling up on handle until string fits into nock. If bow does get loose, it flies away from you.

Several ounces of prevention can be carried in this fanny pack, one of the many available which either hook onto a belt or come equipped with integral straps for attachment.

you are lost, even if only temporarily, and it can happen to even the best of hunters. Nothing will abate panic as quickly as knowledge of direction, and even the simplest style of compass will give that. Be sure that you know how to read your style of compass.

One of the better styles of compass on the market is the lensatic compass, similar to the military compass and relatively inexpensive and easy to use.

The lensatic compass features a fine degree of graduations along the dial, and a sighting system that allows for sighting on a landmark and plotting a course of direction.

By now it may seem as if the hunter is completely bogged down by extra equipment, since he should be carrying a spare bowstring — perhaps taped directly to the bow — some type of signaling device, a compass, topographic maps, food, matches, a knife and water. Where does he store it all? Good hunting jackets feature numerous pockets and the needed items for hunting, safety and survival can be stored in the jacket itself. It's amazing just how much gear can be stored inside a properly made hunting jacket.

When all the gear required cannot be carried inside the jacket, many hunters carry a small pack popularly called a fanny pouch. This pouch attaches directly on the belt, or is tied around the middle of the body, resting behind the hunter in the small of the back. While extremely compact,

For overnight trips, the Adventure 16 ruck sack accommodates just about everything needed except a sleeping bag and fits snugly to the back, allowing you to shoot while wearing it.

Spare bow and arrow parts always should include, at the minimum, a spare string with nocking point in place, some extra broadheads and a good broadhead sharpener.

the minipack will carry food, survival gear, signalling systems, spare string, some extra broadheads, a sharpener for field use, and even a light rain jacket or windbreaker.

There is one debatable item left to carry or leave behind: water. If hunting near a running stream, a canteen probably isn't necessary. However, in dry areas, or areas where purity of the water is questionable, it is a must. How much water to carry is dependent on the individual hunter, as well as on the climate of the hunting area. Altitude, temperature and physical exertion are all factors to consider in determining the amount of water to carry. A particular hunter might never touch his canteen while hunting at 10,000 feet in Colorado, but may become extremely thirsty at 6000 feet in New Mexico in similar terrain. Each hunter should know his physical needs and be able to gauge his requirements accordingly.

There is one last category to consider when discussing bowhunting safety. It pertains to technique when in the field. Excitement of a hunt should never dull technique. Nothing is more frightening than to see a hunter, beginner or advanced, in the field with razor-sharp steel sticking up from a bowquiver unprotected, or on the bowstring itself. The majority of bowhunting accidents, and fortunately there are extremely few of them, are due to hunter carelessness. Chances are, with the use of a little common sense, they might never have happened at all.

Each year new items appear on the market, new ideas are formulated, and more is added to the equipment list as older items are deleted. Even the basic survival gear, though standard, goes through a constant updating. How much to carry, how much to leave in camp, these decisions are part of the fun of hunting. Change is part of hunting and the joy of going into the field.

Statistics indicate there are fewer bowhunting accidents than in any other sport. The wise hunter will enter the hunting field educated and prepared, keeping accidents to a minimum and kills to the maximum.

Additional items to carry into the field, particularly when planning to stay overnight or longer, include (above photos): black, 600-pound nylon cord; wire-type hand saw (in plastic container); whistle and signaling mirror for emergencies; a good compass; hip-flask liquid container; extra matches in a waterproof container; and several shotgun shells filled with paraffin and a wick for ease in starting fires. All can be carried in fanny pack (below), including nylon windbreaker.

BOWHUNTING BOWS OF DISTINCTION

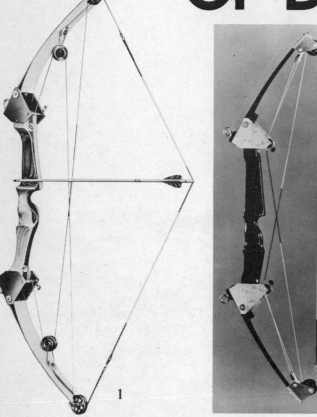

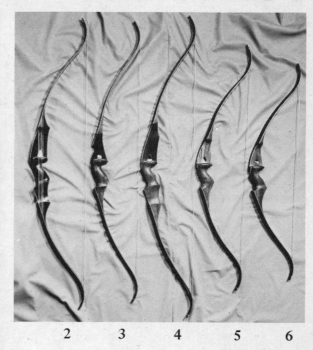

1 ALLEN COMPOUND HUNTER — Black, solid glass limbs with brown hardwood handle in 50 to 60-pound draw weights. Special Black Hunter with black hardwood handle in 40 to 50-pound weights.

AMERICAN V.I.P. SUPER HUNTING TAKE-DOWN — Comes in 58 and 60-inch lengths with exclusive fast limb-coupling, no tools required. In weights from 30 to 65 pounds, features 6-inch sight window, super flex core, exotic hardwoods riser and position stabilizer insert.

2 AMERICAN ALL PRO CUSTOM — Seven-inch sight window is featured on this 60-inch hunting bow in weights from 40 to 75 pounds. Has tropical hardwoods riser with laminations, capped with black and white overlay. Super slim taper core, built-in hunter's grip, positioned stabilizer insert and flannel bow case.

3 AMERICAN CHEETAH HUNTER SPECIAL — This 58-inch bow has built-in reminder grip, super slim taper core, 6-inch sight window and riser of tropical hardwoods with capped overlay. Draw weights from 40 to 75 pounds.

4 AMERICAN CHEETAH 64 — In draw weights from 25 to 75 pounds, featuring 8-inch sight window, super slim core, positive hunter's grip, tropical hardwoods riser and laminations.

5 AMERICAN SUPER NITRO — Brush-country deer bow, 54 inches long in draw weights from 35 to 75 pounds. Tropical hardwoods riser and capped overlay, super slim core, reminder grip with 5½-inch sight window.

6 AMERICAN X-48 — Same features, except for sight window, of Super Nitro, but in 48-inch length and draw weights of 40 to 55 pounds.

AMERICAN HUNTER — Features 6-inch sight window and is available in weights from 35 to 70 pounds. Length, 56 inches.

BEAR VICTOR KODIAK — Medium length sight window makes this magnesium bow equally at home on shooting line or on the hunt. Vinyl arrow rest, Kodiak adjustable arrow plate, Converta-Accessory insert and pistol grip are standard equipment. Routed for 5-inch Bear field model hunting bowsight. In AMO lengths of 60, 62 and 64 inches; draw weights from 25 to 70 pounds. Available in 7 different colors.

BEAR VICTOR MAGNUM — Lightweight magnesium handle with ironwood finish. Comes with vinyl arrow rest, Kodiak adjustable arrow plate, Converta-Accessory insert, pistol grip, and is routed for 3¾-inch Bear field model hunting sight. AMO lengths of 56, 58 and 60 inches; draw weights from 25 to 70 pounds. Seven different colors.

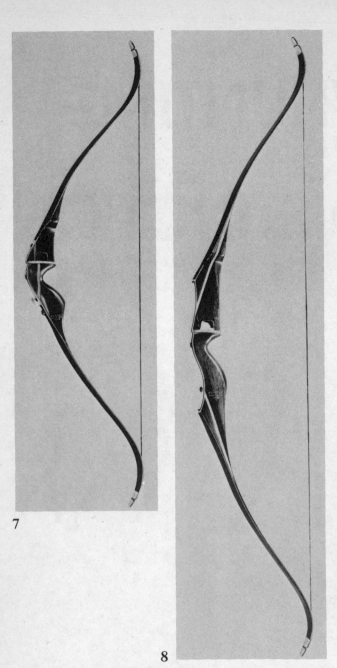

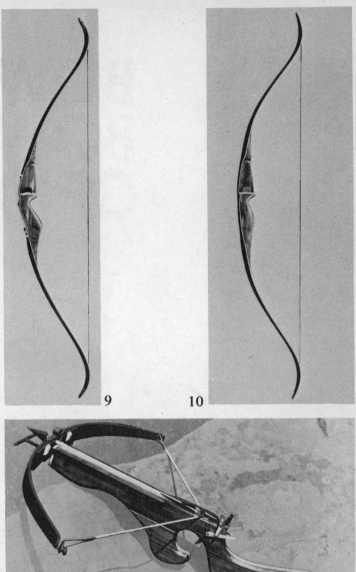

BEAR VICTOR SUPER GRIZZLY — Standard on this distinctive bow, featuring the Team Bear Crusader Red regimental stripe and bow tip, are Bear's "Prefurred" Silent arrow plate and Bearhair arrow rest, Converta-Accessory insert, reinforcing and protective Futurewood overlays on tips, hand-contoured grip with thumb rest, Fascor powered limbs and Universal Temper Strand black dacron bowstring. AMO length of 58 inches in right-hand draw weights from 40 to 55 pounds; left hand, 45 and 50 pounds.

8 BEAR VICTOR SUPER KODIAK — In midnight black Futurewood with distinctive Crusader red stripe and tips. Comes with Bear "Prefurred" Silent arrow plate and Bearhair arrow rest, Converta-Accessory insert, Fascor powered limbs, Futurewood overlays on tips and 3-ply fiber overlays on back of handle, hand-contoured grip with thumb rest. AMO length of 60 inches, stocked in 40, 45, 50 and 55-pound weights; can be ordered in 35, 60, 65 and 70-pound weights.

7 BEAR VICTOR SUPER MAGNUM 48 — Designed for hunting from tree stands or in heavy cover, this 48-inch bow has features similar to other Bear hunting bows. Available in either right or left-handed models in weights from 40 to 55 pounds; other weights on special order.

9 BEAR KODIAK HUNTER — Forest green Futurewood with green accent tips make this 60-inch bow fit in anywhere. Equipped with Silent arrow plate, Bearhair arrow rest, Converta-Accessory insert, hand-contoured grip with thumb rest. Weights from 40 to 55 pounds; other weights on special order.

BEAR KODIAK MAGNUM — Similar to Hunter, except 52 inches in length.

BEAR GRIZZLY — In draw weights from 40 to 50 pounds — others on special order — this 58-inch bow is designed for the two-season hunter. Features leather arrow plate, Bearhair arrow rest, Converta-Accessory insert, reinforcing and protective Futurewood overlays on tips, hand-contoured grip with thumb rest.

10 BEAR BLACK BEAR — 60-inch Black Bear for beginners is at home on the range or in the field. In draw weights from 25 to 50 pounds.

11 DAVE BENEDICT BLACK KNIGHT — Based on "True Center" shot design principle, comes in draw weights from 20 to 140 pounds. No bolts and nuts required for holding interchangeable recurved limbs. Select black walnut stock, fully automatic safety, and geared rear sight adjustable for windage and elevation.

DAVE BENEDICT CARBINE SK-1 — Laminated walnut stock, arrow lock, foot cocking stirrup and automatic safety. Has 140-pound pull and can be ordered with 4-power Weaver scope.

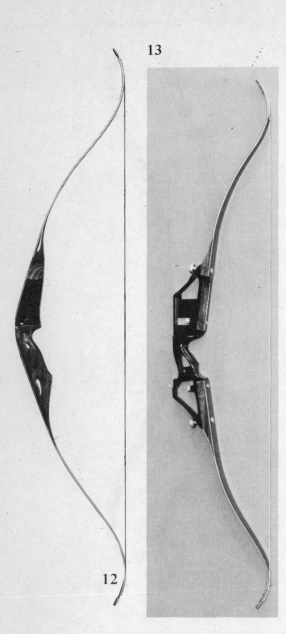

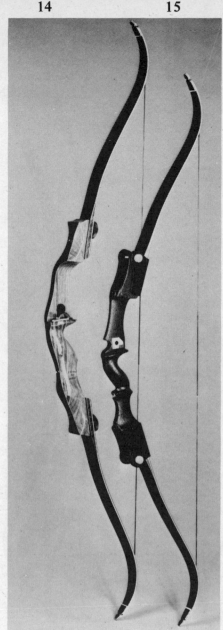

12 BLACK HAWK SHORT BEE — Mid-length bow for beginners and experts alike. Stable limb design and dark hardwoods combined with rich finish. Comes with rug rest and leather plate in 60 or 62-inch lengths.

BLACK HAWK HORNET SPECIAL TD — Hardened steel studs and knurled thumb nuts make setting up and taking down a hand operation. Flat, black handle and camo limbs with tapered maple core. 58 and 60-inch lengths.

BLACK HAWK SHORT HORNET — Riser of 6 contrasting woods on this now longer, 58-inch bow.

BLACK HAWK MARS — Ideal brush or tree bow, 52-inch Mars features colorful handle, nock overlays and rich finish.

BLACK HAWK AVENGER — Dark hardwoods handle with maple laminations and redesigned limbs are featured on this 52-inch hunting bow.

13 BLACK WIDOW HUNTER — Patented A-frame design takes down in 30 seconds. Weighs 3 pounds and comes in 60 or 64-inch lengths, draw weights from 35 to 65 pounds.

14 BROWNING BACKPACKER — In two models, I and II, for hunter, backpacker or any shooter who demands portability. One is a 54-inch bow that takes down to 19 inches; the other a 60-inch bow that knocks down to just over 22 inches. No tools required, each limb is locked onto riser by metal index pin and hefty through bolt. Locking holes reinforced by close tolerance metal insert bushing with nylon washer cushioned between knurled knob and limb. Shedua handle riser with bubinga lamination stripe. Full center-shot sight window, whisper arrow rest and full pistol grip with contoured thumb rest. Comes with 3 accessory insert bushings and weatherproof finish. Draw weights from 35 to 70 pounds in either model.

15 BROWNING FOLDING HUNTER — Balanced and matched jet black, composite hardwood and fiberglass limbs. Precision cast alloy handle riser with full pistol grip fitted with 3 accessory insert bushings. Drilled for use with Berger Button or adjustable arrow rests, comes with Browning Sure-Fold arrow rest. Folds up into compact 26-inch by 8-inch bow bag for ease in carrying. Draw weights from 35 to 70 pounds. Folding Hunter I, 56 inches; Folding Hunter II, 60 inches.

16 BROWNING EXPLORER — Available in two models — 56-inch Explorer I and 62-inch Explorer II — each featuring East Indian rosewood handle risers that taper into limbs of black fiberglass, with lamination stripes the full length of riser section. White overlays accent limb tips and riser. Sculptured with full pistol grips and thumb rests, plus full center-shot sight windows. Draw weights from 35 to 70 pounds.

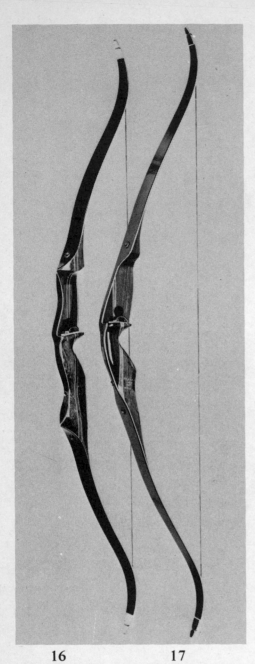
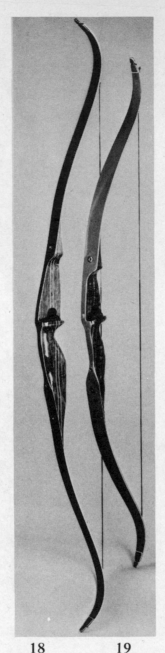
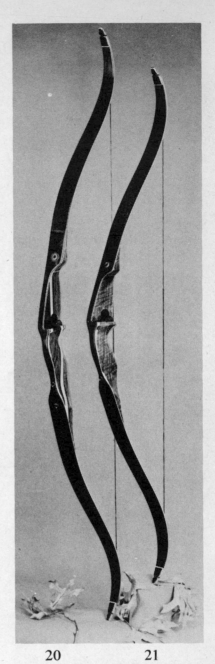

16   17   18   19   20   21

17 BROWNING COBRA — Broad limbs with face and back of jet black, unidirectional fiberglass. Additional fiberglass bonded to bow tips for strength and protection. Handle riser, featuring pistol grip with thumb rest, formed from laminations of deep grained East Indian rosewood and hi-density, black phenolic. Available in 50-inch — Cobra I — and 38-inch — Cobra II — lengths, draw weights from 35 to 70 pounds.

20 BROWNING FURY — Fury I is 54-inch bow that handles easily in thickest brush. Fury II, at 60 inches, has slightly smoother draw and more range. Bubinga wood handle riser has maple and black fiberglass lamination stripes complemented by midnight black fiberglass limbs, touched off with white overlays on riser back and limb tips. Full-working recurve limbs. Full pistol grips with thumb rests and full center-shot sight windows. Three accessory insert bushings accept Browning's new Piranha Bowfishing Reel and all popular hunting stabilizers as well as popular double-arm quivers. Hard, clear, weatherproof finish. Draw weights from 35 to 70 pounds.

21 BROWNING'S NOMAD STALKER — Full pistol grip handle riser sculptured from select hardwoods. Extra broad limbs laminated with layers of maple veneer and black unidirectional fiberglass. Nock reinforced with fiberglass overlay. Durable weatherproof finish. Equipped with 3 accessory insert bushings. 52-inch Stalker I, 58-inch Stalker II. Stalker I Hunting Set comes with 6 fiberglass olive drab hunting arrows, camouflage arm guard, Kwikee bow quiver, 6 field points and 6, 3-blade hunting points plus stick of Ferr-L-Tite cement.

18 BROWNING ROVER — Fast shooting 64-inch bow suitable for hunting or field archery. Black and white laminated fiberglass limbs, exotic hardwoods riser with maple lamination strips rubbed to high polish. Three accessory insert bushing. Draw weights from 25 to 60 pounds.

19 BROWNING WASP — Tuned for tight groups, 56-inch Wasp is easy to maneuver in thick cover. Exotic hardwoods handle riser tapers into limb laminations of maple veneer sandwiched between unidirectional fiberglass. Full-working recurve limbs protected at string nocks with fiberglass overlays. Comes with 3 accessory insert bushings. Draw weights from 35 to 70 pounds. Wasp Hunting Set contains 6 olive drab Port Orford cedar arrows with 6 field points and 6 interchangeable 3-blade hunting points, all-purpose arm guard, top grain shooting glove, slip-on 6-arrow bow quiver, 24-inch deer target face and Ferr-L-Tite point cement.

BROWNING COMPOUND HUNTER — Only 48½ inches from tip to tip, handle is lightweight, precision cast magnesium with durable, baked-on vinyl finish for non-slip grip. Riser equipped with over-draw cutout. Adjustable for draw length and draw weight.

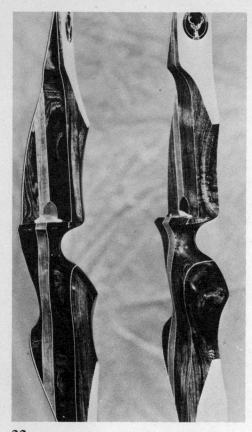

22

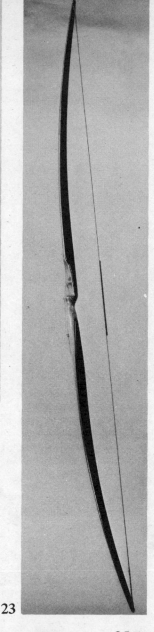

23

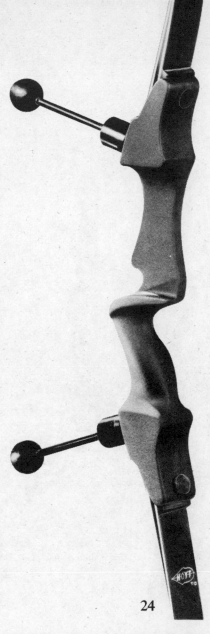

24

Comes with Sure-Fold arrow rest, 3 accessory insert bushings and weighs 4¼ pounds. Available in 4 pre-set draw lengths: 28, 29, 30 and 31 inches with slight adjustments. Draw weights from 45 to 60 pounds.

22 HOWARD GAMEMASTER JET — Guaranteed to be the world's fastest bow, the Jet features controlled limb recovery for truest arrow flight possible. Recurves designed for quietness, eliminating need for silencers. Glass spine method allows accurate gauge of strength for exact and proper wood-to-glass ratio for each bow weight and draw length. Handle is composite of Brazilian rosewood, African vermillion and decorative white strips. Bow finish is tough, durable plastic. Length is 66 inches in draw weights up to 65 pounds.

23 HOWARD HILL LONGBOW TEMBO II — Tempered, split bamboo, surfaced on back and belly with layer of Gordon's fiberglass, featuring recurved styled, reverse handle. Model 6001 in 68 and 69-inch lengths, draw weights to 75 pounds. Also available with conventional handle.

24 HOYT PRO MEDALIST HUNTER T/D — Lightweight, magnesium handle with special recess for broadhead overdraw. Limbs snap in and out without tools, AMO lengths of 58, 60 and 62 inches with up to 70-pound draw weight at 28 inches. Equipped with stabilizer inserts, Action-cor powered limbs and tear-drop tip overlays.

25 HOYT SUPER HUNTER — Superwood handle with Action-cor powered limbs in AMO length of 62 inches, delivering up to 70 pounds at 28-inch draw. Equipped with dual stabilizers and bushings for mounting optional bow quiver or bow reel, Pro rest, Ply-O-String bowstring, deluxe bow case, tear-drop overlay bow tips.

JENNINGS COMPOUND — Impregnated ash wood in 4 adjustment ranges: 40 to 50, 45 to 60, 50 to 65 and 55 to 70 pounds. Draw lengths from 25 to 34 inches.

26 JENNINGS COMPOUND — Light, aluminum alloy handle section. Full wrap-around grip. Available in 4 adjustment ranges: 40 to 50, 45 to 60, 50 to 65 and 55 to 70 pounds. Draw lengths from 25 to 34 inches.

27 MARTIN KAM-ACT MK-2 — Camming action bow with variable adjustments to allow peak draw weights from 30 to 65 pounds. Comes with Torrington roller bearings, stabilizer insert, 3/8-inch Berger Button hole, tapped for sight mount and hunting quiver.

BEN PEARSON EQUALIZER — Wide, laterally stabilized Hyper-Kinetic limbs on this 48-inch hunting bow give flat, accurate cast. Similar to Pearson's other hunting bows except 4-inch center-shot sight window.

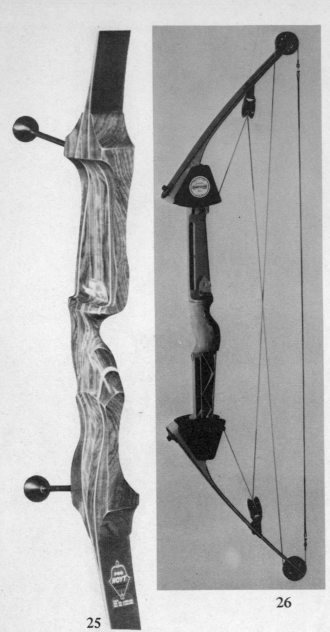

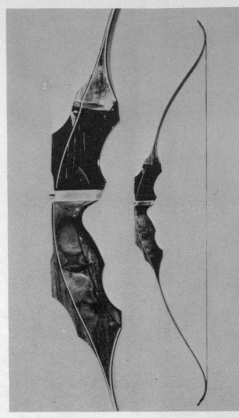

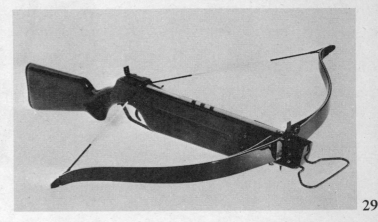

25

26

27

28

29

BEN PEARSON SPOILER — Easy handling 52-inch Spoiler has same features as rest of Pearson hunting bows, except center-shot sight window is 4½ inches.

28 BEN PEARSON MARAUDER TD — Modified handle riser with contoured thumb rest provides flat planes for easy sight mounting. Equipped with full working recurve Hyper-Kinetic limbs of black Gordon Bo-Tuff fiberglass with reinforced tips, mohair arrow rest, and Serv-Weld custom dacron string. Length, 60 inches AMO; draw weights from 40 to 50 pounds.

BEN PEARSON SILENCER TD — Hand-finished marblewood handle with Rigid-Lock aluminum alloy knuckles and Hyper-Kinetic full working recurve black Pearsonite fiberglass limbs with reinforced tips. Mohair arrow rest, 5½-inch center-shot sight window and Serv-Weld custom dacron string. Length, 58 inches AMO; draw weights from 40 to 55 pounds in right or left-handed models.

BEN PEARSON RENEGADE — Black marblewood handle with Hyper-Kinetic full working recurve limbs of black Pearsonite fiberglass with reinforced tips. In draw weights from 40 to 55 pounds, 60-inch AMO hunting bow comes with mohair arrow rest, 5½-inch center-shot sight window and Serv-Weld custom dacron string.

BEN PEARSON ROGUE — Hyper-Kinetic, full working recurve

limbs of black Pearsonite fiberglass with reinforced tips. Handle of hand-finished marblewood and select hardwoods. Center-shot sight window, 4¾ inches. Length, 58 inches AMO; draw weights from 40 to 55 pounds.

29 BEN PEARSON CLASSIC — This 36-inch bow with Pearsonite fiberglass backing and double reinforced tips features a cherry stained hardwood stock, checkered pistol grip, black polyvinyl butt plate and metal foot stirrup. Brace height of 4¾ inches, 75-pound draw weight.

30 SABO PAC-KING FIELD GRADE — African shedua handle reinforced with glass overlays, complete center-shot sight window and sculptured grip. Limbs, attached with unique fold-down idea, feature inlaid tip wedges to minimize limb mass while reinforcing tip area. Tapered limb core and fadeout provide uniform limb stresses. Handles are offered in two lengths and when fitted with standard limbs provide 60 and 64-inch bow lengths. Standard model has shedua inlay accentuated on either side by a maple/walnut laminate, sandwiched between contrasting exotic hardwoods with multiple glass overlays. Includes bow quiver inserts, center-shot window and hand-sculptured grip.

31 SHAKESPEARE QT — Quick take-down and put-together without use of tools. Wedge-type design assures positive alignment of

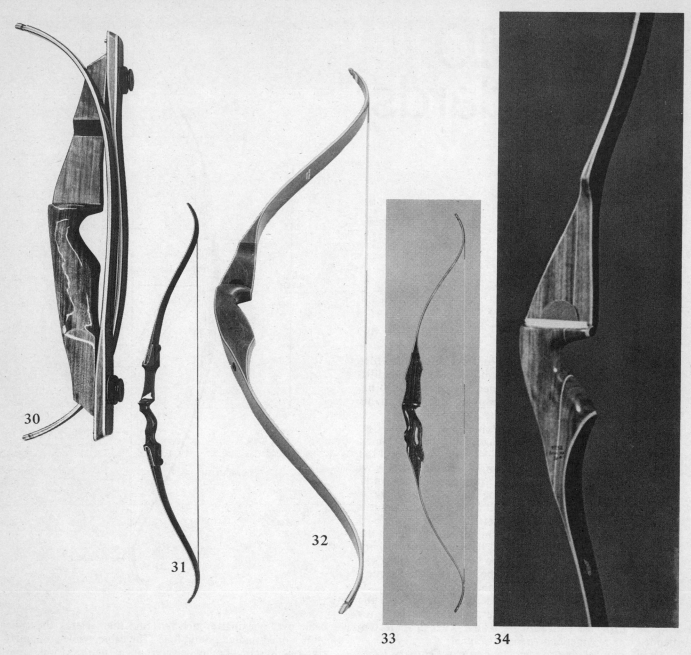

30

31

32

33   34

limbs and aluminum/magnesium handle. Wide-limb design gives extra smooth draw and super penetration. In three lengths: 56, 58 and 60 inches, right-hand only. Weights: 40, 45, 50 and 55 pounds. In gray or green.

SHAKESPEARE X32 SUPER NECEDAH — Duo-flex designed midnight black fiberglass limbs and sculptured handle of Wonderwood are prime features of this 54-inch hunting bow. Available in right or left-hand models in draw weights of 40, 45, 50 and 55 pounds, it comes with Hunter rest and dacron bowstring.

SHAKESPEARE X-28 NECEDAH — Same features, except limbs are green fiberglass, has rug arrow rest and is 58 inches long. Also available in right or left-hand models in same draw weights as X32.

SHAKESPEARE X-18 SIERRA — Field-grade bow for beginner or economy-minded hunter, 52-inch Sierra offers choice of 20 to 50-pound draw weights. Handle of random, exotic imported woods. Comes with rug arrow rest, 4-inch sight window and dacron bowstring.

33 SPARTAN HUNTER — Small, torque-free handle has sight window cut 3/16-inch past center. Bow is crafted of bubinga hardwood and eastern hardwood maple in black 3M glass. Comes in lengths of 58 and 62 inches, draw weights from 25 to 75 pounds.

STEVENS — Only 29 inches when strung, bow features seasoned, air-dried Ozark walnut stock, hand-forged hardware inset with blued finish, push-in safety, specially designed rear sight and stirrup. Draw weight of 140 pounds.

WING JOHN WILLIAMS TAKEDOWN — Black, lightweight magnesium handle and fiberglass limbs in draw weights from 40 to 55 pounds. AMO lengths, 62 and 66 inches. Weighs approximately 2 pounds, 10 ounces.

32 WING RED WING HUNTER — In AMO lengths of 52 and 58 inches featuring WingWood risers and special inserts for Wing's bow quiver and quick-attach fishing reel. Draw weights to 70 pounds. Brown fiberglass limbs.

34 YORK THUNDERBOLT — Pioneer of short hunting bows, 54-inch Thunderbolt is available in draw weights of 45 to 60 pounds in right or left-handed models. Handle is constructed of contrasting imported and domestic hardwoods.

YORK TRACKER — American walnut handle is feature of this 58-inch hunting bow available in draw weights from 40 to 55 pounds.

AMO Standards

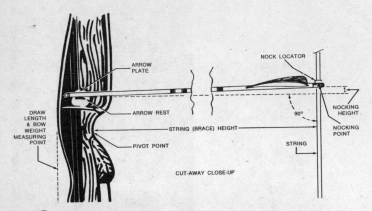

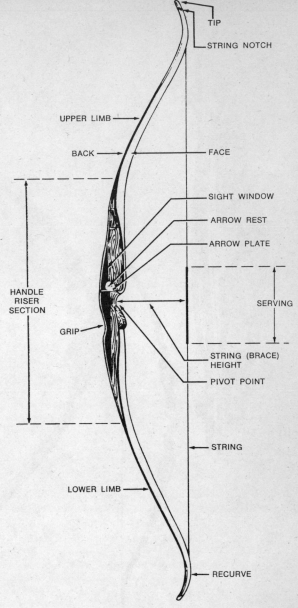

ANYONE WHO HAS ever stumbled through the first year of high school Latin can readily appreciate the difficulties encountered by the foreigner who tries to fight his way through the maze of homonyms and heteronyms generously sprinkled throughout the English language.

From words pronounced the same but spelled differently and having different meanings — homonyms, knock and nock — to those pronounced differently but spelled the same and having different meanings — heteronyms, bow and bow — not to mention those pronounced differently and spelled differently but having the same meaning — synonyms, release and free — well...it's a wonder we ever really know what we're talking about.

Some sort of this same situation was evident among the bow and arrow fraternity until 1968, when the Archery Manufacturers Organization led the way in simplifying and lessening the confusion brought about by the use of interchangeable words such as fistmele and string height.

Deciding that common, simple terms were the best, the AMO drew up and adopted industry-wide standards for bow and arrow nomenclature — standards which are recommended by the American Archery Council.

Until approval of the new standards in February 1968, every bowmaker had his own method of measuring the length of a bow; a practice which caused enormous confusion among archers when it became necessary to buy a new bowstring. Invariably, when the purchaser got home and attempted to string his bow, he would find that the string was too short or too long and didn't provide the proper string (brace) height.

It was to solve this inherent problem and standardize bow and string lengths that the AMO Standards Committee developed a systematic method of measuring bow lengths. As a result, the length of all bows manufactured to AMO standards are designed to have the proper string height when braced with a standard one-sixteenth-inch diameter steel cable. To accomplish this end, the cable must be exactly three inches less than the marked length of the bow. For example, the cable for a sixty-six-inch bow is sixty-three inches long.

Naturally, measurement of the steel cable's length must be precisely determined; that is exactly what the AMO does. First, they place the 1¼-inch loops on each end of the

cable over one-quarter-inch pins and then stretch the cable with a one hundred-pound load. The cable, while still under this one hundred-pound tension, must then measure, from the outside edge of each one-quarter-inch pin, its marked length with a tolerance of only one-sixteenth of an inch.

The AMO makes available to all bow manufacturers a complete set of twenty-five master cables — one for each bow length from forty-eight inches to seventy-two inches — in one-inch increments. Subtracting the three inches required for proper string height, actual length of the cables are from forty-five to sixty-nine inches.

Now nearly universally used in the bowmaking industry, these standards for bow length have materially improved bow comparison and string fitting. Since most bows made to AMO standard lengths are marked as "AMO Standard" and with the correct bow length, archers are not so apt to find themselves in the field, or on the range, with a busted string hanging from their bow and a useless piece of string in their pocket.

And, just to make sure we're all communicating in the same language, the illustrations displayed on this page contain the standard nomenclature as approved by the AMO and recommended by the AAC.

Glossary Of Bowhunting Terms

Arm guard: This shaped leather protector is worn on the inside of the forearm of the bow hand. Purpose is to protect this section of the arm from the bowstring.

Arrow plate: This is a protector, often inlaid, just above the bow handle, on the side where the arrow passes as it is launched in flight.

Back: This is the surface of the bow that is farthest away from the shooter, when the bow is held ready to shoot.

Backing: This can be any one of a number of materials that are glued or affixed to the back of the bow to improve cast. Included have been such materials as fiberglass, rawhide, sinew and various synthetics of modern manufacture.

Backed bow: This is a bow which has had some type of backing material glued to it.

Barb: Part of the hunting arrowhead or broadhead that is fashioned to keep it from being shaken out or pulled from the wound. Illegal in many states.

Barreled arrow: A shaft which is tapered, starting in the middle and becoming smaller at the ends. The greatest cross-sectional area is in the middle.

Bast: This is the coil of twisted straw that is behind the target and to which the target face is attached.

Belly: The side that one sees, closest to him, when the bow is held in the standard shooting position.

Bend: Bracing or placing the bowstring in the nocks of the bow.

Blind: A place of concealment for the hunter. May be constructed of natural or artifical materials near a water hole or along game trails.

Bobtail arrow: One that has the greatest cross-section at the pile and tapers toward the nock.

Bolt: The missile-like shaft that is shot from a crossbow.

Boss: The same as bast.

Bow lock: A finger release of single-unit construction.

Bow stave: This is the billet of wood from which a bow is made.

Bowyer: One who makes bows; in this era, more often used in connection with one who builds custom bows to order.

Brace: To string the bow, using any of the accepted methods.

Brace height: Distance from pivot point on the bow handle to the bowstring after bracing.

Broadhead: A hunting head, usually made of steel, that is triangular in shape. Originally, it had only two blades, hence the name, but the same term is used to describe more complicated heads now.

Butt: A backstop, such as straw bales, to which the target can be attached.

Cast: The ability of the bow to propel an arrow and the degree of efficiency with which this is achieved.

Chested arrows: One that has its greatest cross-section area near the nock, tapering both toward the nock and pile.

Clout target: A standard target of four feet, which has been enlarged twelve times and is laid out on the ground for clout shooting.

Cock feather: Fletching feather on the arrow at right angles to the nock. In commercially made arrows, this usually is the bright-colored feather.

Crest: This incorporates bands of varying colors and widths, which are painted around the arrows, often by the individual shooter, for identification.

Crossbow: A short bow set on a stock, which usually must be drawn by a mechanical device. It was used primarily for warfare during the Middle Ages. It discharges a bolt by means of a trigger. Numerous sporting models are built today.

Curl: This is a natural swirl in the grain of the wooden bow stave.

Draw: To pull the bowstring the full length of the arrow, ready to shoot.

Draw fingers: Normally the first three fingers of the hand. These are used in pulling the string to full draw.

Draw weight: The force — measured in pounds — required to pull the bow to a full draw.

Drift: The movement to one side or the other of the arrow in its flight, caused by a crosswind.

End: The number of arrows used in scoring a particular target event. In most instances, an end is considered to be six arrows.

Eye: The loop in the end of the bowstring.

Field captain: The official in charge of a target archery tournament.

Field point: Metal arrow tip used for small game hunting. Also designed to give the bowhunter the same tip weight as a broadhead for purposes of practice.

Finger tips: Sewn leather finger stalls that are worn over the tips of the shooting or drawing fingers to protect them against the string.

Fistmele: This is the distance from the base of the clenched fist to the tip of the extended thumb. This distance is used as a measurement of the proper distance from the bow handle to the string, when the bow is braced.

Fletch: A verb, often confused with a noun; it concerns actual placement of the feathers on the arrow shaft.

Fletching: This is the noun that often is confused. It is the term to describe the feathers that guide the arrow in flight — after they have been fletched — as in the verb — to attach them.

Flight arrow: This is a light arrow with little in the way of fletching that is used in the distance shooting event.

Flirt: A jerky or jumping movement of an arrow in its normal line of flight. This also is decribed by some shooters as "porpoising."

Flu-flu: An arrow that is used in shooting birds, usually on the wing. It usually is fletched with a complete spiral and, in recent years, rabbit fur has been tried rather than feathers. The size and shape of the fletching are determined in such a way that the arrows travel only a short distance and can be retrieved easily. Also: floo-floo.

Footing: Little used except in special instances today, this is a spliced section of hardwood at the pile end of a wooden arrow.

Gold: This is the bullseye in the four-foot regulation circular target. The actual circle is 9-3/5 inches in diameter.

Grip: The section of the bow, which is held in the shooting hand. It also is called the handle; however, grip also can refer to the manner in which the bow is held.

Hen feathers: Usually of the same color, these are the two feathers that are not at a right angle to the arrow nock.

High brace: According to the Archery Manufacturers Organization, this is when the fistmele distance is more than seven inches. It generally is accepted that it is better to high brace a bow, than to use a low brace.

Hold: This is a pause by the archer, while at full draw, and is just prior to release of the arrow, aligning the arrow with the target.

Lady paramount: Assistant to the field captain, this is a woman who is charged with the women's shooting segment of a tournament.

Laminated bow: A bow that is created from superimposed layers of materials. This can be different types of wood; wood in combination with other materials such as fiberglass or even metal.

Limb: This is the section of the bow from the handle to the tip. Each bow has an upper and a lower limb; these usually cannot be interchanged in the more custom type of bows.

Longbow: The type of bow, without recurve, that usually was fashioned of a single piece of wood without laminations. It gained its reputation during the Middle Ages, but has been replaced almost entirely by bows of more modern design and efficiency.

NAA: This abbreviation refers to the National Archery Association, which is made up entirely of target archers. It also controls United States' participation in all international competitions, insofar as archery is concerned.

NFAA: This abbreviation refers to the National Field Archery Association. Its members, primarily bowhunters, sought a course on which they could compete, using animal targets at varying distances. Although much younger than the NAA, it also has become much larger in membership.

Nocks: This has a double meaning in archery. First it is the slot behind the fletch into which the bowstring fits. It also is used to denote the groove at the tip of each bow limb into which the loop of the bowstring fits, when the bow is strung.

Nocking point: This is the section of the bowstring where the nock of the arrow rests. There is a specific point on the string at which efficiency of the arrow is best when shot.

Over-bowed: This term is used to indicate the instance wherein the draw of the bow is more than an individual archer can draw and shoot with any degree of comfort and efficiency.

PAA: These initials refer to the Professional Archery Association, an organization made up primarily of those who compete in contests for money, but the competition must be recognized by the membership; it also includes others who make their livelihood from archery, including qualified instructors and others. It is a young, but aggressive organization.

Petticoat: This is that section outside of the last ring of the target, which has no value in scoring.

Pile: This also is spelled "pyle" in Old English references. It is metal tip attached to the head of the arrow shaft; the arrow point. It comes from the Anglo-Saxon term meaning dart, which is "pil."

Pinch: To squeeze the arrow between the fingers, when drawing.

Pinhole: The exact center of the gold ring in the target used in competitive events.

Point of aim: This is the point or the object at which the archer aims, when he sights over the tip of his arrow.

Quiver: The size, shape and style varies considerably, but this is a holder for arrows so that they may be transported, ready for quick use. The quiver may be slung over the shoulder on the back, hung from the waist, or special designs attached to the bow. In target archery, a device called a ground quiver often is used on the shooting line. This is a rod about twenty inches in length with a loop at the top. The sharp end is stuck into the ground, then arrows are dropped through the loop, standing ready to be withdrawn as they are used.

Recurved bow: This is a bow that is bent back from the straight line at the ends of the limbs.

Reflexed bow: If the recurve bit didn't throw you, watch out for this one: According to the Archery Manufacturers Organization, "when the bow is unstrung and is held in the shooting position, the limbs curve outward, away from the shooter."

Release: This is an artificial device that is about as old as archery, but recently has been rediscovered in sundry forms. It is used to draw and release the bowstring without the fingers actually doing the work. It has been responsible for higher scores in many cases, since it tends to afford more consistent shots. It is considered illegal in some types of competition.

Round: This designates the number of shots taken at a give distance or standardized series of distances.

Run: When one of the strings in a bowstring frays, stretches or even breaks, this string is said to have a run much as one might refer to a similar situation in hosery.

Self: This refers to a bow or arrow that is made from a single piece of wood, thus they are called self bows and self arrows.

Serving: The wrapping around the bowstring at the nocking points, which protects the string from normal wear at the stress points.

Shaft: This is the body of the arrow — wood, fiberglass or aluminum — to which the fletching and arrowhead are attached.

Shaftment: The section at the rear of the shaft to which the fletching or feathers are attached.

Shake: A crack running with the grain in a bow stave.

Shooting glove: The partial glove with three fingers used to protect the fingers in shooting.

Spiral: The curved manner in which the fletch is attached to the shaft of the arrow.

Spine: The bending quality of an arrow that allows it to spring out as it passes the bow upon being shot, then return to its original straightness, when free in flight.

Stacked bow: A bow in which the thickness of the limbs is little greater than the width; this type of bow usually is oval in cross-section.

Stalk: To move cautiously and stealthily toward sighted game to get within shooting range.

Still-hunt: Move quietly and slowly through hunting area, pausing often to stand or sit motionless and look for game. Usually employed during midday, after making a morning stand or blind-hunt.

Tab: A piece of leather, which is worn across the shooting fingers for protection much as is the shooting glove.

Tackle: A collective phrase to cover all of the archer's equipment, including bow, arrows, strings and accessories.

Take-down: The type of bow that has limbs that can be removed for transportation or even to change the weight of the bow by a switch in limbs.

Tiller: This involves shaping the bow, usually in the limb sections.

Under-bowed: The situation wherein an archer has a bow that is too light in draw weight.

Unit: The fourteen targets on a roving field archery course.

Upshot: The final shot in an archery competition.

Vane: This originally referred to the flat expanded segment of the feather fletching. In recent years, however, it has come to be used more in connection with the flat pieces of plastic that are cemented to shafts in place of feathers. These are used primarily in target archery.

Wand: A piece of wood, six feet long and two inches in width. It is driven into the ground and serves as a shooting mark.

Whip-ended: Description of a bow of which the limbs are too weak in the tip area.

Directory of the Archery Trade

BOW MANUFACTURERS

Allen Archery, 805-E Lindberg, Billings, Missouri 65610

American Archery, P.O. Box 100 Ind. Park, Oconto Falls, Wisconsin 54154

Archery Engineering Company, Tice & Watts, 309 Belvidere Drive, Huntsville, Alabama 35830

Archery Research, Incorporated, Route 3, Big Rapids, Michigan 49307

Bear Archery Company, Rural Route 1, Grayling, Michigan 49738

Browning Arms Company, Route 1, Morgan, Utah 84050

Bro-Ken Arrow Archery, 1620 S. 81 Street, West Allis, Wisconsin 53227

Carroll's Archery Products, 59½ S. Main Street, Moab, Utah 84532

Cravotta Brothers, Incorporated, Third Street, East McKeesport, Pennsylvania 15132

Eicholtz Archery, 7075 Mission Gorge Road, San Diego, California 92120

Groves Archery Corporation, 5200 San Mateo Boulevard, N.E. Albuquerque, New Mexico 87109

Herter's Incorporated, Rural Route 1, Waseca, Minnesota 56093

Howard Hill Archery, Route 1 Box 354-C, Hamilton, Montana 59840

Jack Howard, Washington Star Route, Nevada City, California 95959

Damon Howatt Archery, Route 8, Yakima, Washington 98902

Hoyt Archery Company, 11510 Natural Bridge Road, Bridgeton, Missouri 63042

Indian Industries, Incorporated, Evansville, Indiana 47717

Magna Flight Archery Company, 1822 S. Timber Court, Peoria, Illinois 61607

Mahackamo/Brave Archery, P.O. Box 218, Forestville, Connecticut 06010

Martin's Archery Company, Route 5 Box 127, Walla Walla, Washington 99362

Old Master Crafters Company, 130 Lebaron Street, Waukegan, Illinois 60085

Olympus Archery Company, 1128 W. 19th Street, Houston, Texas 77008

Ben Pearson, 2912 W. Second Street, Pine Bluff, Arkansas 71601

Plas/Steel Products, Incorporated, Walkerton, Indiana 46574

Roberts Archery Shop, 118 E. Main Street, Mt. Sterling, Illinois 62353

Root Archery, Route 3, Big Rapids, Michigan 49307

Sabo Archery Company, 9311F Kramer Avenue, Westminster, California 92683

S&J Archery, (Jennings Compound Bow) 10945 Burbank Boulevard, North Hollywood, California 91601

Shakespeare Archery, Kalamazoo, Michigan 49001

Shankland-Saxon Corporation, 9115 26th Avenue, Kenosha, Wisconsin 53140

Spartan Archery Company, 2465 Fourth North, Seattle, Washington 98109

Staghorn Archery, Merrill, Wisconsin 54452

Stewart Archery, Route 1, Box 1, Harrah, Washington 98933

Tice And Watts Archery, Incorporated, 11813 W. Gateway Drive, S.E., Huntsville, Alabama 35803

Wilson Brothers Manufacturing Company, Route 8 Box 33H, Springfield, Missouri 65804

Wing Archery Company, Division of Head Ski, Route 1, Jacksonville, Texas 75766

Woodcraft Equipment, (York Bows) P.O. Box 110, Independence, Missouri 64051

ARROW MATERIALS, EQUIPMENT

Acme Wood Products Company, Box 636, Myrtle Point, Oregon 97458 (Port Orford cedar shafts.)

Arizona Archery Enterprises, 310 N. Crismon Road, Mesa, Arizona 85207 (plastic vanes.)

Bingham Archery, P.O. Box 3013, Odgen, Utah 84403 (arrow shafting, feathers, points, nocks.)

Henry A. Bitzenburger, Route 2, Box M-1, Sherwood, Oregon 97140 (fletching jigs.)

Calcoast Suppliers, 803 Washington Heights Road, El Cajon, California 92020 (two-blade broadheads.)

Covy Arrow Straightener, P.O. Box 498, Moraga, California 94556

James D. Easton Incorporated, 7800 Hashell Avenue, Van Nuys, California 91406

F/S Arrows, Box 8094, Fountain Valley, California 92708

Golden Arrow Archery Lanes, 1410 S. Main Street, Las Vegas, Nevada 89104

Gordon Plastics, Incorporated, 5334 Banks Street, San Diego, California (fiberglass arrow shafts.)

Max Hamilton, Route 2, Box 333, Flagstaff, Arizona 86001 (plastic vanes.)

J. Dye Enterprises, 1707 Childerlee Lane, Atlanta, Georgia 30329 (arrow guides.)

J.C. Manufacturing Company, 6435 West 55th Avenue, Arvada, Colorado 80002 (Tel Tale nock points.)

King-Tool-Company, 5925 9th Street, North, Arlington, Virginia 22205 (arrow straightener.)

Little Shaver Company, Box 543, West Unity, Ohio 43570 (two and three-blade broadheads.)

M.J. Log Corporation, 1921 14th Street West, Billings, Montana 59102 (aluminum, fiberglass and cedar arrow shafts.)

Mark V Industries, 4 Hyder Street, Westboro, Massachusetts 01581 (fletch waterproofing compounds.)

McKinney Arrow Shafts, Oakland, Oregon 97462 (cedar shafts.)

Miller Masterfletchers, P.O. Box 395, Orem, Utah 84057 (fletching jigs.)

Norway Archery, Incorporated, Norway, Oregon 97460 (cedar shafts.)

Pacific Archery, Route 3, Box 912, Coos Bay, Oregon 97420 (hand-spined cedar arrow shafts.)

Pioneer Sporting Goods, Route 12, Bloomington, Indiana 47401 (Game Tamer hunting points.)

Precision Shooting Equipment, Route 1, Mahomet, Illinois 61863 (plastic vanes.)

Pro-Tec-To-Tip, 228 Cavlin Court, Hartland, Wisconsin (broadhead protectors.)

R and D Products, P.O. Box 154B, Euless, Texas 76039 (arrow holders.)

Rose City Archery, P.O. Box 342, Powers, Oregon 97466

Chester A. Stem, Incorporated, Grant Line Road, New Albany, Indiana 47150 (wooden arrow shafts, exotic woods.)

Sweetland Archery Products, 2441 Hilyard Street, Eugene, Oregon 97405 (Forcewood shafts, fur fletch.)

Texas Feathers, Incorporated, Brownwood, Texas 76801 (fletching feathers.)

Tofco, 1842-44 Dorchester Avenue, Boston, Massachusetts 02124 (Tourney-Flite fletches.)

R.C. Young Company, Manitowoc, Wisconsin 54220 (feather burners.)

Ultra Products, Limited, Box 100, Fairfield, Illinois 62837 (plastic vanes.)

Utah Feathers, P.O. Box 396, Orem, Utah 84057

MAIL ORDER DEALERS

Anderson Archery, Grand Ledge, Michigan 48837

Archery Wholesale, 2007 High Street, Alameda, California 94501

Archery Wholesaler, 2701 South Dixie Highway, Dayton, Ohio 45409

Arrow Manufacturing, 1245 B Logan Avenue, Costa Mesa, California 92626

Bingham Archery, Box 3013, Ogden, Utah 84403

Cabela's Incorporated, Sidney, Nebraska 69162

Deercliff Archery Supplies, 2852 Lavista Road, Decatur, Georgia 30033

Feline Archery, R.D. 1, Greensburg, Pennsylvania 15601

Finnysports, 9571 Sports Building, Toledo, Ohio 43614

Golden Arrow Archery, 1410 S. Main Street, Las Vegas, Nevada 89104

Herter's Incorporated, Waseca, Minnesota 56093

Howard Hill Archery, Route 1, Box 354C, Hamilton, Montana 59840

Kittredge Bow Hut, P.O. Box 598T, Mammoth Lakes, California 93540

Martin Archery Company, Route 5, Walla Walla, Washington 99362

Roberts Archery Company, RFD 1, Palmer, Massachusetts 01069

Robin Hood Archery Company, 215 Glenridge Avenue, Montclair, New Jersey 07042

Saunders Archery Company, Columbus, Nebraska 68601

Southeast'n Archery, 4718 S. Orange Avenue, Orlando, Florida 32806

Vick's Archery Center, 938 S. Cooper, Memphis, Tennessee 38104

BOW, ARROW CASES

Challanger Manufacturing Corporation, 94-28 Merrick Boulevard, Jamaica, New York 11433

Gateway Luggage Manufacturing Company, Incorporated, 820 W. Tenth Street, Claremore, Oklahoma 74017

Gun-Ho, 110 E. Tenth Street, St. Paul, Minnesota 55101

Paul-Reed, Incorporated, P.O. Box 227, Charlevoix, Michigan 49720

Penguin Industries, P.O. Box 97, Parkesburg, Pennsylvania 19365

Protecto Plastics, Incorporated, 201 Alpha Road, Wind Gap, Pennsylvania 18091

Sloane Products, P.O. Box 56, Saugus, California 91350

Sportscase, Incorporated, 204 Central Avenue, Osseo, Minnesota 55368

Sylvester's Archery Supplies, 212 Hawthorne Circle, Creve Coeur, Illinois 61611

VARMINT & GAME CALLS

Burnham Brothers, Box 110, Marble Falls, Texas 78654

Electronic Game Calls, 210 W. Grand Avenue, Grand Rapids, Michigan 54494

Faulk's Game Call Company, Incorporated, 616 18th Street, Lake Charles, Louisiana 70601

P.S. Olt Company, Pekin, Illinois 61554

Penn's Woods Products, Incorporated, 19 W. Pittsburgh Street, Delmont, Pennsylvania 15625

Scotch Game Call Company, Incorporated, 60 Main Street, Oakfield, New York 14125

Johnny Stewart Game Calls, Incorporated, 5100 Fort Avenue, P.O. Box 1909, Waco, Texas 76703

Thomas Game Calls, P.O. Box 336, Winnsboro, Texas 75494

Western Call & Decoy, P.O. Box 425, Portland, Oregon 97207

LEATHER GOODS

J. M. Bucheimer Company, P.O. Box 280, Airport Road, Frederick, Maryland 21701

Hobby-Horse Crafts, 1811 Sixth Street, Wyandotte, Michigan 48192

King Sport-Line Company, 328 S. Cypress Avenue, Alhambra, California 91801

Kolpin Brothers Company, Incorporated, 121 S. Pearl Street, Berlin, Wisconsin 54923

Swiss-Craft Company, Incorporated, 33 Artic Street, Worcester, Massachusetts 01604

BOWSIGHTS

Accra Manufacturing Company, 1226 S. Norwood, Tulsa, Oklahoma 74112

Eryleen Products, 361 Cambridge Street, Burlington, Massachusetts 01803

Full Adjust Products, 915 North Ann Street, Lancaster, Pennsylvania 17602

Goodyear Company, Box 265, Lincoln City, Oregon 97367

Merrill Bow Sights, 3830 Orleans Lane, Minneapolis, Minnesota 55427

Miletron Products, 1851 South Orange Avenue, Monterey Park, California 91754

Moto Miter Company, Prairie du Chien, Wisconsin 53821

Pro Line Company, P.O. Box 370, Hastings, Michigan 49058

Range-O-Matic Sight Company, 35572 Strathcona, Mt. Clemens, Michigan 48043 (bowsights and arrow holders.)

Scanner Products, 3 Hawthorne Road, Gibbsboro, New Jersey 08026

Schneider Enterprises, 11245 South Thompson Drive, Wind Lake, Wisconsin 53185

Sprandel's Bowsight Company, 19 Brookside Drive, Monroe, Connecticut 06488

CROSSBOWS

Benedict Crossbows, P.O. Box 343, Chatsworth, California 91331

Midwest Crossbow Company, 9043 S. Western Avenue, Chicago, Illinois 60620

Stevens Crossbows, Box 72, Huntsville, Arkansas 72740

MISCELLANEOUS ACCESSORIES & EQUIPMENT

A & W Archer, Box 1219, Garden Grove, California 92640 (bow quivers.)

Avery Corporation, P.O. Box 99, 221 N. Main Street, Electra, Texas 76360 (varmint calling lights.)

Auto-Quiver, P.O. Box 771, Wayne, New Jersey 07470 (bow quivers.)

Baker Manufacturing Company, Box 1003, Valdosta, Georgia 31601 (tree stands.)

Belke Company, 2308 Pleasant, New Holstein, Wisconsin 53061 (saw-knife.)

Joe Bender, Stoddard, Wisconsin 54658 (No-Glove finger protectors.)

Vic Berger, 1019 Garfield Avenue, Springfield, Ohio 45504 (Berger button.)

Brownell, Incorporated, Moodus, Connecticut 06469 (bowstring material.)

Buck Knives, 1717 N. Magnolia Avenue, El Cajon, California 92022 (hunting knives.)

Buck Stop, Incorporated, 3015 Grow Road, Stanton, Michigan 48888 (insect repellent, deer lure.)

C/J Enterprises, 410 S. Citrus Avenue, Covina, California 91722 (one-piece aluminum release.)

Camillus Cutlery Company, Camillus, New York 13031 (hunting knives.)

Camouflage Manufacturing Company, 9075 Atlantic Boulevard, Jacksonville, Florida 32215 (camouflage hunting clothes and accessories.)

Camp-lite Products, Incorporated, 1408 W. Colfax, Denver, Colorado 90204 (lightweight back pack and camping tents.)

Camp Trails, P.O. Box 14500, Phoenix, Arizona 85031 (back packing and camping equipment.)

Colorado Outdoor Sports Company, 1636 Champs Street, P.O. Box 5544, Denver, Colorado 80217 (lightweight packing equipment.)

Cutter Laboratories, Incorporated, Fourth and Parker Streets, Berkeley, California 94619 (insect repellents, snake bite kits, first aid kits.)

D&D Rods, Box 206, Comstock, Michigan 49041 (stablizer rods and weights.)

Deer Me Products, Box 345, Anoka, Minnesota 55303 (tree steps, tree stands, deer drags.)

Dolch Enterprises, Incorporated, Box 606, Westlake, Louisiana 70669 (telescopic bowstringer.)

Federal Instrument Company, 93-36 65th Avenue, Rego Park, New York 11374 (range finders.)

Fleetwood, 902 Ogden Avenue, Superior Wisconsin 54880 (general line of accessories and bow racks.)

Game Winner, Incorporated, 2940 First National Bank Tower, Atlanta, Georgia 30303 (camouflage and hunting clothes, accessories.)

General Recreation Industries, Fayette, Alabama 35555 (sleeping bags.)

Gordon Plastics, Incorporated, 5334 Banks Street, San Diego, California 92110 (fiberglass shafts.)

Gutmann Cutlery Company, Incorporated, 900 South Columbus Avenue, Mt. Vernon, New York 10550 (hunting knives.)

Indian Ridge Traders, P.O. Box X-50, Ferndale, Michigan 48220 (hunting, skinning knives.)

Jet-Aer Corporation, 100 Sixth Avenue, Paterson, New Jersey 07524 (insect repellents, game lures, fabric and leather treatments and waterproofing.)

Kelty Pack, Incorporated, P.O. Box 639, 10909 Tuxford Street, Sun Valley, California 91352 (pack bags, pack frames, soft packs.)

Killian Chek-It, 12350 S.E. Stevens Road, Portland, Oregon 97226 (competition string release.)

Kwikee Kwiver Company, 7292 Peaceful Valley Road, Acme, Michigan 49610 (bow quivers.)

Lawson Manufacturing Company, Route 3, Oregon, Illinois 61061 (tree stands.)

Len Company, BT-101 Brooklyn, New York 11214 (survival knives.)

L&M Cork Products, Mokena, Illinois 60448 (cork target backstops, mats.)

Magna-Flight, 212 Hawthorne Circle, Creve Coeur, Illinois 61611 (bowstring releases.)

Mac's Archery Supplies, Incorporated, 6336 W. Fond du Lac Avenue, Milwaukee, Wisconsin 53218 (bowfishing reels, arrows, points.)

Marco's Enterprises, 2120 Ludington Street, Escanaba, Michigan 49829 (deer soap.)

Mini Bow, 1880 Century Park East, Suite 315, Los Angeles, California 90067 (novel system for living room archery.)

Mountain Products Corporation, 123 S. Wanatchee Avenue, Wenatchee, Washington 98801 (lightweight camping gear.)

National Packaged Trail Foods, 632 E. 185th Street, Cleveland, Ohio 44119 (freeze-dried camping foods.)

Natural Scent Company, 1170 Elgin Avenue, Salt Lake City, Utah 84106 (animal scents.)

New Archery Products, 107 Berrywood Drive, Marietta, Georgia 30060 (flipper rests.)

Nock Rite Company, 3720 Crestview Circle, Brookfield, Wisconsin 53005 (bowstring attachments.)

Old Master Crafters Company, 130 Lebaron Street, Waukegan, Illinois 60085 (bow laminations.)

W.C. Phillips, 2515 Magnolia, Texarkana, Texas 75501 (tree stands.)

R&D Products, P.O. Box 154, Euless, Texas 76039 (arrow holders and bowfishing points.)

Ranger Manufacturing Company, P.O. Box 3386, Augusta, Georgia 30904 (camouflage clothing.)

Ranging, Incorporated, P.O. Box 9106, Rochester, New York 14625 (range-determining devices.)

Razor Edge, Box 203, Butler, Wisconsin 54007 (hunting knives.)

Ron's Porta-Pak Manufacturing Company, P.O. Box 141, Greenbrier, Arkansas 72058 (tree stands.)

Rorco, Box 1007, State College, Pennsylvania 16801 (shaft spiders.)

S & K Manufacturing, 1707 S.E. 136th Avenue, Vancouver, Washington 98664 (hunting release.)

San Angelo Die Casting Company, Box 984, San Angelo, Texas 76901 (bow racks and holders.)

Saunders Archer Company, P.O. Box 476, Industrial Site, Columbus, Nebraska 68601 (complete line of archery accessories.)

Schrade Walden Cutlery Corporation, New York, New York 12428 (hunting knives.)

Shockalator, 12122 Monter, Bridget·   ·i 63044 (mercury bow stabilizers.)

Smiths Sports Products, 925 Hillcrest Place, Pasadena, California 91106 (bow slings.)

10-X Manufacturing, 100 S.W. Third Street, Des Moines, Iowa 59309 (camouflage and hunting clothing.)

Trail Chef Foods, P.O. Box 60041, Terminal Annex, Los Angeles, California 90060 (lightweight foods.)

Trophyland USA, Incorporated, 7001 West 20th Avenue, P.O. Box 4606, Hialeah, Florida 33014 (trophies.)

Trueflight Manufacturing Company, Incorporated, Manitowish Waters, Wisconsin 54545 (string silencers, nock locators and assorted accessories.)

Wilson-Allen Corporation, Box 104, Windsor, Missouri 65360 (brush nock.)

L.C. Whiffen Company, Incorporated, 923 S. 16th Street, Milwaukee, Wisconsin 53204 (bow quivers.)

R.C. Young Company, Incorporated, Manitowoc, Wisconsin 54220 (feather trimmers.)